My very best to Denna.

12-17-01

"Big Ed"
and the
Haggar Family
Behind an Apparel Giant

Ed R. Haggar

EAKIN PRESS Austin, Texas

For CIP information, please access: www.loc.gov

FIRST EDITION
Copyright © 2001 By Ed R. Haggar
Published in the U.S.A.
By Eakin Press
A Division of Sunbelt Media, Inc.
P.O. Drawer 90159
Austin, Texas 78709-0159
email: eakinpub@sig.net
website: www.eakinpress.com
ALL RIGHTS RESERVED.
1 2 3 4 5 6 7 8 9
1-57168-590-1

Contents

Preface	v
Acknowledgments	vii
1. The Joseph Marion Haggar Family	1
2. My Early Years	24
3. Notre Dame	39
4. The War Effort and Military Service	60
5. Haggar Corporation	74
6. Haggar Corporation (Postscript)	117
7. Presidents We've Known	133
8. Work, Directorships, and Other Business Interests	152
9. My Wonderful Family, Special Friends, and Favorite Pastime	161
Appendix	191
Index	195

The J.M. Haggar, Sr., Family

J.M. Haggar, Sr.

Rose Mary Wasaff Haggar

Edmond Ralph Haggar

Joseph Marion Haggar, Jr.

Rosemary Haggar Vaughan

Preface

Joseph Marion Haggar was born in 1892, in the remote mountain village of Jezzeen, Lebanon. At age thirteen, with little money in his pocket, this young boy left home, bound for North America.

Known as "The Chief," J.M. Haggar was a whirlwind. Working side-by-side with his two sons, Ed and Joe, Jr., he founded a company bearing his name in 1926. Fifty years after its founding, Haggar Corporation was the largest manufacturer of men's dress pants in the United States. Seventy-five years after its founding, Haggar is one of the largest apparel manufacturing companies in the industry.

"Big Ed" and the Haggar Family Behind an Apparel Giant is the story of this extraordinary dynasty that made Haggar a household word. In fact, oldest son Ed and Morris Hite coined the term "slacks" to describe the company's products.

Haggar changed the way men dressed in 1970 with the introduction of double-knit slacks. Known worldwide for producing apparel of high quality and value, J.M. Haggar possessed a keen eye for design and an uncanny sense of style.

The Haggars were friends of U.S. presidents, celebrities, and a roster of athletes that reads like a universal hall of fame. It's worth mentioning those who endorsed the products as well those who were personal friends.

From the White House: Presidents Johnson, Nixon, Ford, and both Bushes.

From the baseball diamond: Nellie Fox, Mickey Mantle, Phil Rizzuto, Eddie Matthews, and Robin Roberts.

From the gridiron: Cloyse Box, Frank Gifford, Otto Graham, Sam Huff, Bobby Lane, Johnny Lujac, Don Meredith, Roger Staubach, Hank Stram, Pat Summerall, and Doak Walker.

From the links: Dow Finsterwald, Doug Ford, Ben Hogan, Byron Nelson, Tommy Nieporte, Bobby Nichols, Arnold Palmer, Charlie Sifford, and Art Wall, Jr.

From the tennis courts: Arthur Ashe, Bjorn Borg, Rod Laver, Ille Nastase, John Newcombe, and Stan Smith.

From the Formula 5000 Road Racing Association: David Hobbs and Carl Hogan.

From basketball: Bobby Knight, Digger Phelps.

Celebrities: Bob Hope, Danny Thomas... And the list goes on and on...

There is also a concrete connection between the Haggar family and the University of Notre Dame, both on the gridiron and off!

Personal acknowledgments are offered by Ambassador Walter Annenberg, President George H. Bush, President Gerald Ford, Father Theodore Hesburgh, and Father Paul Schott.

Ed Haggar has encompassed his memoirs in this book — an eyewitness account of one of America's great corporate success stories, told with wit, wisdom, insight, and humor.

Acknowledgments

The writing of this book was completed in April 2000 with revision made in March 2001. Working on this project has been enjoyable and remarkably rewarding. I was fortunate to have the assistance of family, friends, and co-workers in assembling the book. Their generosity of time and recollection is truly valued.

Abundant thanks for their input and inspiration to my family: Patty, Patty Jo, Eddie, Jimmy, Mary Alice, and John.

Written recollections of their early years by my brother Joe and sister Rosemary Haggar Vaughan bring color and warmth to this book.

Special thanks for their written contributions and assistance with recalling the history of Haggar Corporation go to our corporate executives: Joe Haggar III, Frank Bracken, and former executives Kevin Chisholm, Charlie Martin, Jack Smith, Ted Sullins, and Hal Tehan.

And finally, a special note of gratitude to my current secretary, Jimmie Morin, and my former secretary, Dolores Campbell, for their assistance and input.

The text for both books was compiled through a collaborative series of taped interviews with Linda Krull of "Memoirs," Palm Desert, California.

CHAPTER 1
The Joseph Marion Haggar Family

JOSEPH MARION HAGGAR

He never threaded a needle in his life, and chances of finding tailor's chalk on his fingers were slim-to-none, but my father, Joseph Marion (Jim) Haggar, innately knew about the design, manufacturing, and especially the sales and marketing of men's pants. Drawing from his experiences on the road for Ely & Walker Company in 1914 and D.M. Oberman Company in 1923, Dad started the Haggar Company in 1926.

He was feisty, smart, tenacious, God-fearing, and most of all, Jim Haggar had an extraordinary ability to judge people.

Dad went to work for the Ely & Walker Company in 1914. In essence, Ely & Walker was a retail distribution business, focused primarily on dry goods. Dad worked as both an inside and outside salesman. There were only a few salesmen out on the road in those days, mostly because automobiles were scarce and road conditions were poor. Rather, the merchants came to the big cities such as St. Louis, Dallas, or Kansas City and bought their wares from companies such as Ely & Walker.

In early 1917, Ely & Walker Company had an opportunity to acquire 700,000 dozen spools of "Lacadena" thread, manufactured by the J.P. Coats Company of Glasgow, Scotland. It was a type of thread seldom used in this country, but Dad remembered seeing this variety when he lived in Mexico. Indeed, the thread was manufactured with the intention of sending it directly from Glasgow to Mexico. However, just prior to shipping, Great Britain clamped down an embargo on shipment of goods to most of South America, and the deal was off. The director of J.P. Coats cabled Ely & Walker, desperate to unload the order. Somehow, Dad got his hands on that cablegram and convinced the president of Ely & Walker, a Mr. Calhoun, to buy the entire lot on consignment. "I can sell it all in Mexico," he assured Mr. Calhoun. Knowing his customers, and able to speak the language, by communicating over the telephone and through Western Union telegrams Dad sold out the entire inventory of 700,000 dozen spools in one day! He bought the thread at sixty cents per dozen and sold it in Mexico for $1 per dozen.

Once again, cablegrams crossed the Atlantic Ocean and the inventory was loaded onboard a freighter leaving Scotland, bound for New Orleans, where it was to be forwarded to Laredo, Chihuahua, and Monterrey. The return cable from Coats assured Dad the thread was on its way. The following day, every newspaper from New York to San Francisco, including St. Louis, exploded with the headline: "United States Enters World War I."

The recipients in Mexico were ordered to wire their payments directly to a St. Louis bank. Everything was going Dad's way. The shipment arrived in New Orleans, dodging the submarine-filled seas, and the local bank was collecting the money. Suddenly, without warning, every Mexican merchant stopped payment or canceled orders. Pancho Villa and his guerrilla army had commandeered a bloody raid and massacre in the city of Torreon. In fact, Dad's brother-in-law was attacked and nearly murdered in his dry goods store.

Dad's brain must have clicked into warp speed. He picked up a telephone and, in Spanish, began calling merchants in Mexico City and Guadalajara, which were not under Villa's threat. For the second time, Dad managed to resell all 700,000 dozen spools at the same price of $1 per dozen. He cabled the freighter to deliver the shipment to Tampico instead of New Orleans.

Rumors of Dad's success had skyrocketed the size of the shipment to two million dozen, and Dad made a bunch of money in commissions from this deal. It also made him a really big man with Ely & Walker. It was at this time that the company opted to take my father off commission sales and offered him a weekly salary. But Dad knew that his potential income based on his sales abilities far outreached the salary being offered by the company, and he left Ely & Walker.

(A little aside to this story: After reading President George Bush's autobiography *Looking Forward,* I learned that his maternal grandfather was the Walker of Ely & Walker—hence the name George Herbert *Walker* Bush. I sent President Bush the story from Dad's book about his big coup with the thread at his grandfather's company. President Bush really got a big kick out of Dad's story.)

¤ ¤ ¤

Jim Haggar's life was a complicated and finely woven tapestry. Father–husband–businessman–industry innovator–civic leader–philanthropist... so many threads, so many intricate patterns.

It was a long and arduous journey from the small village of Jezzeen, in the mountains of southern Lebanon, to the bustling metropolis of Dallas. This story really begins in 1892, the year of my father's birth, in the mountains of Lebanon.

Colon Thurbron, author of *The Hills of Adonis,* offers this picturesque history :

> Jezzeen is typical of the pretty towns and villages of the Mountain, built out of limestone and roofed with pink European tiles. Down its ravine two waterfalls glisten for a hundred and thirty feet before their rivers run together in a flower-filled valley. Its people are Maronites—Christian mountaineers—and are well known for their cutlery and stone-work.[1]
>
> Here the mountain history begins: vestiges of families grown to power through courage and intrigue, who sometimes ruled the Lebanon independent of the Ottomans, building forts and palaces in the hills for their brief years. At Jezzeen the emir Fakr ed Din took refuge in a gorge and defied the Turks with scarcely a friend beside him.

---

1. The name "Haggar" in Arabic means "stone cutter" or "stone mason."

Thinking three centuries ahead of his time, the emir envisaged a "Greater Lebanon," free from Turkey and oriented westward. Under his rule the Roman Catholic missions first entered the Mountains and the ports became depots for European merchants—Florentine, Venetian and French—where Lebanese silks, olive oil and cereals were exported for profit.

My father was the youngest of seven children, two boys and five girls. His father was named Kahlil Abou Chacra El Hajjar and his mother was Mrs. Kalil (Maney) Hajjar, born in 1852 and died March 1928 in Dallas, Texas.

At the time of Dad's birth, nearly half the population of Lebanon was Christian. Lebanese Catholics were affiliated with either the Maronite or the Orthodox church; both were affiliated with Rome. One of Dad's parents belonged to the Orthodox church, whose patron saint was Nicholas, and the other parent belonged to the Maronite church, whose patron saint was Marion. With the birth of each son, my grandparents argued like cats and dogs: "I'd rather name the boy Mohammed than Marion" or "I'd rather name the boy Mohammed than Nicholas!" To honor both saints, my grandparents bestowed these two names on their two sons: my father, Joseph Marion, and his brother Nicholas.

Dad told me that he got his basic education studying under a fig tree near his home. His only schooling, in Lebanon, was limited to just a few years.

In 1906, at the age of thirteen, with little money in his pockets, speaking Lebanese and a bit of French, Joseph Marion Haggar was packed into steerage and sailed to North America. As the twentieth century unfurled, many immigrants from Dad's part of the world began their new lives in Mexico. Dad was no exception.

He worked as a peddler in Mexico, which is where he developed his skills as a salesman par excellence. With a good ear for language, Dad was soon fluent in Spanish. It was only a matter of time (about four years) before he was able to speak English fluently, and eventually he entered the United States. He would become a naturalized citizen of the United States on January 22, 1923.

Entering this country at New Orleans, Louisiana, Dad took any kind of work he could find—dish washing, window washing, etc. He gradually worked his way to St. Louis, Missouri, which was home to a large Lebanese immigrant community.

Many of Dad's friends during those early days in St. Louis were members of the Maronite church and shared the same immigrant background. In fact, in those days, all of his friends from the old country called Dad "Maroun" (the Arabic pronunciation). In English, Maroun sounded like the girl's name "Marion." In any event, Dad never liked that part of his name. When he signed his name, as JM Haggar, the JM looked like Jim, and that's what he was called for the rest of his life.

When he first arrived in St. Louis, Dad worked as a window washer alongside a young Greek immigrant named Spyro Skouras. Both young men were eager entrepreneurs. Spyro invested his money in a motion picture theater in St. Louis and eventually became president of Twentieth Century Fox Films in Hollywood.

In the meantime, while conducting all the machinations of big business in St. Louis, Dad fell deeply in love with a girl named Rose Wasaff, who sang in the church choir at the Maronite church. Dad was smitten and endeared himself to Rose's entire family. When Rose's father left St. Louis and moved to Bristow, Oklahoma, Dad followed. Hoping for Rose's hand in marriage, Dad worked hard at a variety of jobs in Bristow, eager to convince Mr. Wasaff that he could offer Rose a secure future. While in Bristow, Dad worked in a grocery store, bought and sold oil leases, and classified cotton.

Dad and Mother were married August 22, 1915, in Bristow.

By 1921, Dad's creative and assertive sales abilities were at their peak. He went to work for the D.M. Oberman Company, selling their King Brand Overalls throughout the Southwest, and moved his family to Dallas, Texas, to set up a showroom at the Southland Hotel in downtown Dallas. But he spent a great deal of his time on the road.

By the time he was twenty-nine, Dad had honed his uncanny ability to read people and react on the spot. In fact, Jim Haggar was already becoming somewhat of a sales legend known by most of the rural shopkeepers in his desolate, rustic territory of rural Texas, Louisiana, and New Mexico. Looking back at those early years, Dad liked to brag that he rarely opened up his sample cases without selling something. But he would face one of his greatest challenges in 1923 in the Panhandle town of Hale Center, Texas.

At the time, that dusty dot on the Texas map was most easily accessed by train. All salesmen, whether peddling carpet sweepers, canned edibles or, in Dad's case, King Brand Overalls, arrived on the early morning train and departed on the 7:00 P.M. train, the only outbound train of the day. Dad recalled:

> The old man who owned the general store in town always sat in the back of the narrow store. In order to get to him, I'd have to drag my sample cases, each weighing about fifty pounds, down the long narrow aisle in the center of the store. Two glass showcases, filled with bandanas, celluloid collars and pocketknives lined each side of the aisle. Even though I stopped in to see him three or four times a year, the old merchant never remembered my name or the merchandise I was carrying. And when I carefully maneuvered those bulky cases to the back, I'd open them up, spread out the goods, only to be told, "I'm not interested today. Come back again." It was time to get tough. So on my way out this particular day, I nonchalantly gave two firm wrist flips and the bags shot out of my hands, shattering the glass showcases on each side of the aisle.

The sound of splintering glass brought the old man to the front of the store in seconds. Acting mortified by the terrible accident, Dad contritely offered to hire a carpenter to make the repairs. He had to stay in town all day anyway, until the 7:00 train.

Well, two hours and $6.50 later the glass was replaced, the floors were swept up, and the displaced merchandise was neatly replaced in the showcases. The storeowner was greatly impressed by Dad's concern and once again asked Dad to open his sample cases. An ear-to-ear grin covered Dad's face. He was probably thinking to himself, "He's hooked!" In fact, the merchant bought $300 worth of overalls. And whenever Dad returned to Hale Center, the old man always greeted him: "Here comes Haggar, the fellow that broke my showcases!"

Dad never lost the ability to switch into overdrive. Always eager for success and dedicated to hard work, he built a company that assured a secure life for his beloved Rose and their three children. In doing so, he eventually employed thousands of workers, enriched the cultural life of Dallas, educated and trained scores of people (many of whom were disadvantaged), and set new industry standards.

¤ ¤ ¤

The year was 1933. I was seventeen years old and driving the family car on a month-long vacation along the West Coast. Dad was recovering from a three-week hospitalization for ulcers, and therefore, on strictest orders from his doctors, Dad and the family "got away" for a while. After a harrowing week in San Francisco, where the city was experiencing a general strike, all of us settled down for some relaxation in a rented cottage in Beverly Hills. During this sojourn, Dad taught me a very special life lesson, and it had to do with gambling.

Herbert and Clarence Grunsfeld were the company's top salesmen at that time. The brothers both lived in Los Angeles, and when they heard that Dad was vacationing for a week in the area, they made every opportunity to visit with Dad and the family. One night Dad, the Grunsfeld brothers, and I drove to Tijuana, Mexico, to visit the Agua Caliente Casino. The casino looked like a big castle. All of us enjoyed a sumptuous five-course dinner. The cost was $1 per person. After dinner, Dad and the Grunsfelds enjoyed some games of chance. Clarence looked up from the blackjack table and noticed General Johnson standing a few feet away. General Johnson headed the National Recovery Act under President Roosevelt. Next to the president, Johnson was the most powerful man in the country at the time. Clarence, whose hot-under-the-collar-temper was well known, turned to Dad and said, "I'm going to bust Johnson in the face!"

Dad was mortified. "What the hell are you talking about?" he protested.

Clarence replied, "Just think of the publicity Haggar Company will get!"

At midnight Dad was down about $2,500 — a significant sum in those days. We had a two-and-a-half-hour drive ahead of us. Mother, Rosemary, and Joe were waiting for us in Beverly Hills. Dad was a great gambler and refused to leave the casino until he had a chance to recover some of his losses. By 1:30 A.M., Dad turned that deficit into a small profit and we headed back to Los Angeles. Not wanting to awaken anyone at such a late hour, Dad decided not to call Mother. We finally rolled in at 4:00 A.M. That was the only time in my life that I remember seeing Mother hopping mad at Dad. She was worried, and rightfully so. Dad looked at me, silently acknowledging his response to the anguish he had caused Mother, and I just knew what he was thinking: "Gambling doesn't pay!"

Dizzy Dean began his dazzling career as a pitcher for the St. Louis Cardinals in 1932. Over the next three years, he led the National League in strikeouts. Dizzy's brother, Daffy Dean, also played for the Cardinals. In the late 1950s, well after retiring from major league baseball, both Dizzy and Daffy moved to Dallas and joined Lakewood Country Club. One afternoon, Dad met Dizzy and Daffy in the clubhouse and expressed an interest in playing golf with them. Dizzy replied, "Well, Mr. Haggar, we usually play a $50 Nassau." Leaning forward, toward Dizzy's ear, Dad whispered, "That's fine with me, just don't tell my boys!" Dad was a good gambler and he liked to gamble, but he never wanted to set a bad example for his sons. Earl Summers, a great and longtime friend, related this golf story to me.

It is believed that the game of backgammon was born in the Middle East. Whatever the origin and wherever he learned the game, backgammon was one of my father's passions. For years he played with many of his friends from the Old Country.

Later, he played poker on Monday nights at Lakewood Country Club. For years Joe and I tried to entice Dad to join Preston Trail Golf Club. But Dad wanted to remain at Lakewood because of his golf, backgammon, and poker friends. Subsequently, I told Dad that some of the new members at Preston Trail were playing backgammon. With no hesitation at all, he turned to me and said, "Okay, I'll join!"

Dad eagerly anticipated those Monday night poker games at Lakewood. One time, Mother's parents were visiting and their

"Jezzeen is typical of the pretty towns and villages of the mountain, built of limestone and roofed with pink European tiles. Down its ravine, two waterfalls glisten for a hundred and thirty feet before their rivers run together in a flower-filled valley." From Hills of Adonis by Colin Thurbon.

Joe with Dad's cousin, Joseph Marion Hajjar, at Dad's birthplace in Jezzeen, Lebanon.

Mother's parents, Kalil and Maggie Wasaff

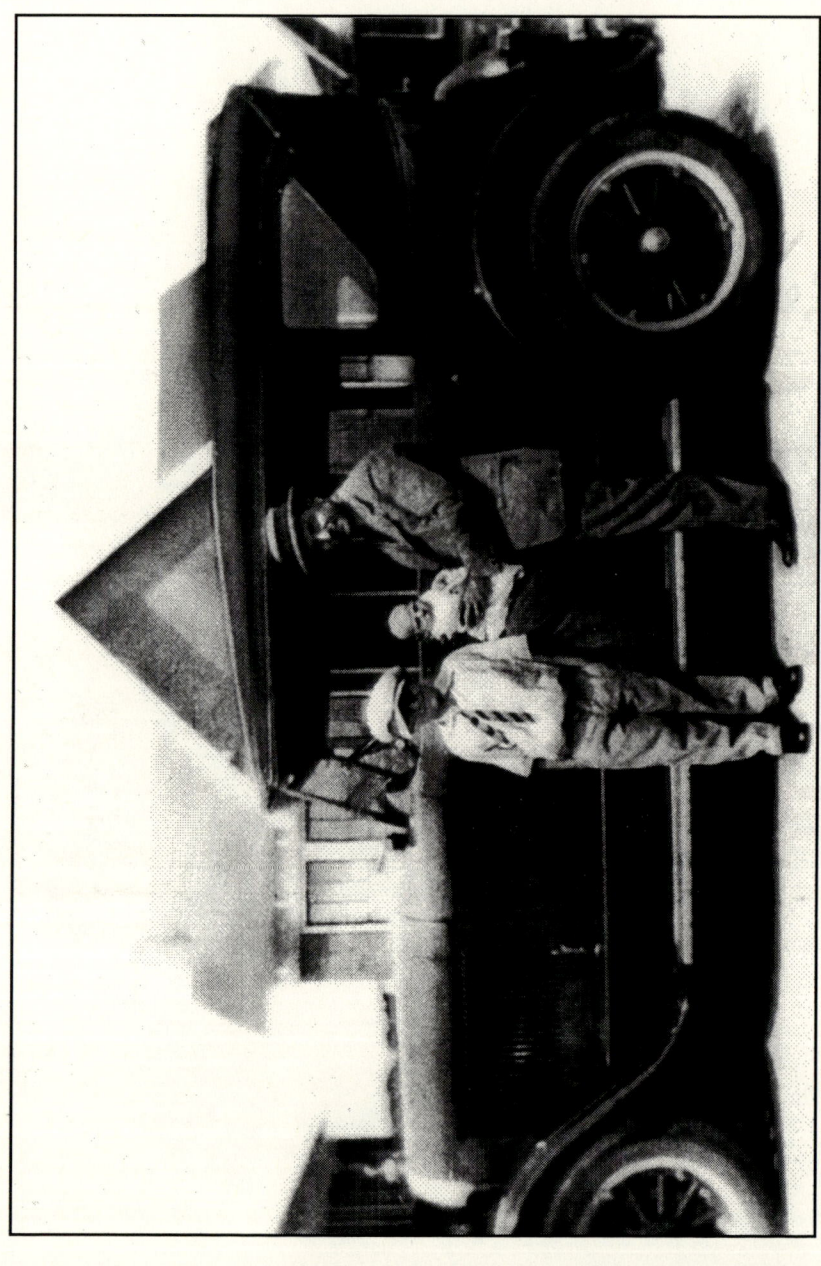

Standing in front of Dad's Peerless with the "Hollywood Top." House on Garrett Avenue in background. L-R: E.R.H., Joe, Jr., Dad. Circa 1925.

*Fourth Unit of the Santa Fe Building.
Site of our first manufacturing facility and headquarters.*

Celebrating Dad's eightieth birthday – December 1972. First row, seated, L-R: Patty Haggar, Isabell Haggar, J.M. Haggar, Sr., Rosemary Vaughan, E.R.H.

Second Row: Vicki Vaughan, Robert Rumble, Marty Rumble, Mary Lynn Vaughan, Marian Haggar, J.M. Haggar, Jr., J.M. Haggar III, Eddie Vaughan, Jr.

Third row: Ann Haggar, Lydia Novakov, Mary Alice Stedillie, Patty Jo Turner, Lee Haggar.

Fourth Row: John Daley Haggar, Eddie Vaughan, Eddie Haggar, Dan Novakov, Terry Stedillie, John Turner, Jimmy Haggar, Jimmy Vaughan.

Haggar Highlights

JUNE 1976

Celebration 50

Celebrating our fiftieth anniversary – Texas barbecue style!

stay coincided with Dad's poker night. Knowing how much Dad enjoyed the company and the game, Mother sent him off to the club and entertained her parents. There must have been some heavy action that night, because the hours slipped away and Dad stayed late at the club. He was very surprised to find Mother awake when he came home. "Dear, pour me a glass of bourbon, please," Mother requested. This was a very unusual request from Mother, who rarely imbibed. She drank the bourbon and went to sleep. The next morning, she offered no arguments about Dad's late hours—only the silent treatment.

¤ ¤ ¤

With all the demands of running a business, Dad managed to find a little time to follow professional sports. He was a great fan of baseball and football. The strenuous physical work of his youth provided him with a tough physique. He was a fair golfer and an excellent hunter.

The energy of running the dogs and shooting quail and dove was an ever-present part of his life. He remained active in the sport until his ninetieth birthday. West Texas offered some of the finest bird hunting in the country. As a young boy, I enjoyed Dad's company on some of these expeditions, but was never eager about hunting itself. Many years later, my son Jimmy, who loved to go hunting with Grandpa Haggar, asked my mother one day, "Why did you make my dad a sissy?"

Mother replied, "Your dad's no sissy!"

"Well, he is too, because he doesn't like to hunt!" Jimmy replied.

Starting in his pre-teens, my younger brother, Joe, acquired the same love of hunting as Dad and accompanied him on many hunting trips. To this day, I am forever grateful to Joe. After Joe's first hunting trip with Dad, I was excused from all outings, much to my pleasure.

¤ ¤ ¤

Joseph Marion Haggar was a highly respected man in Dallas. Throughout his lifetime Dad had many close friends. Some of them, such as Gene McElvaney and Nathan Adams of the First National Bank in Dallas, were acquired through business. Both men respected Dad's abilities and were eager to help him with financing and banking. Weldon Bomer and Joe Shadid were hunting buddies.

Here's a postscript regarding Gene McElvaney and Nathan Adams. More than a quarter century after the founding of the company, Joe III's office was scheduled for redecorating and renovation. During the mayhem, Joe III found a letter written by Gene McElvaney to Nathan Adams stating, "I have checked out Jim Haggar. He is a very astute businessman. Enclosed please find a copy of his statement showing net worth of $75,000. We should do business with him."

As a rule, Dad avoided politics and political friends. Needless to say, he was never a big fan of Lyndon Johnson—until the barbecue at the ranch. Actually, Dad first met Lyndon at a civic luncheon in Dallas on April 23, 1963. He heard from the vice president four days later, when nearly 100 United Nations ambassadors visited the LBJ Ranch for a traditional Texas barbecue. In addition to the international delegation, Vice President Johnson invited Dad and a few other businessmen from Dallas. Lyndon knew Dad was from Lebanon and seated him with several dignitaries from the Middle East. Dad was delighted and spent the afternoon conversing in Arabic with these distinguished gentlemen. It was quite a day. After that, Dad was infatuated with Lyndon Johnson. Both were superb salesmen.

It was Dad's custom to send several pairs of pants along with a thank-you note to his host after any party. He sent several pairs of PIMALON pants to Vice President Johnson. These pants were 35% pima cotton and 65% polyester. Fine pants, indeed.

Seven months went by and Lyndon Johnson became president of the United States. One Sunday afternoon my brother Joe got a call from the White House. A secretary's voice announced that the president of the United States was calling for Joe Haggar, Jr., and asked Joe to hold for the president! Convinced that I was playing a joke of some kind, Joe sent his kids next door to my house, to make sure I wasn't on the other end of the line. Joe's wife, Isabell, got on the extension phone.

Finally, Lyndon was on the phone. "Joe, your dad sent me the best damn pants I've ever worn and I'd like to have some more." Well, Dad was out of town, but Joe was pretty sure which pants were sent to the White House. A few minutes of silence followed. Finally, President Johnson spoke up. "Joe, those are the best pants, but I would like you to make two changes for me. I need deeper pockets and more room... down where your nuts hang!" In essence, Lyndon was asking for pants cut with more rise. After that, any pants we styled with a deep rise were always referred to as the "LBJ Cut."

¤ ¤ ¤

Dad passed away on December 15, 1988, in his ninety-fifth year, at St. Paul's Hospital, following surgery that removed a cancerous part of his colon. A second operation was performed shortly after the first. Dad was hospitalized for six months and never recovered from the two surgeries. Earlier in his life, he had been hospitalized two or three times—nothing very serious. He always bounced back stronger than ever. Haggar Corporation records note that Jim Haggar commandeered the company for sixty-two years. In fact, Dad never retired. He worked right up until the day before he entered the hospital.

¤ ¤ ¤

ROSE WASAFF HAGGAR

Excerpts from a letter written by my Uncle Sam Wasaff (Mother's brother) from his law practice in Ranger, Texas, serve as a fitting introduction to Mother's origins.[2]

> Grandpa Wasaff was born Kalil George Wasaff, May 17, 1872 in Bazoun, Lebanon. A twin and one of several children, the son of George Wasaff and Rose Debs of Bazoun. Grandpa Wasaff left Lebanon when 12 years of age for the British West Indies remained there for about 2 years and them came to St. Louis, Missouri, when he was about 15 years of age. Grandpa Wasaff met and married Maggie Alban in St. Louis, Missouri, July 20, 1895.

---

2. These excerpts were taken from a letter written by Sam Wasaff in 1969. The spelling "Kerry" may be a typo.

Grandma Wasaff was born in Batroun, Lebanon, April 20, 1877. She was one of 6 children, the daughter of J. Frederic Alban and Norma Kerry. Her family came to St. Louis when she was 10 years of age.

Grandpa Wasaff was a tall man, about six feet. He was a handsome gent who always sported a black mustache. Grandma Wasaff was short—barely five feet—and as round as she was tall. More than physical appearance, what I remember most about Grandma Wasaff was her cooking and her great personal warmth. She was a loving, loving lady. If several days went by without a visit from me, she would remark, "Honey, I haven't seen you in so long, I don't know how you look like!"

Mother was the eldest of seven children. She had one sister, Marie, and five brothers—Sam, Harry, Alex, Fred, and Amil. Most of the boys were fairly tall, just less than six feet, which is where I gained my height, I am sure. Although they were my uncles, Fred and Amil were only four or six years older than me and felt more like my big brothers.

Mother was a first-generation American, born in St. Louis, Missouri. When the family was quite young and much smaller (Mother, Harry, and Sam), Grandpa Wasaff took them to Lebanon, where they lived for almost three years. Mother went to school and learned to read and write Arabic. She remained fluent in the language all her life. Both my grandparents spoke English very well. However, they spoke a great deal of Arabic around me. And to this day I can speak it fairly well.

In St. Louis there was a notorious group of mobsters called the CooCoo Gang. This was a group of tough Irish, Lebanese, and Italian guys. Only Al Capone in Chicago rivaled their Mafia-type organization. Mom went to school with several of the Lebanese boys from that dreaded gang. She knew them quite well.

St. Louis always held a special place in Mother's heart. She remained a Cardinals' fan all her life. I, too, became a fan of the Cardinals when I was about five years old—there were no other choices in our household. Whenever Mother got to bragging about her hometown, we were always eager to remind her of her CooCoo Gang schoolmates.

At one time or another, all the Wasaff brothers worked for

Dad. Uncle Alex worked for the company in various capacities until his retirement. Sometimes there were misunderstandings and hard feelings. Uncle Sam also spent some time working for Dad but later opened a law practice in Texas. After many years of working for my father, Uncle Harry opened his own business, called Wasoff Pants Company. *Ripley's Believe It or Not* was so tickled with the name that they listed it in their book—a company that manufactured pants that "Was-off!"

Mother enjoyed traveling with Dad during the summer months. I stayed with my grandparents quite a bit while Mom and Dad were on the road. Those were wonderful summers for me. Grandma and Grandpa lived in a one-story brick house on West Broadway in Muskogee. The house sat on nearly an acre of land, and Grandma raised all kinds of vegetables in the backyard. I learned to swim at a place called Stem Beach. There was an airfield called Hatbox Field not too far from the house. Airplanes were just coming into vogue. Uncle Fred or Uncle Amil often took me out there to watch the airplanes take off and land.

Aunt Marie was a favorite relative. She loved the movies and always took me to an afternoon show whenever I visited my grandparents in Muskogee. A vivid memory: I was about six years old. Aunt Marie and I came out of the show and the Ku Klux Klan was marching in front of the movie theater. Clad in white robes, the men silently marched down the main street of town. I asked Marie who the men were and she explained, as best she could, about hate groups. She told me their targets were blacks, Jews, and Catholics. The unreality of seeing those men parading in hoods and robes with lighted torches scared me terribly. I never forgot that incident.

Raised within the precepts of the Catholic church, Mother remained a religious Catholic woman all her life. She never missed Mass and made sure we never missed either.

Both Mother and Dad taught us right from wrong. They taught us by example. They were good people, never gossipy or caustic.

I can hear her saying: "Don't laugh at a crippled person. Because if you do, God will punish you." She gave us other good advice: "When you are in an elevator and a lady enters, take off your hat... If you're riding in a crowded streetcar and you see a lady standing, always offer her your seat... Always say 'Yes, sir' and 'Yes, ma'am'... Respect your elders, teachers, and people in authority... When you shake hands with somebody, always shake the hand firmly and look them straight in the eye... If you can't say anything good about a person, don't say anything at all... Don't brag about yourself or something you accomplished." I never recall Mother saying anything bad about any person she ever met.

Some of my fondest childhood memories occurred in my mother's kitchen. Like her mother, Mom created some of the finest Lebanese cooking this side of the Mediterranean. She was a great cook of American dishes, too. Dad often relied on her ethnic culinary talents when he entertained customers. On many occasions, Mr. J.C. Penney, the founder of the J.C. Penney Stores, dined at our home and savored Mother's food. She loved to cook and took great joy entertaining family and friends. My sister Rosemary is also an excellent cook—skills she learned from Mother.

Throughout her adult life, Mother was active in many civic, religious and social organizations. She was the first president of the Syrian-American-Lebanese Educational Association (SALEA). She was also an active participant in the Dallas Symphony, Dallas Opera, Catholic Charities, St. Paul's Hospital, and the University of Notre Dame.

My sister Rosemary (Mother's namesake) recalls Mother's charitable work:

> Mother was always involved in charities—aiding people who needed help; buying paintings from struggling artists; helping support musicians and singers. Her greatest joys were her family and helping others. My Dad always referred to her as "Our Guiding Light"... and she was!

Music and art were both passions and talents possessed by Mother. She was one of the early backers of the Dallas Symphony Orchestra and the Dallas Opera. At home, she played piano and loved to sing.

¤ ¤ ¤

Mother was hospitalized for a colon lesion on October 10, 1965. She was in her late sixties at the time. I will always remember the day we took her to St. Paul's Hospital. When she was settled in her room, Mom said to us, "I'll never leave this hospital." We assured her that she would indeed recover. She had surgery for colon cancer on October 14. She withstood the operation; however, she had several complications when her kidneys failed to function following the surgery. Her doctors moved her to Parkland Hospital, where she underwent dialysis. The dialysis machine looked like an extremely large, industrial Maytag washing machine. (Today dialysis machines are small and portable.) The procedure failed, and her doctors held out no hope. Hanging to life by the slenderest of threads, she survived a full week until November 1, 1965—All Saints' Day. Mother truly was a saint. Maybe the good Lord was trying to tell us something by taking her on All Saints' Day.

In later years, I was asked to chair the Kidney Foundation of Texas, which I did in memory of Mother. Our objective was raising money to research more successful means of dialysis and treatment for kidney-related diseases.

¤ ¤ ¤

ED R. HAGGAR

I was born September 18, 1916, in Bristow, Oklahoma, and remained an only child for the next eight years. Dad used to tell the story that on the day I was born, he invested in some oil leases, which he later resold for a healthy profit. He always said I was a good omen and brought him good luck!

About six months after my birth, Dad was at the town square, where traders did their business. He saw a nice horse and buggy and wanted to buy them for my mother. Dad only had $50, and the asking price was $60. Being a good trader he bought the horse for $50 and took it home. The next morning he went out to feed it, and the horse was on its side having an epileptic seizure. Well, he took it right back to the square to get rid of it. He ran into a farmer who had a blind cow. They ended up striking a deal—Dad traded the horse and received $10. When he took the cow home he figured he had a great deal; a cow he would use to get milk for me. To make a long story short, the cow kept running into things, tearing up the yard, and Dad decided the cow had to go. He went back to the square to sell it. He sold it several times, but the next day the cow would be returned to him. He finally decided to charge $10 if he was going to get it returned each time. He sold the cow three different times; each time it was returned with a $10 handling charge. Finally, he sold it for $30 and got out of the cattle business. If you do the math, his original investment of $50 (horse and buggy) turned in a profit of $30, or a 60% return. He learned at an early age about negotiation, compassion, knowing the merchandise and the return on investment. The lesson he recited from his story was "never invest in something that eats while you are sleeping."

¤ ¤ ¤

JOSEPH MARION HAGGAR, JR.

All the love, respect, hopes, and aspirations that my parents shared were manifested in their family. I am the eldest child followed by my brother Joe and sister Rosemary.

Joe was born February 6, 1925. I was eight and a half years old when Joe arrived. It was a lot of fun having a new baby in the house. "Ed, watch the baby," Mother said many, many times after Joe and Rosemary were born. By age ten, I already had housemaid's knee from making beds, washing dishes, mopping, and sweeping the floors!

Dad liked to stay at the Pennsylvania Hotel whenever he went to New York City on business. The Pennsylvania had one of the biggest lobbies in the city. In 1928 Dad made a trip to New York and took Mom and Joe along. Joe came into the hotel carrying a rubber ball. At one point he threw that ball clear across the lobby. The hotel manager was present at that exact moment and assured Mother and Dad that Joe had set some sort of notable record. This became a favorite story in our family.

As he grew up to the fourth and fifth grades, Joe was more studious and more serious than I was at that age. He was an excellent student all through his school years. Joe was a doer. He woke early every morning (and still does) and tended to any task at hand. Mother always called Joe "my little industrious man."

Joe recalls those early years:

As a youngster, about thirteen years old, I remember working in the Santa Fe Building. One of my first jobs was working in the thread room. That job entailed keeping the ladies on the sewing lines supplied with thread, buttons, zippers, etc. One of the ladies decided to test my knowledge one day and asked me to bring her a box of buttonholes. Earlier, I had befriended the woman that operated the buttonhole machine. So, I asked my friend to make up a whole bunch of buttonholes, which I then stuffed in a box and delivered to the lady on the sewing line. She was surprised and amused when I delivered the box of buttonholes.

Joe excelled in all sports. After several lessons at the Lakewood Country Club, he became an excellent golfer by the time he was fourteen. Joe always had lots of friends and lots of fun.

But don't get the impression that Joe was all work and no play. In high school Joe was the star football player at St. Joseph's Academy. During the last game of the season of Joe's senior year, he suffered a major concussion and our family doctor forbade him from playing any college football. That was the end of Joe's football career.

Dad was delighted when Joe developed both an interest and skill in hunting. Here are some of his recollections about hunting with Dad:

When I was about fourteen years old, Dad, along with two of our sales associates, Jake Henson and Archie Fowler, went quail hunting in West Texas. As the only child on the expedition, I was the guy doing all the work. But I did get to do a lot of shooting as well. We ran into more quail than I had ever seen. In fact, we shot so many quail that we were over our limit. Afraid of being caught, we discussed what to do with our extra cache. Somebody in the group finally came up with the idea of putting the quail in a large milk can filled with ice. Being the youngest and most inexperienced in the group, I volunteered to put the milk can on the Dallas-bound train. Before boarding the train, I called Mother and she made arrangements to have someone meet me at Union Station in downtown Dallas. I got on the train, found an out-of-the way compartment and placed the milk can there. "If anyone asks about the milk-can, just tell them it will come off the train in Dallas," I told the porter. The train arrived in Dallas on schedule, and I got off the train carrying the milk can. For years afterward, I always liked to remind Dad, Jake and Archie that they owed me a lot of money... because I saved them from getting a steep fine for overshooting their limits.

The next story occurred many years later, but while we're on the subject of hunting...

Johnny Horany, a customer from Olney, Texas, arranged a quail hunt for Dad, my son, Joe III, and my nephew, Jimmy Haggar, and myself. We hunted all morning and never saw a single bird. Driving back to Olney, we passed the Buckalew Ranch. "That looks like a good ranch for hunting quail," Dad remarked. Back in Olney, Johnny Horany told Dad that the Buckalews didn't allow any hunting on their ranch... and that Mr. Buckalew was a pretty tough guy. "They can't shoot us," I told Johnny. We drove back out and I rang the doorbell at the ranch house. "We're three generations of the Haggar family. We spent the entire morning out in the countryside and didn't see a single quail. My dad spotted your ranch and thought it would be a good place to teach the boys about quail hunting," I told Mrs. Buckalew. She agreed to let us hunt on one part of the ranch. We had a great hunt.

At the end of the afternoon, we stopped back at the ranch house. I thanked the Buckalews, Joanne and Don, and told them how much the boys enjoyed the experience. "Where are you hunting tomorrow?" asked Don. He invited us back the next day, all three generations, and set us up at a premium spot on the ranch. I thought I had died and gone to heaven... This goes back thirty-five years, and we've been good friends and enjoyed many fun hunts together since then.

¤ ¤ ¤

Our country was in the throes of World War II when Joe, Jr., graduated from Notre Dame. He was in a special unit called the V-12 Program, where he studied aeronautical engineering and graduated with the rank of ensign. For the remainder of the war Joe served as a catapult officer aboard the aircraft carrier USS *Sicily* in the Pacific.

Joe married a beautiful Lebanese girl from Gulfport, Mississippi, named Isabell Salloum. They have three children: Lydia, Joe III and Marion. Following in our footsteps, Joe III worked all around the plant. Lydia graduated from St. Mary's and is a housewife, married to Dan Novakov, a partner in the law firm of Novakov and Davis. She is very active in Dallas civic affairs. Marion is happily married to George Bryan, president of Southwest Business Graphics & Forms. She has three children and still finds time to work at the company part-time.

Joe's pride in his own family is evident:

> When we were raising our children, we always attempted to participate in everything they did, including plays, athletic events, recitals, etc. I can always remember spending Sunday afternoons at Fair Park in Dallas, where the girls' basketball games were played. As a result, there was never any hesitation when they had any problems to come and talk to us and ask us certain things. Our children were always supportive of everything that either Isabell or I did. As an example, when I was chairman of the 1967 bond program, which was the largest bond program in the State of Texas, the children were very supportive and wanted to help in every way they could, because they were proud of the fact that I was involved in the campaign.
>
> The bond drive was extremely successful. We won all thirteen of the issues in the election. One issue was the creation of the Dallas/Fort Worth Airport that became a tremendous engine for economic growth in the North Texas area, creating thousands of jobs and many new businesses.
>
> After the successful conclusion of the 1967 bond drive, I was approached by many people and asked to run for City Council, with the thought of eventually running for mayor of Dallas. At the time, I was just beginning to accomplish a lot of things at the business and declined. However, in the late 1970s I decided to run for City Council. I agreed to run under two conditions: 1. If Morris Hite, a close personal friend and president of Tracy-Locke Advertising Agency, would be my campaign

manager and 2. Dolores Campbell, my great secretary, agreed to stay with me during my years on the Council. I served two terms; one under the leadership of Bob Folsom and the other under the leadership of Jack Evans, two longtime friends.

Fortunately, all three of our children grew up to be responsible citizens who understood to get something out of life, you have to put something into it. They also understood the importance of community service and helping people who needed help or could not help themselves. We are very proud of what they have done, and what they continue to do.

Both Ed and Rosemary's families were also blessed with good children. None of our children were ever in any serious trouble.

Joe first traveled to Lebanon as a member of the "Task Force for the Rebuilding of Lebanon." On that particular trip he visited Dad's birthplace in Jezzeen. To celebrate his fiftieth wedding anniversary, in 1998, Joe took his entire family — his wife, Isabell, their children and grandchildren — to Lebanon.

That visit remains fresh and vivid in Joe's mind:

Special arrangements were made to travel to Jezzeen. I met with a member of the Parliament and chairman of the Finance Committee, Mr. Samir Azar. He was kind enough to invite me to a luncheon at his home, where we met some of Dad's relatives. There was a young man present whose name was the same as mine: Yousef Maroun Hajjar (the Arabic spelling).

We visited Dad's birthplace. Dad always told us that he was born in a cave. Actually, it was a stone structure that was built up against the side of a mountain. It wasn't exactly a cave, but it wasn't much more improved than such. It had a dirt floor. The roof had come off the house. I decided to put the house back in good repair and it is now being lived in by some of our relatives.

After seeing Dad's home, we were taken to the church, "Notre Dame d'Liban," which is French for Our Lady of Lebanon. I found it very interesting that J.M. had no formal education, yet he received an honorary doctorate degree from the University of Notre Dame. Perhaps it was more than a coincidence that Dad was baptized in a church dedicated to Notre Dame, Our Lady.

ROSEMARY HAGGAR VAUGHAN

Rosemary was born December 18, 1926: A beautiful baby girl came into our lives. Graceful and agile, Rosemary was a great dancer. She and Joe used to entertain family and friends by dancing tangos and other popular dances. Mother always called Rosemary her "Little Hunsie."

Rosemary's grammar school education began at the Ursuline Academy. She attended St. Mary's, the sister school of Notre Dame, in South Bend and attended Southern Methodist University.

Rosemary recalls some special incidents from her early childhood:

> My youth was so happy and fun-filled. I remember Dad coming home at night and wrestling with Joe and me. I also remember "Fig men" (little men made out of dried figs) and yard-long chocolates that Mama brought home from the Hotel New Yorker when she traveled with Dad.
>
> Dad had a cousin living in Brooklyn, New York. Mama used to call him "Om" (Uncle in Arabic). He was in the knitting business. When I was a little girl, Mother, Dad, and I traveled to New York. We took the subway over to Brooklyn and visited with Om, who was quite a bit older than Dad. On that visit, I remember Om telling Mother that he had a sister living in Mexico City. In 1945, at age seventeen, Mother and I traveled to Mexico City during the summer months. Mother had a letter of credit from the First National Bank. Needing some extra cash, she took the letter of credit to a bank nearby our hotel. The woman in the teller's cage took Mother's letter to show to one of the bank officers. "The president of the bank would like to see you," she told Mother. We were introduced to the bank president and the first words he said were, "My mother was a Hajjar." His family owned several banks, cotton mills, and a number of other businesses throughout Mexico City and its environs. At that time there were a number of very wealthy Lebanese in Mexico City, and they were very, very prominent in business circles.
>
> In the early fall of 1944, I accompanied Dad to a men's wear convention (now known as M.A.G.I.C.) in Palm Springs,

California. We had a lovely suite with a great patio, where we enjoyed breakfast every morning, at Charlie Farrell's Racquet Club. On this particular morning, Dad stared and stared at me and finally said, "Rosemary, it looks like you want something." In my own mind I thought, "This is just as good a time as any to tell Dad that I'm smoking." And I told him that I wanted a cigarette. I really started smoking two years earlier, while in high school, but never told anyone except my close girlfriend, Fran McCleod, from Lakewood Boulevard, who shared this vice with me. Dad asked me what brand, and I said, "Pall Mall." (I didn't want to say Dad's brand, because it was too strong.) Dad called room service and had a pack of Pall Malls delivered to our suite. I didn't know what kind of reaction Dad would have, but he handled it quite well... believe it or not! His only comment was, "Is this what I sent you to St. Mary's for... to learn to smoke?"

After attending SMU, Rosemary married Eddie Vaughan, who was originally from Kentucky. Rosemary and Eddie had five children: Mary Lynn, Eddie Jr., Martha (Marty), Vicki, and Jimmy.

When my children were grown and settled, Dad and my brothers asked me to serve as executive director of the Haggar Foundation. I had done tons of charity and civic work since the age of fourteen, but this was the first time I really worked outside my home.

My daughter Marty at one time was the executive director of the Foundation. She has three wonderful sons, Graham—14, Robert—12, and Sydney—9. Marty attended the University of Houston and graduated in Dallas from the Northwood Institute. Ed, my oldest, is running an investment business and doing a great job. Eddie received his undergraduate and an M.B.A from SMU. Mary Lynn attended St. Mary's for one year and then finished her college education at SMU. She runs a remodeling business and really does a "man's job"—all her employees are male. Vicki, who also attended St. Mary's for a year and graduated from SMU, owns a children's shop called "Goodnight Moon," and her children (Mathew—6, and

Rosemary—4) are great models. Jim is in the cattle business and has a ranch in South Texas. His first year in rodeo, 1996, Jim was named "Rookie of the Year" for calf roping. Before returning to the ranch, Jimmy worked as a Haggar marketing associate for a couple of years on the West Coast. Both boys are still single. The married names of the girls are: Mary Lynn Vaughan De Ore, Martha Ann Rumble, and Vicki Vaughan Miller.

CHAPTER 2
My Early Years

I was born September 18, 1916, in Bristow, Oklahoma. What was happening in the world at that time?

The Measurement of Intelligence (1916) by Stanford University psychologist Lewis Madison Terman introduced the term I.Q. (intelligence quotient) and presented the first tests for measuring intelligence. A mechanical home refrigerator was marketed for the first time in the United States. Pancho Villa raided Columbus, New Mexico, March 9, and killed nine Americans. A U.S. punitive expedition was moved to Mexico March 15 under the command of Gen. John J. Pershing. Pershing had orders to "capture Villa dead or alive!" (Some of Dad's relatives living in Mexico were almost killed by Villa's men.) Albert Einstein introduced his Theory of Relativity that revolutionized the science of physics in 1916.

After their marriage, Dad moved the family to St. Louis. We lived on the second floor of a two-story duplex. As a toddler, I kept myself busy by banging whatever pots and pans Mother had in her kitchen. A German man downstairs complained every day: "That boy yust keep yumpin, yumpin, yumpin." I continued to "yump" there until 1921, when we moved to Dallas.

"The New York of the South" was the way many people described Dallas. It was a very cosmopolitan city and has remained so. I remember watching the first skyscraper—the Magnolia Building—being built downtown. Thirty-two stories... it seemed awesome. The Adolphus and the Baker were the two finest hotels in Dallas. They were located catty-corner from each other. There was a public streetcar system that connected the downtown area with the residential areas.

¤ ¤ ¤

The year 1921 found the Haggar family living in an apartment on Forest Avenue, near Colonial. We lived in another apartment at the corner of Leonard & Ross in 1922. The year 1923 found us in still another apartment on State Street, and in 1924 we were at 207½ Fitzhugh.

Dad scheduled a business trip to St. Louis in 1921. I was about five at the time. Besides Mother and myself, we took along one of Dad's customers, Joe Shadid from Paducah, Texas. We were driving on the road through Missouri when Joe spotted an apple orchard. Dad pulled off the road, and he and Joe grabbed as many apples as they could handle. "God will punish you for stealing apples!" Mother warned them.

Well, sure enough, the car broke down outside of a little town called Otterville, Missouri. We stayed at a little boardinghouse, the only one in town, for a few days while we waited for a part to be delivered from Springfield. The owner took us in. "One dollar for you and your wife," he said, "and we will throw in the little boy." We wandered through town, Dad spoke with some of the neighbors, and we became known as "The Folks."

Dad traveled throughout Texas, Oklahoma, and New Mexico when he worked for the D.M. Oberman Company. At the time he was driving an old Ford Model-T. We got stuck in the sand in a small town called Muleshoe, Texas. A filling station, small general store, and a post office were the only buildings standing on the dirt road intersection at the center of town. Not able to budge the Model-T out of the sand, Dad walked three or four miles down a dusty road looking for help. Mother and I waited in the car. He returned a few hours later, unable to find assistance. Daylight was beginning to fade and we slept in the car that night. About 3:00 in the morning Dad was awakened by voices right outside the vehicle. He opened his eyes and two men were staring directly at him.

At first Dad was frightened; he thought these men were going to rob us. But the men introduced themselves as ranchers from a well-known and respected West Texas family, the Waggoners. By this time I was wide awake. Looking out the car window, we saw a big Cadillac parked by our car. Later, Dad said, "That was the biggest Cadillac I have ever seen!" Using a strong rope, they pulled us out of the sand and we were on our way.

Nogales, Arizona, on the U.S.–Mexico border, was a destination for Mother and me in 1922. We visited with Dad's first cousin, Solomon Saba, and his family. Solomon had a successful dry-goods business. The family lived in a big home. Being a border town, it seemed that everyone was bilingual. After four weeks in Nogales, I really picked up a lot of Spanish.

In 1923 Mother and I traveled by train to visit with my maternal great-grandmother in St. Louis. When it was time to leave, my grandmother packed what seemed like a never-ending feast for us to enjoy on the long return trip to Dallas.

Both of my parents were religious people, and so it was important to have a church and school nearby. I made my first Holy Communion in 1923 and was confirmed in 1926 at the Sacred Heart Cathedral. Joe and Rosemary also made their Holy Communions at Sacred Heart.

In those days we learned to serve Mass early. I became an altar boy in the second grade and learned the prayers and duties of Server, then Vestment Carrier for the Bishop, and finally top Acolyte. Being an Acolyte was the highest honor one could attain—it was my duty to assist the Bishop with his Crosier and Miter. Major Marsh, Charlie Manicchi, and George Linskie were three friends who shared these responsibilities with me. We remained friends throughout our lives. Serving Mass required us to memorize many, many prayers in Latin. I served Mass once a week. Wedding and Funeral Masses (my personal favorites) often awarded the Server a nice tip—sometimes as much as $5. Joe later became an altar boy in the same church.

My education began in 1923 at the Sacred Heart School, located at Ross and Pearl streets. The Sacred Heart Cathedral was a beautiful red brick structure. The school stood immediately behind the church and was housed in a building that constituted one and a half stories. The basement level was partially subterranean and housed the school cafeteria. Eight classrooms, a library, and principal's office occupied the top floor.

On a warm, autumn afternoon in 1923, during the first grade, our teacher asked one of the boys to open the classroom windows. I was one of three or four boys who stood on the windowsill and leaned against the heavy window. I lost my balance — or was accidentally pushed — lunged forward and fell out the window, down one and a half stories, and broke my fall at the bottom of a concrete staircase. The fall broke my arm and leg and fractured my skull.

Mother was walking to the corner to meet me when she heard a siren. She had a premonition that something happened to me and hastened her pace to the schoolyard, where she found me lying on the concrete. I was laid up for several weeks, but was still promoted to the second grade. Two significant events resulted from this catastrophe: first, heavy iron screens were installed on all the windows. Second, because of the skull fracture, I was not allowed to play any contact sports for a number of years.

In the second grade the family moved to 207½ North Fitzhugh Street and I transferred to St. Edward's. Mother was never happy about the school or the parish at St. Edward's. Father O'Grady, the pastor, had one of the thickest Irish brogues this side of the Atlantic. The subject matter of his sermons was always questionable. He usually began with an elevating topic such as the Blessed Mother and ended up instructing the congregation on how to bake the best devil's food cake. Such silliness was too much for Mother. We moved to a home at 2316 Garrett Avenue so that I could return to Sacred Heart. It was a red-orange brick veneer house with three bedrooms, dining room, living room, and two baths.

That same year, 1927, Dad brought his mother over from the Old Country. We called her "Sitte," which is Lebanese for "Grandmother." Sitte lived with us for a year or so before she died. She was quite senile. I remember Mother had to hide candy — Sitte's only uncontrollable vice. She spoke very little English, but I remember her gentle, sweet manner.

I remember only two of my father's siblings, a sister, Barbara, and Dad's only brother, Nick. I never met Dad's two sisters who lived in Mexico, but I did know two of their sons, Antonio and Baltazar, who visited with us in Dallas on several occasions.

After moving to Garrett Avenue, I rode the streetcar to Sacred Heart every day. Remembering Mother's orders to give my seat to any woman who might be standing, I rose and offered my seat to a woman passenger who was hugging a pole in the center aisle. Acknowledging my politeness, she started up a conversation by asking where I went to school.

"Sacred Heart. It's a Catholic school," I replied.

Well, this woman looked at me as if I had horns! Back in those days there weren't too many Catholics in Dallas.

The schoolyard at Sacred Heart was simply a wide-open graveled surface. During recess we usually played soccer. In the fourth grade, I remember getting badly shinned by a sixth-grader. My leg swelled up like a pumpkin; Mother put cold, raw beefsteaks on the injury to reduce the swelling.

Sacred Heart had a baseball team that played against other Catholic grammar schools in Dallas. One afternoon we played Holy Trinity (the very richest parish at the time). The pinstriped uniforms worn by our opponents awed all the boys on our team. We looked like "Raggedy Andies" in our mismatched knickers and shirts. Huddled in a group after the game, I was elected by my teammates to speak to the pastor about getting uniforms. At that time, Monsignor Diamond was the pastor of Sacred Heart and principal of the school. Monsignor was a very fine man but much feared by students and parishioners because he looked tough and talked tough. "I don't want to see any coppers!" were his instructions to the congregation before beginning the collection.

Anyway, my knees were shaking when I asked him for baseball uniforms, but I learned that his bark was worse than his bite. Monsignor listened patiently to my plea and said, "If Holy Trinity has uniforms, we'll have them too!"

One day during the fourth grade I got into trouble by participating in a food fight in the cafeteria. The perpetrators were gathered together in the principal's office and scolded, then dismissed for the day. Instead of going home, we all walked downtown and went to the movies. I arrived home at the usual time, thinking that Mother wouldn't know about my dismissal. However, she had received a phone call from the principal right after we left school. Dad was on the road at the time, so it was up to Mother to discipline me. We sat together and talked about what I had done and why it was wrong. I promised her no more trouble and kept my word. In turn, she promised not to tell my father, a strict disciplinarian, and kept her word.

The first historic event of great significance that I remember occurred on May 21, 1927. Garrett Park was four blocks from the house. The park had a public swimming pool, which I frequented along with my buddies. The school year had just ended and I remember walking home from the park on that sunny afternoon in May. Within a matter of seconds the streets were suddenly filled with newsboys hawking the headlines at the top of their voices: "Extra, extra... Read all about it! Charles Lindbergh crosses the Atlantic and lands in Paris!" LINDBERGH LANDS IN PARIS... those four words filled the entire front page.

Also in 1927, Dad bought a Peerless Touring Car, which was one of the premier automobiles of the day. The top came off, and in inclement weather there were removable isinglass curtains (a sort of fiberglass-like material made from mica) that hung where our conventional car windows are now placed.

I first listened to the world around me on one of the earliest manufactured commercial radios. Later on I built a crystal set, which was a primitive contraption made with a piece of quartz, some copper wire, earphones, and a wire called a "cat's whisker." The copper wire was tightly wrapped around a round cardboard Quaker Oatmeal box. When the wire touched the crystal, various radio stations could be heard through headphones. Eventually, Dad bought a Philco radio that was placed in the living room. Mother loved the musical programs. I loved the comedies like "Amos and Andy" and "Fibber McGee and Molly." After dinner Mother turned on the radio, and our evening's entertainment began with, "Good evening, Mr. and Mrs. America, and all the ships at sea, this is your New York correspondent Walter Winchell..."

Movies were also a major entertainment. In the summer months silent movies were shown outdoors at Garrett Park. Many of the movies were westerns featuring the greatest cowboy star of them all, Tom Mix. There was an area downtown on Elm Street where all the movie theaters were located. Starting on the west side there was the Queen Theater, the Old Mill, the Capital, the Palace Theater, the Melba, and the Majestic. The

Majestic was built on three levels: orchestra, balcony, and upper balcony. The top balcony was always an afternoon hangout for kids. The Majestic also hosted some of the country's top vaudeville stars, like Will Rogers. I remember the slapstick comedians, dancers, and magicians—all vaudeville troupers.

Quiet moments were spent with some favorite books. I read the *Hardy Boys* series, the *Tom Swift* books, and almost everything written by Mark Twain. I kept up with sports and the news through the Dallas newspapers and local radio stations.

Lawson Long lived across the street from us on Garrett Avenue. We were both the same age and good friends. One summer when I was twelve years old, we became the neighborhood entrepreneurs and opened a soda pop stand. A case of Coca-Cola (containing twenty-four bottles) cost us seventy-two cents. We sold each bottle for a nickel apiece and made two cents profit on each. I stood on that corner and shouted, "Ice Cold Soda Water. Curls your hair and freezes your teeth! Makes you feel like a millionaire." One of our best customers that summer was a yardman, who stopped by at least once a day. Standing over six feet tall, but looking even more awesome in his overalls, he used to say, "I want it colder than ice, or colder... and not hotter than piss, or hotter."

By 1928 the business was much healthier and our family was growing. Dad bought a house at 6712 Lakewood Boulevard. At that time there were two prime residential areas in Dallas and two fine country clubs. Lakewood drew its membership from the Lakewood–Swiss Avenue area. The Dallas Country Club drew most of its membership from Highland Park. Our family had a membership at the Lakewood Country Club, which was very near our home.

In 1928 I accompanied Dad on a business trip to New York. I was twelve at the time. We traveled by train to Chicago and then to Detroit, where we visited with Aunt Barbara. We took an overnight boat trip across Lake Erie and visited Niagara Falls. In Buffalo we boarded the "Twentieth Century Limited" and rode the rails to Manhattan. Dad took me to see the Woolworth Building, which was the tallest building in the world at that time, and Coney Island.

After we moved to Lakewood Boulevard, I played a game

called "Association" with some of my buddies from the neighborhood. This game is very similar to the current game "Pass, Run and Punt." There was no physical contact. Two of the kids I played with became great football players. Davey O'Brien became the star quarterback for TCU and later won the Heisman Trophy. Raymond "Tessy" Keeling, a big and clumsy kid, became a star player (tackle) at the University of Texas (1935–1937).

The first family vacation I remember was in the summer of 1930. Mother, Joe, Rosemary, and I traveled by rail to Manitou Springs, Colorado, a resort outside of Colorado Springs. Dad rented a small cottage for us near the Cave of the Winds. I have two vivid memories from that sojourn. There was a boy my age living in the next cottage, and we struck up an immediate friendship. Shortly thereafter, Mother found out that this boy had tuberculosis, which was highly contagious. There were no vaccines or cures in those days. For the rest of the vacation and even after we returned to Dallas, Mother was highly fearful that we were at risk of being stricken with TB. My second memory of that vacation is much more pleasant. We took in all the local sights—the Cave of the Winds and the cave dwellings of the ancient peoples of that land. In 1930 the United States manufactured three luxury touring cars: Cadillac, Packard, and Pierce Arrow. Mother hired a driver who took us to the top of Pike's Peak in a brand new Pierce Arrow. It was a magnificent ride. There was a marker indicating the elevation—14,109 feet. I still remember that number to this day. We descended the mountain on a cog-train. That was a wonderful experience I will always treasure.

The Dallas University and Academy, located in Oak Lawn, was a very impressive and imposing two-year college preparatory school. The school was founded and operated by the Vincentian Fathers. Classrooms were housed in a beautiful red brick building on the upper part of the campus looking down onto Turtle Creek Boulevard. On the lower level were several playing fields and a track course. Each year the Dallas Academy hosted a citywide track meet for the Catholic grammar schools. I participated in the 100-yard dash and the high jump events.

After graduation from Sacred Heart in 1930, I looked forward to attending high school at the Dallas Academy. However, the Dallas Academy was one of the first victims of the Great Depression and closed its doors in 1929, before my freshman year ever started.

Instead, my parents sent me, and later my brother Joe, to St. Joseph's Academy. I began my schooling at St. Joe's in 1930 and graduated in 1934. Prior to the closing of the Dallas Academy, St. Joe's had been a grammar school, with a girls-only high school. However, with no other Catholic high school in town, St. Joseph's expanded their facilities and faculty. The school was run by the Sisters of Divine Providence, which was headquartered in San Antonio. It was really a makeshift school for about 150 students—75 boys and 75 girls. The school was located almost downtown on the corner of Swiss and Texas avenues. The old Southern Pacific Railroad yards were located right behind the school. St. Joseph's did not have the best academic reputation in town. However, during the depression, good grades and the ability to pay college tuition were all the requirements needed for almost any college in the country.

Had we attended the Dallas Academy, we would have been quartered in one of the finest residential areas in the city. The same cannot be said of St. Joseph's. Several black bawdy houses were tucked between the railroad yards and the campus, and we were often hustled on our way home from school.

Two years of a foreign language were required in school. We were offered our choice of French, Latin, German or Spanish. I was in a quandary about which language to study. Neither of my parents had much formal schooling in this country. Being practical, Dad suggested that I take Spanish. In hindsight, I regret not studying Latin, the origin of so many other languages and the language of the church. However, I did learn some Latin through osmosis. Being short of classroom space, study halls were conducted in the back of the classroom while lessons were being taught in the front. I can still remember Sister Sacred Heart as she stood in front of the class and drilled her students on the conjugation of the Latin verb "to be": *eram, eras, eret.* I followed along, ignoring my math and science homework. Later on, I suggested to Joe that he study Latin, which he did for four years.

Because of my head injury in the first grade, I was not allowed to play any contact sports. Finally, in my junior year

(1933) the doctors told my parents it was okay and I went out for football at St. Joseph's. We played with second-hand equipment and were coached by Father Zachary, who taught Bible History. He was a wonderful man but did not know very much about football or coaching. Our school did not have enough boys to field a team and reserves, so we brought in some ringers. What are ringers? We recruited boys from the public high schools who weren't eligible to play on their teams because of failing grades. The star kicker of the team was a young man in his twenties named Cooter, who worked for the Dallas Fire Department. He was the first place kicker I ever saw who kicked shoeless. We gathered for practice after school and really learned the game and planned our strategies among ourselves while Father Zachary sat on the bench and studied the Bible.

Playing with ringers was not illegal on our part because we were not in any type of organized league in the city. We played the second-string teams from the top high schools in Dallas. Some of our games were played against teams from small neighboring towns, such as Richardson, Mesquite, Plano, Farmers Branch, DeSoto, and Wiley. Ira "Snag" Shepherd, from Forrest Avenue High School, coached our team during my senior year. He was an excellent coach, and I learned a lot about the game.

Not the most knowledgeable football coach, Father Zachary had the reputation of being a good handball player. I used to play at the YMCA and thought of myself as a pretty good player. One time I challenged the padre to a friendly game. Living up to his excellent reputation in this game, he turned me every way but loose!

In the mid-1930s Southern Methodist University was the largest and most prestigious institution of higher education in the area. The school had a fine football team and competed with all the major colleges and universities throughout the country. Football coach Ray Morrison led his team to many victories. Known for their great passing, the team was called the "SMU Aerial Circus."

¤ ¤ ¤

Being the oldest child, I was the first of the second-generation Haggars to work alongside my father in the plant. Starting in my early teens, it seemed I worked from one end of the plant to the other. Zipper flies were not commonly used until the mid-1930s. Buttons were used prior to zippers. Using a red grease pencil, my first job at the plant was marking the fabric where the buttons were to be placed. In addition to being a button marker, I was a bundle boy and later worked spreading cloth for the cutters.

Men's pants are constructed from four parts: two backs and two fronts. After the pants were cut, they were put into bundles of thirty to forty pairs or more. The individual pants within the bundles were marked by size and numbered accordingly. An operator received one bundle at a time. After her part of the process was completed, she passed the bundle to the next operator for finishing work. Dad employed several men who moved the bundles from one operator to another. I was one of the youngest bundle movers.

I spent the summer of 1932 between the pressing and shipping departments. Two very colorful Lebanese fellows named Bill Razook and Meled Joseph were my cohorts that summer. Bill was born in the United States, a first-generation American. Meled Joseph came over from the Old Country and settled in Dallas. A friend sent him to my father for employment. "Mr. Hajjar (Arabic pronunciation) will give you a job, go see him." And Meled got a job as a presser. Bill became Meled's unofficial custodian at the plant. There were some pretty tough fellows in the pressing department, and Meled picked up some pretty interesting colloquialisms from these guys.

One morning a truck driver pulled into the loading area. He got out of his truck and said, "Good morning." Meled smiled and replied, "You cott-damn son of a bitch." Whereupon the driver jumped on Meled. Fortunately, there were other men in the department who averted a fight between the two men. Apparently, Meled thought the phrase "Good morning" was a particularly nasty insult! Another time, Meled got into an argument with some of the fellows. He shouted: "You think my money is like cabbage leaves." One day Bill nearly slammed Meled's hand in his car door. "You cott-damn Dego, you almost bruke my hand!" screamed Meled. To which Bill replied, "You call me 'Dego,' what kind you?"

The men in the pressing department were paid by the number of finished pieces they handled, rather than an hourly wage. I sized the pants and stacked them at the end of the line. Bill and Meled worked ahead of me on the pressing line. It seemed like Bill and Meled went into overdrive during the summer months. The hotter the day, the faster they worked. But there was a method to their madness. When all the jobs were finished, we left the plant together and went skinny-dipping in the old gravel pits in West Dallas. Dad caught me and Meled and some of the other pressers shooting craps one day in the piece goods department. Dad had the ability to verbally scare the hell out of anyone not doing their jobs, including me!

During the depression years a lot of the migrant workers started picking cotton in South Texas and then did farm work all the way up to Oklahoma and Kansas. The merchants in these areas ordered their products to coincide with the travels of these migrant workers. To avoid cancellations, the shipping department worked until 10:00 at night, to be sure that all our orders were filled on time. Dad paid extra money to his people and furnished dinner when they worked over forty hours. We used to eat at a place called the Young Street Café, which was right next door to the Santa Fe Building. A Greek man by the name of Gus Alexander operated the café. People sat at a U-shaped counter and Gus stood in the middle, hashing out the orders. He called all the waitresses "Suzy." Throughout dinner, Gus's voice rang out, "Step on it, Suzy."

Dad taught me to drive when I was fifteen. On the way to work, he slid over to the passenger seat and let me drive the car. On my sixteenth birthday he bought me a new Chevrolet coupe. Many responsibilities came with the car. Dad was out on the road selling the product and building the business. Mother didn't drive. Just about the time I got the car, Joe and Rosemary were in the first and second grades. So my day included taking them to school, picking them up after school, and depositing them at their various music and dance lessons, etc. Every time I left the house and walked toward the car, Joe and Rosemary were always just a few paces behind me. This became a real problem, especially when I had a date. Rosemary never quite understood why she couldn't ride along! I was also the designated chauffeur on family vacations.

Mother, Joe, Rosemary, and I vacationed in the northeast during the first part of summer in 1933. I was sixteen, Joe was eight, and Rosemary, six. I did all the driving on that long haul. We went to the World's Fair in Chicago, Aunt Barbara's house in Michigan, Niagara Falls, Old Orchard Beach in Maine, and then down the Atlantic Coast to Boston and New York City. All along the road we saw billboards reminding us of the Great Depression—the blue eagle, a symbol of the National Recovery Act.

The J.C. Penney department store chain, headquartered in New York City at 34th Street and 8th Avenue, was Dad's largest and most valued customer in those days. A gentleman by the name of E.E. Cummings was the buyer of men's pants for all their stores across the country. "When you get to New York, I want you to visit Mr. Cummings in his office," Dad instructed me. "Be pleasant and be polite!" Dressed in a cream-colored linen suit, white shirt, and tie, I introduced myself to Mr. Cummings. He asked the usual questions about school and summer jobs. Then he asked me about my future plans. "One of these days, I hope to be back in New York working with both you and Dad." Mr. Cummings called Dad in Dallas after I left and told him how impressed he was with me. After that visit, I think Dad had me tagged as a marketing man.

Dad's dear friends and family physicians, Dr. Hill and Dr. Samuel, were treating Dad for ulcers in 1933. Dad plowed along in business despite the doctor's warnings of serious complications. Eventually the ulcers overpowered his ability to work. Doctors Hill and Samuel hospitalized Dad for about three weeks.

When Dad was on his feet again, the doctors ordered, "Take a month's vacation... get away from the business!" To show his gratitude for their concern and good advice, Dad gifted some shares of Haggar stock to Hill and Samuel, the first non-family members to own stock in the company.

After Dad's hospitalization, I drove the family (in Dad's Buick sedan) from Dallas to Colorado Springs; Cheyenne, Wyoming; Yellowstone Park; Salt Lake City; all the way up to Seattle, Washington; Vancouver, British Columbia; then down the coast through Portland, Oregon; and on to San Francisco and Los Angeles, California. The Kappa Gamma sorority was holding their national convention in the campgrounds at Yellowstone when we arrived. Hundreds of beautiful college coeds greatly enhanced the natural beauty of the park. Although only a high school junior, I looked old enough to be a collegian, which enabled me to have a few good times with some of the girls.

The San Francisco longshoremen went on strike just before we arrived. In sympathy, every union joined the longshoremen for a general strike that crippled the entire city. It was impossible to get any kind of service at all. I remember we stayed at the famous Fairmont Hotel. The elevator operator's union was on strike, and we had to walk up and down six flights of stairs to our rooms. Bellboys, waiters, and taxi drivers... the city was at an absolute standstill.

Dad rented a cottage in Beverly Hills for a week. It was a welcome retreat after our struggles in San Francisco. A few days later Dad returned to Dallas on a Ford Tri-Motor plane. These were the earliest days of commercial aviation. We drove him to the airport in Pasadena and watched him board the twenty-passenger plane. Dad was thrilled with the whole process. Instead of a forty-hour drive, Dad returned to Dallas in just ten hours! I drove Mother, Joe, and Rosemary back to Dallas.

¤ ¤ ¤

Joe Stevens, one of my best friends and a neighbor at that time, attended Woodrow Wilson High School, part of the public school system of Dallas. I was not a student at Woodrow Wilson and therefore not really eligible for the Woodrow Wilson High Y (which was affiliated with the YMCA). Joe was president of the High Y, and since we were best friends, he decided I should become a member, which I did. To this day, I have never set foot in Woodrow Wilson High School. Several years ago, when Woodrow Wilson had their fiftieth reunion party, several people asked why I didn't attend! My answer, "I didn't know about the reunion! If I did, I would have attended!" Later, Joe and I attended a High Y convention in Austin and were infatuated with the city and the University of Texas. We both decided that was the school for us.

Besides Joe Stevens, my high school buddies were Trammel

Crow, James K. Wilson, Louis and Tommy Maher, Philip Schnitzius, C.D. Danna (his actual name was Cosmos Damien, having been named after two prominent Italian saints), Lucille Love, Bill and Oscar Lalla, Jack Lalier, and Roberta Palms.

Trammel Crow is one of the preeminent real estate developers in Dallas and throughout the country. As kids we ran around together on the east side of Dallas. Trammel came from a poor family and was not in a high school fraternity at Woodrow Wilson High School. However, we took great delight in crashing a great many fraternity and sorority parties. After our high school years, we used to sail together on White Rock Lake. We are still the closest of friends, both in our mid-eighties.

In the spring of 1934, St. Edward's Academy[3] in Austin sent Father O'Donnell (who later became president of Notre Dame) and Father Boland (who later became the prefect of discipline at Notre Dame) to Dallas to recruit students for their school. I was invited by both these distinguished gentlemen to attend St. Edward's after my graduation from St. Joseph's. During my football days at St. Joe's, we played the underclass (high school preparatory level) team of St. Edward's a few times. This may only be hearsay, but St. Edward's had the reputation of including a few of their college freshman players on their high school team. However, I informed Father Boland that my plans were to attend the University of Texas in Austin. As this story unfolds the reader will find that I did not attend St. Edward's or the University of Texas. But there were some amazing coincidences that occurred. Jack Chevigny, who coached at St. Edward's, became the head coach at the University of Texas in 1935. Johnny "One Play" O'Brien, who later ended up coaching me at Notre Dame, coached a couple of my teammates, Pat Bell and Fred Moses, who did go to St. Edward's.

---

3. St. Edward's was part of Notre Dame, but at the time I didn't know that.

CHAPTER 3

Notre Dame

The University of Notre Dame was founded in November 1842 by a priest of the Congregation of Holy Cross, Reverend Edward Sorin. His original land grant of several hundred acres was the site of an early mission to Native Americans, but included only three small buildings in need of repair. The land had been purchased by Reverend Stephen Badin, the first Catholic priest ordained in the United States, and left in trust to the Bishop of Vincennes, Indiana, for anyone who would found a school on the site. Father Sorin and his companion Brothers of St. Joseph (later the Holy Cross Brothers) called the fledgling school, in their mother tongue, L'Universite de Notre Dame du Lac. The University was officially chartered by a special act of legislature of the State of Indiana on January 5, 1844.

Notre Dame's dramatic post-World War II flowering began under Father John J. Cavanaugh, C.S.C., who raised entrance requirements, increased faculty hiring, and established the Notre Dame Foundation to expand the university's development capabilities.

The explosive growth of the university, both in size and stature, gained national prominence during the thrity-five-year tenure of Father Theodore M. Hesburgh, C.S.C., who himself became an internationally distinguished figure for his work in education, the church, human rights, and world affairs. The Hesburgh era saw the doubling of Notre Dame's enrollment, faculty, and degrees awarded; its library volumes increased fivefold; its endowment raised from less than $9 million to more than $1.5

billion; its physical facilities increased from forty-eight buildings to eighty-eight buildings; its faculty compensation increased tenfold; and its research funding expanded more than twentyfold.

¤ ¤ ¤

UNDERGRADUATE YEARS (1934-1938)

Stepping off the streetcar and seeing the campus for the first time, I was entranced by the grandeur and beauty of the famous "Golden Dome," which is still the same today as it was in 1934. The Old Main Building and the Sacred Heart Church stood at the center of the campus. Labor and building supplies were pretty cheap during the Great Depression. Notre Dame took advantage of these circumstances and built several new buildings during my student tenure. However, concrete was one commodity that was both expensive and rare during the depression. Without resources for concrete sidewalks, boardwalks were constructed throughout the campus. When it rained, the campus turned into a real quagmire! Dillon Hall, a newer dormitory on campus, was home during my freshman year.

In 1934 there were approximately 2,700 students—all male, most from the Midwest and Northeast. However, every state in the Union was represented on campus. Tuition, room, and board for my freshman year totaled less than $1,000. Today those fees are close to $33,000 per year!

One of the easiest courses I ever took at Notre Dame was an advertising course taught by Father Lahey. I learned more about advertising and marketing from this padre than I thought possible. "Keep it simple," he taught. "If you've got a good product, advertise it. Let the customers know that your product is in the store because they are in there to buy." He used to say "fast nickels are better than slow dimes." I told Dad about "fast nickels," and he just loved it because he gave his customers fair values at fair prices. Dad really liked the phrase and *he really made it famous*. It is a great statement to this day.

During my junior year at St. Joseph's Academy, I took a class called "20th Century Bookkeeping." The German nun who taught the class said over and over, "Boys und girls, der are tree rules in a nutshell: Debit vhat comes in, credit vhat goes out.

Credit dose who give to the business, debit dose who take from the business. Debit vhat costs the business. Credit vhat contributes to the business." One of the toughest business courses at Notre Dame was "Principles of Accounting" taught by Professor Stan Price. Because of my experience with 20th Century Bookkeeping, I passed the course with flying colors, while many of my fellow classmates dropped out like flies.

¤ ¤ ¤

My wife Patty likes to tell this tale on me: "Ed went off to Notre Dame not knowing a soul. Four years later, everyone on campus was his friend." There is *some* exaggeration to this story—but I did make tons of friends during my four years.

New England born and bred Joe Cochran and Chick Gallagher were close friends of mine. The best of friends and roommates, they were still prone to some pretty heated arguments. Sometimes several weeks went by without these two speaking to each other—even though they shared the same small dormitory room. An ironic coincidence: A few years later Joe married Chick's sister.

Kenneth Veeneman, my roommate, was from a large family, and every one of the siblings went by a nickname. Ken was known as "Pape," a name bestowed on him by his older brother, whose nickname was "Red." The Veeneman family was part owner of the Frankfurt Distilleries in Louisville, Kentucky. I had my first drink of hard liquor with Pape the day he was notified he had flunked a certain class. We toasted the event with a couple shots of Old Oscar Pepper Rye!

Pape and I began our sophomore year at Morrissey Hall, but midway through the term we transferred to Lyon's Hall. Frankly, we didn't get along with Father George Holdreth, the rector. Unless you were on the golf team or close to it, you were almost persona non grata with the padre we called "Black George." He got this nickname because of the long black cassock he wore—even when he went out to supervise the golf team practice. Alumni Hall was home for my junior year, and senior year I returned to Dillon Hall, which had changed from a freshman to a senior dormitory.

Al Mailhes was nicknamed "Tubby," because as a kid he

was pretty fat. Tubby's father published the *Shreveport Times*. With much of the country still under the yoke of the Great Depression, some of the businesses that advertised in the newspaper paid Tubby's father off in-kind. One such customer was the famous Palmer House Hotel in Chicago. "Tubby," his father told him, "I've got a $200 due bill at the Palmer House. Take someone with you and use it up." That plus the $3.60 fare for the Inter-Urban train to Chicago, and we were off to the big city.

Night after night Tubby came to my room with the same request, "Ed, let's get on that Spanish tonight." After two years of arduous work, the only four words that Tubby mastered were *sí, no, gracias,* and *de nada*. But Tubby sure had the upper hand in English. For starters, he had the most beautiful handwriting I had ever seen. I would struggle for hours writing English compositions, while Tubby knocked off a composition in just a few minutes. All my hard work earned passing grades. Tubby was awarded A's and higher.

Kenny Fox was another friend from Chicago. Kenny's father and his eight uncles ran a large wholesale produce business in Chicago. They also owned a brewery called Fox Deluxe Beer. I had spent so many wonderful weekends with the Fox family in Chicago, Mother and Dad were eager to reciprocate and entertain the Foxes in Dallas. Kenny's parents finally came to Dallas on a business trip. Dad and Mr. Fox had mutual friends in the produce business in Dallas, the Kadane family. Some of the Kadane brothers started a small oil company, and Dad and Mr. Fox joined them for a few ventures in the oil patch. They formed a company called the Big Six Oil Company, with Dad and Mr. Fox being two of the six. Their first venture was a success. They brought in a big discovery well called the KMA Field near Wichita Falls, Texas. Shortly thereafter, Dad sold out his interests. "I better stick to the pants business," he informed the others.

Joe O'Neill, an upperclassman, was one of the first friends I made when I arrived at school. Joe was quite a football legend at Notre Dame. He held the punting record for over twenty years. We attended the Notre Dame vs. Southern California game together in the mid-1950s when some kid finally broke Joe's record!

Billy Castleman, from Louisville, Kentucky, was one of the

few students who attended Notre Dame on a full golf scholarship. After graduation, Billy went to work for Reynolds Aluminum, and Joe went on to Notre Dame Law School and eventually joined the FBI.

A few years after graduation, Joe and Billy were sold some cheap oil leases located in an abandoned oil field. Wouldn't you know it, they hit a major discovery well and overnight they were worth over $25 million! They established the Castleman and O'Neill Oil Company, which started the big oil boom in Scurry County, Texas.

Walter Duncan's family was in oil and banking businesses in southern Illinois. When Walter found out that Dad was in the pants manufacturing business, he started discussing mergers and acquisitions for Haggar Company. At eighteen, Walter read the *Wall Street Journal* from cover to cover every day and followed the Dow-Jones Average, two things which I knew absolutely nothing about at the time. Walter obtained a seat on the Chicago Board of Trade when he was nineteen, and still maintains that seat today! After graduation, Walter got involved with Joe O'Neill and Billy Castleman, and played an integral part in their Scurry County explorations.

Other dear friends of mine from Notre Dame were George Becker, Walter Flemming, Jack Kuhlman, Tom Liston, Bob Magee, Jim Magee, and Al Van Hollenbec.

¤ ¤ ¤

During my junior year, Joe, Chick Gallagher, and I occasionally left campus on Friday nights and enjoyed a good spaghetti dinner at Rosie's Restaurant in South Bend. For less than a dollar each, we dined on a huge plate of spaghetti, garlic bread, and beer. Friday nights were the busiest of the week at Rosie's, and the owners preferred to serve the locals, who ordered more expensive entrees. They never refused service to students, but if the joint was jumping, we seemed to wait an eternity. One night our appetites just got the best of us and we walked out of Rosie's in pursuit of a hot meal. The Miles Avenue Grill, located directly across the street, was declared "off limits" by the prefect of discipline because they served hard liquor. Joe, Chick, and I decided to take our chances, in more ways than one, and have dinner.

Father Boland, the prefect of discipline, had an assistant, a layman named Mr. McCullough, who cruised around the city of South Bend at night and rescued any misled Notre Dame students. Well, on this particular night Chick, Joe and I found the atmosphere and the cuisine at the Miles Avenue Grill to be both warm and friendly. Somewhere between dinner and dessert, Mr. McCullough strolled through the front door: "You boys report to Father Boland on Monday morning at nine o'clock. He'll be expecting you."

I was filled with trepidation for the remainder of the weekend. Acting with much contrition, the three of us explained to Father Boland how we had been pushed around at Rosie's and, nearly crazed with hunger, we had journeyed across the street for our dinners, not knowing that the Miles Avenue Grill was off limits.

"Well, Mr. Gallagher, Mr. Cochran, and Mr. Haggar," Father Boland reprimanded, "I happen to know the three of you enjoy golf. And I am pleased to tell you that you will have plenty of time to enjoy the sport when you are expelled for the spring semester."

My heart was beating so hard I thought it might be visible through my shirt. The one thing I didn't want to do was to explain to Dad and Mother how I got kicked out of Notre Dame. I would be in deep voodoo if I suddenly appeared at home. If Father Boland meant to scare the hell out of us, he certainly succeeded. In the end, our off-campus privileges were suspended for a month and we remained in school.

My summers during those college years were spent working for Dad. At least once a summer Mother, Dad, and I journeyed to New York City for a buying trip. Weekdays Dad and I crisscrossed the city and met with buyers and fabric manufacturer's representatives.

On a particular weekend, while I was still in New York with Mother and Dad, my Notre Dame buddies Charlie Metzger and Ollie McMahon asked me to join them for a weekend at Saratoga Springs in upstate New York. "What's Saratoga Springs?" I asked. "A horse-racing town," they informed me. Each of us had about $20 in our pockets when we drove off. The first night we stayed in a tourist camp, a one-room cabin with two double beds. The cost was $1 per night. Early the next morning we were off to the track. This was my first experience betting on the ponies. We bet on each race and kept doubling up. Charlie, Ollie, and I stood at the rail, clutching our tickets for the eighth race as the horses sped out of the starting gate. With a flourish of pounding hoofbeats and flying dust, our horse, "Sophie Tucker," crossed the finish line first. We were rich!

As soon as we left the track, we checked out of the tourist camp and into the United States Hotel, which was one of the grandest resorts of the day. That night we wandered through the town of Saratoga Springs. There were two dance pavilions, one at each end of the main street. Cab Calloway played at one end of town and Guy Lombardo at the other. We had a ball that night: eating, gambling, and dancing with many of the young ladies staying at the resort.

Feeling very cocky and self-assured, we returned to the track the following morning, ready to pick the winners for the day. Neither luck nor skill smiled on us that day, and within a few hours our resources were wiped out. One of the fellows had an uncle living in Saratoga, and we managed to borrow gasoline money for our trip back to New York. Even though I lost $20, I considered it a cheap lesson in realizing that gambling doesn't pay.

¤ ¤ ¤

In 1988, at my fiftieth reunion, Col. James S. O'Rourke presented me with his book *Reflections in the Dome: 60 Years of Life at Notre Dame*. I had been one of several graduates asked to submit recollections of life at the university.

AN A-TEAM ASSIGNMENT

Believe it or not, I was originally enrolled in the University of Texas at Austin. Mother, however, wanted me to go to St. Edward's. I told her I had seen St. Edward's and she hadn't, and I didn't want to go to St. Edward's!

She said, "Honey, you have to go to a Catholic school." My reply was, "If I have to go to a Catholic school, how about Notre Dame?" I knew nothing about Notre Dame except what I had read on the sport pages or heard on the radio, specifically the Notre Dame–SMU game of 1930.

Well, I applied to Notre Dame. During the depression years, of course, decent grades and money for tuition could get you into just about any school. And, although I applied late, I was accepted.

On my first school trip, I stayed overnight at the YMCA in Chicago and the next morning boarded the New York Central and got off in South Bend with two suitcases in hand. I didn't know a soul, had never been to Notre Dame and never knew anyone who had. I stayed in Dillon Hall that night and made a few freshman and upper class friends the first day.

School hadn't started yet, but I remember a guy by the name of Donohue from the Bronx (he never finished — don't think he stayed more than one semester) and we went to a particular tavern where a lot of the kids gathered. This was a couple of days before school started and, although the place in which we were having a few beers and sandwiches were off limits, we were safe because school had not started. We had a great time and I met a fellow named Joe O'Neill, who was an upper-classman — a junior — and we became good friends. This was during the "hey day" of Max Baer, the World Heavyweight Boxing Champion, and Joe O'Neill had decided I looked like Max Baer. So, for a long time they billed me on campus as Max's younger brother. Because of this, I never did have any problems at N.D., pugilistically. Although I did have a fight in the freshman locker room one afternoon after football practice. It didn't amount to much, though, and as soon as we made up, all was forgotten.

When school actually started, I met new fellows everyday; Notre Dame had students from all over the country and many parts of the world. It didn't take long to realize that lifelong friendships were in the process of being made. Notre Dame didn't stand for any foolishness from the students — there was a great deal of discipline and this discipline made it easy for me to acclimate as an enlisted man, and later an officer, in the Army Air Force. Everyone was in the same boat: no cars, no fraternities. No one knew whether a kid was from a millionaire's family or from poverty row. That's what made it such a great school.

Lights went out in the freshman halls at 10:00 P.M. on weekdays, and at midnight on Saturday nights. A student couldn't stay out later than midnight on the weekend unless there was a special function such as the Sophomore Cotillion, Junior Prom or Senior Ball. Drinking hard liquor was an absolute "no-no," and a student hadn't better be caught in a bar or in a "tipsy" condition when returning to his residence hall. I had to check in with the night watchman whenever I got in, and if I was late or "under the influence," it meant big trouble with the Prefect of Discipline.

The first priest I ran into at Notre Dame—about the second day on campus—was Father John Boland, C.S.C. I first met him at St. Joseph's High School in Texas, where he and Father Hugh O'Donnell, President of St. Edward's University in Austin, were recruiting. At that time, I told Father Boland I wasn't interested in St. Edward's, as I was going to the University of Texas. This man had a memory as broad as his Boston accent; I was surprised to see him later at Notre Dame, and he was surprised to see me. His comment: "As I live and breathe, do my eyes deceive me, Mr. HEY'GER, or is this the University of Texas campus?" I was a marked man with the Prefect of Discipline from that day on.

Almost every kid who entered Notre Dame, if he had any size or football ability, wanted to go out for football. I was no exception. When I hit Notre Dame, I really didn't know very much about football because of a serious head injury I had when I was in the first grade; and, because of this injury, my mother wouldn't let me play football. So, until I was a junior in high school, I never played the game. When I did try the game, it was in a little high school called St. Joseph's Academy. We had a priest who taught religion who was also our coach; unfortunately, he didn't know much about football. Needless to say, I didn't learn much about the game until I got to Notre Dame. I was at a real disadvantage because I was competing with the All-State, All-City, Team Captains, and others as a freshman. During those days, in contrast to the NCAA rules that Notre Dame follows today, there was really no limit to the number of scholarships they could award. They were called "rides" at the time, and today they are limited to fewer than three dozen per year. Between 700 and 800 kids would go out for football, but only a couple hundred could find rides.

It took me about two weeks before I could get a uniform. The equipment manager was an old-timer by the name of "Mac" McCallister; he reminded me of Popeye, principally because he cursed like a sailor. About two or three other Texans were out for football and "Mac" liked to give us a bad time. He didn't really dislike us, he just enjoyed giving us the needle. I guess the only compensation I got out of football, as did most of the other fellows, were the few extra tee shirts, sweat shirts and sweat socks we could spirit home without his knowledge.

Everyday before practice, I would put my old laundry in the hamper and Mac, after cursing his tirades accusing the arriving players of not putting their dirty laundry in the hamper, would then issue clean or new equipment. Most of the time, the dirty laundry wasn't deposited, so I guess I got my share of the little extras.

The only other "freebie"—and I'll never forget this—was when Notre Dame played Navy, my freshman year, at the Cleveland Municipal Stadium in Cleveland, Ohio. We got a free round-trip ticket about 300 miles each way on the night coach. Cleveland was a great Notre Dame town and all you had to do was mention you were from N.D. and from then on you never had to put your hand in your pocket. We really had a great time, and this was probably the first time I was ever in a real bar and we certainly put away a few beers that weekend.

Unlike most other colleges, ours did not play a freshman schedule; as a result, we learned very little about Notre Dame football. About a week or two after the varsity season started in 1934, the freshmen took up the task of learning the opponent's formations and plays so that we could scrimmage the varsity. One of the less attractive features of those practice sessions was the use of freshmen as live tackling dummies. I recall the half-back coaches throwing the football to one of their charges; he would run through a line of four or five varsity players and wasn't permitted to veer out of line more than a couple of feet each way—he was invariably tacked pretty hard.

When the halfbacks had had enough, they would throw the ball to the nifty ends (I was an end, but not too nifty) and we would go through the same procedure. Practice was pretty rugged. I wouldn't take all the money in the world, though, for the great friends I made, freshmen and varsity players included. One of whom I was particularly fond was All-American Bill Shakespeare from Staten Island, New York. We happened to have a class in Politics together and, would you believe the Prefect of Discipline, none other than Padre Boland, was the professor?

Sometimes Bill and I would study together on Sunday evenings. He lived in Alumni, an upper class hall right across from Dillon, then a freshman hall. On Sunday at 7:00 P.M., lights were off in the freshman halls. We were to go over to Sacred Heart Church for a 30-minute Sunday evening service; after that, lights were off for a similar period for upperclassmen. Instead of Bill or I going to church, we would go to each other's room and study Political Science together.

About 25 years after the famous Notre Dame–Ohio State game of 1935, Charlie Callahan wrote an article about the game for *Our Sunday Visitor*, a Catholic weekly. Charlie had been the Notre Dame Director of Sports Publicity for many years before moving on to a similar position with the Miami Dolphins, a team which my brother Joe and I owned for a while. [This statement is incorrect. Joe and I owned only a small percentage of the team for a short time.]

Charlie's article quoted Tony Mazziotti, the quarterback, who bragged that he was the only Catholic who touched the ball on the winning touchdown. The ball was centered by Hank Pojman, a Protestant, to Mazziotti, who was a Catholic, who, in turn, handed the ball off to non-Catholic Bill Shakespeare, who passed the ball to Wayne Millner, who was Jewish. Until I read that article, 25 years after Bill Shakespeare and I would skip evening services, I never knew that Bill wasn't a Catholic. So, he didn't have to go to any of those services—he wasn't obligated—but I was. Funny thing, unless you lived in the same residence hall with a fellow, you'd never know whether he was Catholic or Protestant. I was "goofing off" in my religious duties, but Bill Shakespeare wasn't. I never told Charlie Callahan the true facts because I was afraid he would include me in his next article in *Our Sunday Visitor*.

Elmer Layden, one of Rockne's famous Four Horsemen in the late 1920s, returned to Notre Dame the same year I arrived,

1934. He was a great guy and a good coach, although he didn't look like a football player because he was too thin. We always referred to him as "the thin man," after the title of the popular radio mystery of the day. Since I had intended to study at the University of Texas, would you believe the first game I ever saw Notre Dame play was against Texas? It was during my freshman year. I really didn't know whom to root for. [Texas kicked off to Notre Dame and ND fumbled on their 18-yard line. Three plays later, Bohn Hilliard, the star halfback of Texas, made the touchdown and they made the extra point. Later in the game we made a touchdown but failed to convert the extra point, and as a result we were beaten 7–0.]

Their coach, Jack Chevigny, had just come to the University of Texas from St. Edward's. Jack, of course, was one of Knute Rockne's top assistants and it has been said that had Rockne lived, and picked a successor, Chevigny would have been the man. After his Notre Dame victory, Texas really ruined Jack. They bought him a LaSalle touring car—a status symbol, really, the rich man's sports car of the day. The oil-rich alumni of Texas showered oil deals and many other niceties on him; as a result, he never became a great coach.

Notre Dame, I'm told, gave Jack a beautiful fountain pen set with the inscription: "To Jack Chevigny, a Notre Dame man who beat Notre Dame." I'm not sure if this story is true or not, but Jack was a Naval Officer and was lost in the Pacific. When the peace treaty was signed on the USS *Missouri*, one of the Japanese officers allegedly loaned his pen (part of the Chevigny fountain pen set) to one of the American officers. Makes a great story, true or not.

A story that recently appeared in the Notre Dame magazine about one of the great English professors, Frank O'Malley, reminded me of my experiences in his class. Besides myself, he had several other freshman football players in his class known as "The Novel" which he pronounced as "The No'vil." He could literally chew out the kids without using a curse word; that man had a magnificent vocabulary. I recall turning in a book report—one that I hadn't read, but I had gotten a hold of a synopsis and wrote a report based on that which I thought was pretty good. I was especially proud of the cover page which Professor O'Malley ruined with his red ink remarks and a failing grade. "Too verbose!" "Sounds like wind blowing through dry grass!" "58%"

I'll never forget two very popular strip teasers who performed often in Chicago: June St. Clair and Ada Leonard. Miss Leonard came to South Bend to put on a show at the Palace Theater and the N.D. students were warned not to go to any of the performances. Well, the theater was filled with Notre Dame kids and it looked like Saturday night in Washington Hall. A photo of an old streetcar, from a recent N.D. magazine article, reminded me of this event. Students were hanging out of the windows and on top of the streetcar, making a beeline to see Miss Leonard display her talents.

When players make the football team, it is usually in the spring of freshman year. Because of an appendectomy, though, I missed spring practice entirely, and in my sophomore year I played "B" or reserve football. We had a partial schedule playing reserve teams from such schools as Purdue, Illinois, Michigan, Niagara and Xavier University. I made four of these trips and played in about half of each of the games. That following spring, during my sophomore year, I went out for spring practice and did very well; the new end coach, John "One Play" O'Brien, took a special interest in me because some of my high school teammates were students of his at St. Edward's. O'Brien, by the way, got that nickname because of the pass which he caught in the N.D.–Army game of 1930. It was good enough to win the game for Notre Dame. As a result of his assistance and personal attention, I was called back for varsity football my junior year. Although I was only on the varsity for about 30 days, this was one of the biggest thrills of my N.D. years.

For the first two weeks before classes started, we had very rigorous workouts and practice twice a day with skull practice after lunch. I wouldn't trade anything for that experience, trying and difficult as it was. A couple of weeks into the regular football season, during practice, I banged up my knee. Well, I wasn't all that good and it looked as though I was going to be out for the season, so I figured the only way I could make out was to get Elmer Layden to give me a scholarship. He was very nice and told me that all scholarships were taken (which they were) and, as a result, none was available for me. I guess if I had been better, I'd have received a scholarship. Since I wasn't good enough for a "ride," I felt I would be wasting my time, so I gave up the game.

Although I've been on the Board of Trustees since 1976, which is quite an honor, I was more proud of being on the Alumni Board because I was elected by my peers and not appointed. When I was elected, an article appeared in Joe Doyle's column of the *South Bend Tribune*. "New members of Notre Dame's alumni board," he wrote, "are meeting on campus this weekend, including three 'athletic' names. Edmond R. Haggar, of the Dallas slacks manufacturing family, is the same Ed Haggar who played B-Team football for the Irish in Elmer Layden's tenure as coach." He went on, "Charlie Callahan of Notre Dame says it might be incorrect to label Ed Haggar as a B-team football player. When Haggar left the squad, he was assigned to the A-squad. A hard working player, Haggar is said to have realized his shortcomings, but spirit and desire earned him an A-team assignment. He played with the A-group one night and then resigned from the squad saying, ' I just wanted to prove to myself I could make the varsity for the Fighting Irish.'" Charlie's version made a great story, but like the Jack Chevigny pen story, it's not exactly true.

Times were rough during the depression and kids didn't fly home from school every couple of weeks. I did come home for Christmas on the train, but that was it. Neither Mother nor Dad ever set foot on the Notre Dame campus until the day I graduated in 1938.

POST-GRADUATION YEARS

Mother and Dad were very pleased with the way we all turned out after our individual associations with Notre Dame, and in 1946 began a program of annual support to the university. Dad became very friendly with Father O'Donnell, then-president of Notre Dame, and later with Father John Cavanaugh and Father Hesburgh. The annual funds accumulated by the

Haggar family plus additional special contributions enabled funding for two buildings: the Haggar Hall of Psychology in 1974 and the Haggar Fitness Center in 1988. We also contributed funds for the Haggar College Center at St. Mary's College. Recently, Joe and I established separate scholarship programs for children from disadvantaged families.

¤ ¤ ¤

Joe Cochran eventually became president of the Jones and Vining Shoe Last Company. Even in our student years at Notre Dame, my feet surpassed the largest commonly manufactured-sized shoe. For years, I crammed my aching feet into Thom McCann shoes that were two sizes too small. The year was 1947. Joe, Chick, and I met in Chicago and drove to South Bend to attend the Notre Dame vs. Army football game. After the game, we drove back to Chicago and celebrated Notre Dame's victory at a few choice nightclubs in town. Chez Paree was the last stop of the night. My feet were killing me, and I was limping through the evening. Joe traced my footprint on his white linen napkin. A few days later, he sent a custom designed last to Florsheim, Johnston & Murphy, and Foot Joy shoe companies. From that time on, I have savored the comfort of correctly fitted shoes. I often wonder if I would have been a better football player, if only I had Joe's lasts in my shoes!

¤ ¤ ¤

The Notre Dame football team was the most respected team in the country, and still is. I was serving as president of the Notre Dame Club of Dallas in 1949 when Notre Dame played Southern Methodist University in Dallas. Notre Dame's arrival in Dallas was the biggest thing to hit town since sliced bread or nylon hose. It was a natural occasion to throw the biggest and best party in the Club's and Dallas's history. In addition to the alumni, *we invited Haggar customers from near and far.* As the luck of the Irish would have it, this game turned out to be one of the greatest games of the century.

The Adolphus and the Baker, located directly across the street from one another, were the two leading Dallas hotels of the day. We rented the grand ballroom at the Baker. The SMU alumni rented facilities at the Adolphus. The stage was set for rivaling parties.

An older alumnus, Jim Swift, introduced me to Bob O'Donnell, head of the Interstate Theater chain, who knew just about every celebrity in Hollywood. Through Mr. O'Donnell's help, we got Bob Hope to perform along with Cyd Charisse and Tony Martin. Touting the best entertainment and the best football team, we sold tickets for our party by the truckload.

Bob Hope was scheduled to arrive at the Baker at 7:30 P.M. I glanced at my wristwatch—8:00! "What am I going to tell the audience?" I wondered. Bob walked in a few seconds before 8:00. He apologized for his lateness and told me the SMU alumni and students had kidnapped him. We had the finest program ever and raised a lot of money for the Notre Dame Scholarship fund. That night also marked the beginning of a love affair between Bob Hope and SMU.

¤ ¤ ¤

The outstanding leadership and integrity of Father Cavanaugh, Father Hesburgh, and those who followed enabled the University of Notre Dame to achieve its stature as one of this country's finest and most respected educational institutions.

Father Cavanaugh was, indeed, a great statesman. The Kennedy-Nixon presidential election of 1960 found the country deadlocked at the voting booths. And the question "Who are you voting for? Nixon or Kennedy?" was probably the most discussed topic of the day throughout the country. Father Cavanaugh's friendship with Joe Kennedy (JFK's father) was no secret. As a past president of Notre Dame, Father Cavanaugh was nationally renowned. During a press conference the good father was asked by a member of the press, "Who are you voting for?" His reply, "Half of my friends are for Kennedy and half of my friends are for Nixon. I'm for my friends!" It's only natural that the university would flourish under his leadership.

¤ ¤ ¤

The Alumni Board is the only ancillary arm of the university to which their peers elect members. Joe O'Neill and Mike Layden (Elmer's brother) served on the same board with me. As ever, the university was totally focused on maintaining the highest academic standards for its students and faculty. Admission criteria became tougher and tougher. When I was chairman of the Prep-School Committee, the raising of admission standards was discussed across the boardroom table time and time again.

"I agree that our goal is to admit students of the highest academic caliber, but let's be sure we don't get a bunch of eggheads who have no personality and can't get along with other people," I told the board.

As a result of that particular discussion, arrangements were made for alumni to visit with prospective students in order to evaluate social skills and achievements as well as academic backgrounds.

¤ ¤ ¤

Father Theodore Hesburgh began his thirty-five-year presidency of the University of Notre Dame in 1952. We were both undergraduate students on campus at the same time but never met because the seminarians had separate living quarters.

After completing his studies in Rome, Father Hesburgh returned to Notre Dame. He became vice president of the university and ably served Father Cavanaugh, who served as president. The university experienced its greatest growth, both academically and financially, under Father Hesburgh's able guidance. But it wasn't only Notre Dame that benefited by the Father's dedication and hard work. The whole world came to know Father Hesburgh as a great theologian and defender of human rights.

We are honored by Father Hesburgh's willingness to add his own comments to this volume of memoirs.

> Joe Haggar, Sr., was a very close counselor of my predecessor, Father Cavanaugh, and he became a good friend of mine. We spent a lot of time together, both on campus and whenever I traveled to Texas. I attended his 80th birthday party. When Joe got older and couldn't do as much, his sons, Ed and Joe, stepped in and continued their father's commitment to the University. I have to say, they are two sons worthy of their father.
>
> Ed was always a good counselor and willing to serve the

University in whatever capacity he could. Over the years we spent a lot of time together and discussed a lot of problems together. He is a strong man, who has always maintained strong beliefs. We've always been able to discuss our differences and have a mutual respect for one another. We worked a great deal on development, because a university doesn't get great unless its support is developed all over the world.

Ed Haggar and his brother Joe, and before them their father Joe, Sr., were just superb counselors and supporters of the University.

¤ ¤ ¤

In 1945 Notre Dame's endowment was about $9 million. Today their endowment is over $3.3 billion! Surely, the university has just about the best fundraising arm of any charitable organization in the world. Alumni, friends, and corporations have secured the future of this noble institution.

Art Haley was appointed the first chairman of development for Notre Dame in the early 1940s. At the beginning of his tenure, Art entertained potential donors at his home in South Bend. As alumni and donations increased in number, the Development Committee was restructured into five regional branches, each having a manager who recruited prospects and referred them to the chairman of development. It was Art's firm belief that the asking should be left to the pros! And that policy continued with his successors, James Frick, Bill Sexton, and, most recently, Dan Reagan. All of these guys were really smooth and knew exactly how to cultivate prospective donors and donations. Of course, Notre Dame has a great asset for cultivation—Notre Dame football.

I've had the privilege of working with all the distinguished chairmen of development throughout the years, helping with various fundraising campaigns and recruiting donors. A couple of years ago at Eldorado Country Club, Dan Crossen, one of the great Notre Dame fundraisers, was discussing a potential prospect over the breakfast table in the clubhouse. I looked up from the table and spotted my friend Terry Dillon, also a Notre Dame graduate and great benefactor to the university. At that moment, Dan looked at his watch and realized he was late for another appointment and excused himself. "What was that all about?" Terry wanted to know. I responded, "Terry, he was asking me about a prospect." Then I made the comment, "Those guys, especially Bill Sexton, are so good! They really know how to bullshit the prospects." To which Terry replied, "That's true, but he never gets it on them!"

In honor of the vision of its founder and the outstanding leaders who have succeeded him as president, the University of Notre Dame formally established the Edward Frederick Sorin Society in 1976. Alumni, parents, and friends of Notre Dame were asked to contribute $1,000 to become members of the Sorin Society. Later, a different level was established, which included other privileges, for a donation of $3,000.

In 1986 I received a telephone call from Father Hesburgh, asking me to chair the National Sorin Society. Extensive travels to visit local Sorin Society chapters across the country were duties associated with the chairmanship of this organization. My first thought was to decline this honor, since I was so involved with business and other local civic affairs. But Father Hesburgh was persistent: "Ed, you can arrange the travel and meetings to fit in with your business schedule." Now, I've always enjoyed visiting our customers in different parts of the country, so I called Father Hesburgh and agreed to accept the chairmanship provided I could select the dates and the communities that corresponded to my business travels. I addressed groups in Chicago, St. Louis, Cleveland, Baltimore, and Washington, D.C., just to mention a few.

In addition to the Sorin Society, the Alumni Association, and the Board of Trustees, my father, brother Joe, Joe III, and I have all served on the Advisory Council for the College of Business Administration. Joe was also a trustee. Today, both Joe and I are Life-Members of the Board of Trustees.

FUTURE GENERATIONS OF HAGGARS AND NOTRE DAME

It's been a wonderfully rewarding and fruitful relationship between Notre Dame and the Haggar family. In the next generation, my daughter Patty Jo attended St. Mary's, as did Joe's two daughters, Lydia and Marion, and Rosemary's daughter, Vicki.

Subsequently, Lydia completed her MBA at Notre Dame. My son Eddie and my nephew Joe III graduated from Notre Dame.

Joe III became the first Haggar family member to achieve fame and success playing football for Notre Dame. Joe III was a walk-on player (a player with no scholarship) like I was. As a rule, the coaching staff rarely followed the walk-on players. They remained unnoticed.

Here are Joe III's recollections about the day he was "noticed" on the Notre Dame gridiron:

> The fall of 1969 was like any other fall for the last six years. I was involved in football. The only difference was that I was now at a major university (Notre Dame) and nobody knew my name. How could I get the chance to show the coach and team that I was capable of playing with "the big boys."
>
> I played on the Notre Dame freshman football team. One of our missions was to be human "dummies" for the varsity team. The varsity needed to practice punt coverage. They asked for volunteers to catch and return punts, so the 1st Team could practice tackling. The opportunity to make a name for myself just presented itself.
>
> There were two volunteers that day, myself and Dennis Gutowski (Guts). We both went to the other end of the field to receive punts. The one thing the coach failed to announce when asking for volunteers was that there was to be no blocking or fair catches. It was just Guts and me against eleven other players.
>
> Needless to say, without the two of us blocking for each other, and fair catches disallowed, the practice was just a matter of catching the ball and then being flattened by eleven guys. I was flattened two or three times, and still, nobody knew my name. After the third run down the field, I figured the time had come to make my name known.
>
> The legendary Ara Parseghian (our head coach) was watching from the tower. The punter kicked the ball. It was a beautiful, high spiral, headed to my return partner, Guts. (Remember, I was not supposed to block.)
>
> I looked up the field. Denny Allan (our All-American halfback) was bearing down on Guts, getting ready to absolutely

flatten him. I decided this was the time to make my mark. Within a millisecond of Denny's impact on Guts, I stepped in front and laid a "blind-side" body block on Denny that laid him horizontal.

There was total silence on the field. Finally, Ara Parseghian yelled "WHO IN THE HELL LAID THAT BLOCK?" The other coaches yelled, "IT WAS HAGGAR!" "WHO?" Parseghian shouted again. "HAGGAR."

"Mission accomplished," I thought to myself. But the ordeal was not over.

There were at least fifty people on the field... and there was complete silence. Nobody moved except Coach Parseghian. He climbed down from the tower and started walking in my direction. I thought this was the neatest moment... the legendary Ara Parseghian, striding 70 yards down the field to talk to me... a freshman walk-on.

Well, we didn't exactly carry on a conversation. Coach Parseghian grabbed my facemask and made sure I understood, in *HIS* terminology, what I did wrong. Then, he asked my name again, gave me a kick in the ass and a wink at the same time. From that day on, everyone knew my name.

Joe III played defensive halfback and was one of the fastest men on the team.

In the fall of 1998, another generation of Haggars entered Notre Dame: my grandson Garrett Turner and Joe's granddaughter, Isabell Novakov.

Then in 1999, Dan Novakov, Jr., Joe's grandson and my grandnephew, entered Notre Dame. Dan had a great high school football career as quarterback for St. Mark's in Dallas. Dan was the *only* player allowed to walk on that year. In 1970-71, Dan's father, Dan Novakov, Sr., had been the first string center for Notre Dame. Dan, Sr.'s moment of glory on the field came when he snapped balls to Joe Theisman, one of Notre Dame's greatest quarterbacks.

CHAPTER 4
HAGGAR COMPANY (1926–1943):
The War Effort and Military Service

Jim Haggar possessed an innate sense of style. He loved the feel of fine fabric between his fingers. His ability to judge fabric probably started shortly after he arrived in the United States, when he worked as a cotton classifier for Joe Abraham in Bristow, Oklahoma.

My earliest memories begin about 1922 when Dad was still on the road, selling for D.M. Oberman & Company (under the brand-name King Brand). Based in Jefferson City, Missouri, Oberman manufactured overalls, work pants, and men's dress pants. Much of the manufacturing was done in the Jefferson City Penitentiary.

Driving an old Ford Model-T, Dad traversed the rough and bumpy roads of Texas, New Mexico, Oklahoma, Louisiana, and northern Mexico. He knew the product and his customers, and had become the company's top salesman.

Like many salesmen based in Dallas, Dad worked out of a small office, or "Sample Room," in the Southland Hotel, located directly across from the Santa Fe Building at the corner of Murphy and Commerce streets. I remember sitting in the lobby across from the newsstand and cigar counter, busily reading stories from my first-grade primer to the cashier who worked behind the counter.

When Oberman experienced financial difficulties and was unable to pay my father, the company worked out an in-kind deal to manufacture pants for him in lieu of cash. The year was 1926, and it marked the beginning of Haggar Company.

"Make a good product; sell it at a fair price; do a lot of volume. If you do that, something will stick to your hands." Dad gave me that advice when I was a young boy. He repeated those words of wisdom years later to Joe and Rosemary.

When he was in Dallas, Dad was at the plant every day. I remember on Sundays, after twelve o'clock Mass at the Sacred Heart Cathedral, Dad often took me to the office. He taught me how to judge a fabric. He guided my inexperienced hands across swatches of fabric and showed me how to interpret the "hand" of the cloth. We discussed different styles. It was my first introduction to the business. Later, Joe and Rosemary received the same coaching from Dad.

¤ ¤ ¤

Built by the Santa Fe Railroad, the Santa Fe Building consisted of four units, all connected underground. The first space Dad rented in the building was on the fourth floor of the first unit, which was divided into office space, stock room, and shipping department. My mother's brother, Alex Wasaff, oversaw the operation while Dad traveled, selling to the trade and making trips to New York to purchase fabric, pocketing, thread, and trim. These materials were sent to D.M. Oberman in St. Louis, and the finished pants were shipped back to Dallas. This method of operation was known as "cut-make-trim." Using the popular colloquialism of the day, Dad called his first line of pants "Keen Built." In the mid-1930s we began using the name "Haggar" on our pants.

Another giant step forward for Haggar Company came in 1927. At this point in time, Dad was operating the business as a contract venture. After D.M. Oberman fulfilled their obligation, Dad found another manufacturer. Harry Vogel and John Sidor owned a garment manufacturing business in St. Louis. Dad invited them to Dallas. I remember we were living on Garrett Avenue at that time. Mother cooked dinner—a fine traditional Lebanese dinner. Along with dessert came proposals, deals, and negotiations. My father offered to buy them out if they agreed to relocate in Dallas and run the manufacturing facilities for Haggar Company. I sat at the dinner table along with my parents, Vogel, and Sidor. Harry Vogel was a short, sandy-haired man and a good talker. Sidor, whose original name was Sidornofsky, was the more excitable of the two. My dad labeled Sidor the "Mad Russian." Both men were excellent manufacturers.

Shortly thereafter, Sidor and Vogel moved to Dallas. They brought the necessary machinery and knowledge and started making pants. Dad rented more space in the Santa Fe Building. Harry hired the sewers and cutters and set up the first production line for Haggar. There were several operations, and each sewer did a separate operation like serging, joining, buttonholes, buttons, etc. However, the units were not that well organized. As time went on, there were many modifications, the first of which was the bundle system. Each operator would do her part, such as sew flies, stack them in one bundle, and then the bundle was transported by bundle boys to the next operation.

With the plants going full-steam-ahead producing pants, my father was on the road more than ever. There were trips to the textile mills to buy the fabric and trips throughout the Southwest to sell the finished product. Each night after 6:00 P.M., after the nighttime *low* long distance rates went into effect, he called Mother and wanted the exact figures: orders received, collections and shipments for the day.

Ola Duncan joined the company in the very earliest days. She and Dad were the only two Haggar employees who would never retire. Ola worked as the official bookkeeper and unofficial treasurer of the company until her death at age eighty. Having never married, Ola seemed to devote her adult life to chasing down the source for every penny spent and every dollar received by Haggar Company. Responsible for banking deposits, expense checks and petty cash, Miss Duncan never tolerated any guff or alibis from the employees and executives.

As the company grew, our accounting needs became more sophisticated and Dad hired Jerry Benthal to oversee the factory accounting. A wonderful guy, but kind of a milquetoast by nature, Jerry and Ola were always at odds. R.N. Carr was our able office/credit manager and Beryl Tansil managed sales and service.

The company's first sales force numbered seven men. At the very outset, Dad was the first sales manager. However, with so many demands made from other areas of the business, Dad hired Tansil as sales service manager. He was a pretty mild-mannered guy who had really never been out on the road, per se. However, he did possess good organizational skills and fulfilled his job by keeping the salesmen well organized and up to date on a daily basis regarding prices, changes, and delivery schedules.

¤ ¤ ¤

Twenty-seven-year-old James Cash Penney opened his first store in a small mining camp in Kemmerer, Wyoming, on April 14, 1902. Calling his first endeavor "The Golden Rule Store," Mr. Penney eventually created a retailing empire.

By far, J.C. Penney was our largest customer. How did we get started with Penney's? In the late 1920s, my uncle, Harry Wasaff, and another Haggar Company salesman, Clarence Grunsfeld, started bootlegging our pants to the J.C. Penney stores in their sales territories. Theoretically, all Penney stores were supposed to purchase merchandise through their New York listings. But in some cases, Penney's headquarters closed their eyes to local buying practices. Penney's was, and is, a well-run company, and always was on the lookout for good resources. The stores that bought our product (and eventually there were many of them) liked our pants because they fit well, were styled from good patterns, and represented good value. Dad really jumped on the bandwagon, and subsequently Haggar got a listing with J.C. Penney. Manufactured by Haggar Company, with a Penney label sewn in, our pants were purchased by Penney stores throughout the United States. *Our affiliation with Penney's, begun over sixty-five years ago, marked a significant turning point in the success of our company.* By receiving a listing with Penney's, we added tremendous volume to our business. All of that extra business absorbed a lot of our overhead. Dad always dealt personally with Penney's top management. Therefore, no salesmen's commissions were paid out, which also added to our profitability.

The stock market crashed in 1929 and sent shock waves

throughout the entire country. Many manufacturing businesses came to a virtual standstill. But men needed pants, and we continued to grow.

In those early days most of our company sales were in the Southwest, Pacific Coast, Rocky Mountain states, and the Northwest. The Mel Rose Manufacturing Company of Dallas was one of our biggest competitors. Other regional manufacturers of the day were the Hoosier Pants Company out of Michigan City, Indiana; Rough Rider Pants out of San Francisco, California; Hercules Pants Company from Columbus, Ohio; Rose Brothers from New York City; and Thompson Company of Thomasville, Georgia. For the most part, Thompson and Haggar competed for the lion's share of Penney's business.

In 1933 Dad was in the hospital with ulcers and had a lot of time to think about the business. One recurring thought was about Henry Ford's straight line production method of manufacturing automobiles. Dad figured he could do the same thing with pants. A gentleman named Schmidt, who was schooled and experienced in engineering and sewing production, visited Dad. Sitting up in his hospital bed, Dad shared his dream of this type of production method with Mr. Schmidt. Later on, Dad and Mr. Schmidt did, indeed, design the straight line production method for Haggar Company. The two of them modified Ford's system, and this became a very efficient method for producing pants. The operators worked on a single unit rather than bundles. After they did their work, conveyors then passed along the single items to the next operator. Productivity increased and manufacturing costs decreased.

Throughout the 1930s, Dad was known as the "Mystery Man of the South." Both his competitors and customers couldn't figure out why Haggar products were superior in quality and more competitively priced. Actually, there was really never any mystery at all. With his newly established straight line production, manufacturing became most efficient. Also, Dad had the reputation of being the toughest, shrewdest, but fairest fabric buyer in the market. So, between making his product more efficiently and buying raw materials more competitively, his prices were under the market and the quality superior.

When Dad made the transition from "cut-make-trim" to man-

Haggar Hall of Psychology at the University of Notre Dame.

Haggar College Center at St. Mary's College, Notre Dame, Indiana.

Interior photo of the Haggar Fitness Center at Notre Dame.

Haggar University Center at the University of Dallas.

Notre Dame, 1936, varsity football team. "My friends didn't believe I made the team, until I discovered this old photograph."

John O'Brien, new Notre Dame end coach, was snapped as he took charge of the Irish wingmen in yesterday afternoon's practice session. Tom Conley, making his last coaching appearance on the field, introduced his successor to the end candidates and then stood aside as Johnny took charge. The new coach is shown illustrating a point to Joe Zwers, monogram-winning right end of last year's team, as Len Skoglund, Ed Haggar, Chuck Sweeney and Conley look on. (News-Times Photo.)

DURHAM HAGGAR OUST FAVORITES IN 4-BALL

Giant killers . . . Herb Durham, left, and Ed Haggar, right, upset the favored team of Don Schumacher and Earl Summers, 3 and 2, Saturday in the semifinals of the annual Dallas Golf Association 4-ball championship at DAC Country Club.

—Dallas News Staff Photo.

New 4-Ball champions of the Dallas Golf Association, Herb Durham, left, and Ed Haggar, center, received their trophy from DGA President James S. Hereford Jr., Sunday at DAC Country Club following their 20-hole victory over Shell and Don Holland.

Durham, Haggar Win 4-Ball Title on 20th

From the "Dallas Morning News" – April 20, 1956.

At the Byron Nelson Tournament. L-R: President Ford, E.R.H., and Bob Hope congratulating Mike Massad, who made a hole in one on the fourth hole.

L-R: Bob French, President George Bush, President Gerald Ford, and E.R.H. playing at Ambassador Annenberg's private golf course.

St. Jude's Golf Tournament – 1995. On this particular day, President Ford made a hole in one and Al Geiberger shot a record low of 59. L-R: Don Drinkard, Vernon Bell, Ben Crenshaw, President Gerald Ford, Joe Haggar.

Fishing at Land O Lakes.
L-R: E.R.H., Michael, Marc, our guide, Jimmy, Michael Kidwell.

Shaina and John. Shaina is pointing to a Haggar endorsement by Mickey Mantle at Mickey's restaurant in New York City.

ufacturing, he relocated to the fourth unit and occupied three floors: six, seven, and eight of the Santa Fe Building. Haggar Company was the first manufacturing business in the complex. Some of our early neighbors were the Olmstead Kirk Paper Company, which is still in business; and a book distributor called Hugh Perry and Company. Our space in the fourth unit was divided between piece goods, cutting, sewing, and shipping. Air conditioning, in those early days, had not been invented; however, Dad had the best and biggest fans money could buy.

¤ ¤ ¤

Headquartered in Oklahoma, the C.R. Anthony Department Stores owned and operated stores in Oklahoma, Kansas, New Mexico and other southwestern states. Dad and C.R. Anthony were great friends. Both from similar backgrounds, Mr. Anthony was about five years older than Dad. Like the Penney's accounts, Dad handled all business with C.R. Anthony personally. They argued over price points and this-and-that at their business meetings, then stayed up half the night playing poker. During one business meeting in the middle of the Depression (around 1934) Dad told Mr. Anthony, "The market is down so low. If I only had $50,000 I could sure make a bunch of great deals." A few days later, Dad received a check from C.R. Anthony for $75,000. No note was attached, just a check. Dad returned the check to Mr. Anthony. But this was one of many gestures which showed how much Dad was trusted in the business community. In later years C.R. Anthony became one of the first outside Haggar stockholders.

In the mid-1930s, Haggar salesman George Utsey first sold the Haggar line to the Belk Stores, which marked our first representation in the Southeast. At the time, the Belk family owned 300 or more stores throughout the southeastern United States. (Today there are 200+ Belk Stores.)[4] George enlisted the help of his two brothers, and between the three of them, they managed to sell and service a great many of the 300 stores. This was a time of great growth for Haggar Company, and it seemed like Dad was busy in

---

4. Many stores in smaller towns have been closed or consolidated over the years.

a hundred different areas and never had the time to personally meet the Belk family. In the early 1940s, just before the start of World War II, Dad asked me to make the call on Mr. Henry Belk and his sons. At the same time, I also met Frank Matthews, who was the general merchandise manager. George Utsey and I worked with Mr. Matthews, getting our entire line established in all 300 Belk Stores. (We are still doing business with this fine organization today.) At that initial meeting, Mr. Matthews remarked, "Ed, you're a pretty young fellow. How old are you?"

"I'm twenty-nine, sir," was my reply. Actually, I was only twenty-three. I didn't want to tell him my real age, thinking he might be insulted that the company sent a kid to call on such an important client!

Over the years, Dad got to know all the Belks, and was particularly close with John Belk, Henry's son, who is currently chairman and CEO of the organization. All of the Belks were very fond of Dad, and he was very fond of them. Joe and I also established friendships with this remarkable family. Not only are they wonderful customers, they are also wonderful friends. We've played a lot of golf with the Belk brothers at Augusta National, Eldorado Country Club, and Castle Pines Golf Club.

THE BEGINNING OF MY FULL-TIME CAREER (1938)

Graduation from Notre Dame: June 1938. All my growing-up years and education were completed. Now it was time to join the company as a full-time employee.

On the road in East Texas—driving a light-blue Buick sedan (a graduation gift from Dad and Mother)—that's where my full-time career began. A fellow by the name of Dad Joiner discovered big oil fields in that part of the state in the early 1930s. Most of the oil fields were discovered on agricultural land that yielded cotton, maize, and wheat. Oil brought wealth and employment, and oil workers needed pants.

Shreveport, Louisiana, was the easternmost location. I traveled through such towns as Texarkana, Longview, Gladewater, Tyler, and Gilmer. I also called on Penney stores throughout the Southwest (this was somewhat illegal).

Generally, I made four six-week trips through my sales territory each year, in addition to calling on Penney stores throughout the Southwest. The rest of the time I worked with Dad, by far my greatest teacher, on the inside. "People will like you and respect you if you know your product and can answer all their questions," Dad advised me. My starting salary was $60 per week plus expenses.

Arthur Goodstein joined the sales force in 1934. He was a competent fellow, a good salesman, and my first mentor on the road. Arthur taught me how to show the line, write up orders, deal with deliveries, and answer questions pertaining to our product. "What you want to do is sell the line across the board. Be sure the customer has a good assortment. Don't oversell. The hardest thing is to sell your line for the following season, if the customer has too much merchandise left over." Such was the sagacious advice I received from Arthur Goodstein in those early years on the road.

The people in my territory were the salt of the earth—good old country boys. I enjoyed good relationships with all of them. Stores in these smaller towns were locally owned and operated. At the time, my biggest account was Three Beall Brothers. Headquartered in Jacksonville, Texas, the Beall brothers owned and operated eighteen stores throughout the state. Jake Henson was the merchandise manager for Beall's. Later on, he came to work for Haggar Company. Jake was quite a character, from the "old-time school of salesmen." He had the damnedest ability for telling white lies and getting away with it.

Whenever business took me to Gilmer, Texas, I always ate at the Bell Hotel, which had one of the finest boardinghouse-type restaurants in the state, and a natural spot for business luncheons. Those little towns in East Texas produced the most heated high school football rivalries. Raymond Lademon managed the Beall Brothers stores in Paris, Texas. I always scheduled my autumn business meetings with Raymond late Friday afternoon. I remember attending the big Friday night football game between Paris and Longview. After business was concluded, we had a bite to eat, then went to the game. Trips to Shreveport were the highlight of my territorial travels, because I got to visit with my great friend from Notre Dame, Al "Tubby" Mailhes.

There was always some merchandise left over at the end of the season. The remaining stock was sorted by color and size.

We sold these as "assortments." Just like the retail stores, we offered our overstocked merchandise at sale prices. Pants were sold in quantities by the dozens. Initially, we shipped the summer pants in January, February, March, and April and began selling the closeouts in early July. After a couple of years of being on the road, along with my summer visits, I knew a great many of the managers of the J.C. Penney stores and was able to sell-out the old merchandise over the telephone in just a few days. So by the end of July, the assortments were completely sold out, making room for the fall season lines.

What were we manufacturing in 1938? With the exception of our #118 army twill khaki pants, we manufactured dress pants, although our khakis were constructed with a dress pants make. Our line consisted of 100% worsted, 100% cotton, and blends of cotton and worsted. Our retail prices ranged from $1.49 per pair to $4.98 per pair. We also manufactured quite a number of patterned cotton pants. Patterns were printed on one side of the fabric, and in some cases, for a better look, were printed on both sides of the fabric. A great deal of these fabrics were bought from a converting firm by the name of J.L. Stifle & Company. The base fabric cost was $.22 per yard (36 inches wide), with an additional $.01 per yard for the printing on each side. Sizing ran from boys' pants to extra large sizes for portly men.

By 1938 our manufacturing facilities included six of the eight floors in the Santa Fe Building headquarters, plus a warehouse in the Doggett Building. In addition, Dad leased a facility three blocks east of the fourth unit on Crowder Street, which was strictly a sewing plant.

We had outgrown our space in the Santa Fe Building as the 1930s drew to a close. In early 1939 Dad bought ten acres of land out in the country, on Lemmon Avenue, and plans were made for construction of a new home for Haggar Company.

Except for a nine-hole golf course with sand greens, the remainder of the property on Lemmon Avenue was completely surrounded by farmland. The property was purchased from Carl Whitsel, president of the National Bank of Commerce. The sales price for the total acreage was $11,000, just a little over $1,000 per acre. The building was designed by the architectural firm of Pitsinger and Laine and constructed by the Cowden

Brothers. Built in an "L" shape, the building was designed to accommodate our assembly line production. Piece goods came in at the top of the "L" and moved down to the cutting department. Sewing, pressing, inspection, and shipping were all located on one floor. The facility was exactly one-tenth of a mile in length (528 feet) and totaled 125,000 square feet.

Upon completion, our facility on Lemmon Avenue became the talk of the industry. Certainly it was the most modern plant of its kind. (Air conditioning had not come into play, but several years later the entire facility was air-conditioned.)

Before going into the service, I suggested to Dad that we buy the additional land adjacent to our property on Lemmon Avenue. Dad agreed and arranged a meeting with Mr. Whitsel. Both men were pretty good traders. With the reputation of being a skinflint, Whitsel realized that the potential values of the land could only go upward, and he refused Dad's offer. Instead of a simple refusal, Mr. Whitsel wiggled out of the deal by telling Dad he proposed to dedicate a park on that property. Years went by and the land remained vacant. The final outcome: Mr. Whitsel did build that small park, but nearly a mile from our land, only after selling the adjacent land at much higher prices.

October 19, 1940, 2:00 A.M. The piercing ring of the telephone woke the Haggar household. "The Santa Fe Building is on fire!" Within seconds Dad and I piled into the car and headed downtown. Great billowing clouds of smoke and flames were visible several miles away. An eerie feeling of doom permeated. The cause and source of the fire remain unknown to this day. Our manufacturing facilities escaped damage. However, the offices, cutting room, and stock room were all encumbered by severe smoke damage. Our stock room was filled with merchandise for the upcoming season. About two-thirds of the merchandise in the stock room was destroyed. The company carried plenty of insurance, but in essence, we were temporarily out of business. Sufficient time was needed to manufacture new goods and trace our sales records and payments, before we could resume shipping the merchandise. The company suffered quite a blow.

The most ironic element of this whole story was the coincidence in timing: construction on the Lemmon Avenue factory was nearing completion. We had already begun moving equipment and transferring records out of the Santa Fe Building into the new facility.

¤ ¤ ¤

Europe and Asia were in turmoil in the mid to late 1930s. Despots and tyrants rose to power. Countries negotiated pacts and treaties, which they abandoned shortly after ratification. America's Great Depression of the 1930s loomed even greater in Europe. Currencies were devalued to nearly nothing. Threats of aggression turned into acts of aggression.

Anticipating our entry into the war, the United States government set out to build one of the greatest war machines ever witnessed in history. Laboratories and factories sprang up on the horizon like mushrooms, manufacturing everything from fuses to bombers. Millions of young American men and women enlisted in the military services or were drafted. Most American businesses shifted their production to help with the war effort. At home the civilian population rationed everything from sugar to tires. Even our civilian pants were affected. Because of shortages in just about everything, as an example, the industry was no longer allowed to manufacture pants with pleats and cuffs, because of the extra material required.

Subsequently, we were awarded contracts to manufacture 100% cotton fatigues, khakis and 100% wool, olive drab — both pants and shirts. The Waxahachie Plant was reconfigured for the manufacturing of shirts.

December 7, 1941: The Japanese attacked Pearl Harbor. President Roosevelt declared war on the Japanese, and the United States was in the throes of warfare. By the time these events occurred, 50% of our production was for Uncle Sam. Our sales force at the time numbered fifteen to twenty men. A few men continued selling, while others transferred to the inside and worked production and in the offices. Others went into the service.

As Uncle Sam needed extra military production, we opened plants in Jacksonville and Athens, Texas. About 98% of our operators were women. We did lose many associates who went into heavier labor to replace the young men who had gone off to war.

Early 1940: The United States Quartermaster Corps, headquartered at 21st and Johnson streets in Philadelphia, put out contracts to manufacture military uniforms. It was a competitive bidding process. The government furnished the fabric and trimmings, which they obtained from contracts with various fabric mills. Individual manufacturers were responsible for furnishing the cost of labor. Rigid deadlines regarding turn-around time were established. All in all, it was a fair process. I was very much involved in converting a substantial part of our business from civilian production to military production, and to coordinate matters with the Quartermaster Corps.

The Quartermaster Corps was responsible for feeding, clothing, and equipping every individual in all the American military branches throughout the world. These were awesome responsibilities during wartime, and it was a large and powerful organization. Working so closely with this arm of the military entitled me to six-month deferment. Later, I was offered a direct commission in the Quartermaster Corps, which I refused. Instead, my sights were focused on the Army Air Force Flying Cadet Program. However, I was eventually disqualified because of sinus problems and allergies.

At the onset of the war, Love Field in Dallas was converted to an Air Transport Command Ferrying Division Base. I met Air Force Captain Cal Ledbetter at the YMCA handball courts. At the time, he was stationed at Love Field. "Ed, you better volunteer for enlistment before they get your ass in the walking army!" Cal advised. That was my cue to step up and get active.

WORLD WAR II MILITARY SERVICE

After volunteering for enlistment in the U.S. Army Air Force, I did my basic training in Mineral Wells, Texas, and was assigned to the Ferrying Division of the Air Transport Command at Love Field in Dallas. Two months later, I qualified for Officer's Candidate School at Miami, Florida. After completing the training I was commissioned a second lieutenant, and after two weeks' leave I was sent to Wendover Field,[5] Utah, a Second Air Force base

---

5. Unbeknownst to the personnel at Wendover, this field stationed fifteen B-29 bombers, including the *Enola Gay*, and 800 personnel, for training to drop the atomic bombs on Hiroshima and Nagasaki.

for B-24 bombers. My first assignment there was assistant provo marshal and later I was the civilian personnel officer.

There were very few living quarters for married couples. Wives had to be employed on the base—that was really the only way married couples could live together. It was the job of the civilian personnel officer to assign said quarters to said married couples. We had quite a number of officers, ranking from first lieutenant through colonel, who were assigned to Wendover following overseas duty. My commanding officer filled me in on all the details before I was promoted to civilian personnel officer and promised to back me up 100%. Many of my predecessors had problems handling these officers, especially when they tried to pull rank on them. Fortunately, I was not intimidated and handled them very well.

My next assignment was the 558th Air Force Army Base in Nashville, Tennessee (a Ferrying Division Base), where I served as an assistant personnel officer.

August 6, 1945, the United States dropped the atomic bomb on Hiroshima, Japan, and three days later bombed the city of Nagasaki. The Japanese surrendered within a matter of days, putting an end to the war in the Pacific. There were still many acts of aggression in Germany, but for all purposes, the war was over. Getting our soldiers back to the States and dismantling the gigantic war machine was a huge project for this country.

My last station was headquarters for the Ferrying Division of the Air Transport Command in Cincinnati, Ohio, where I was a personnel officer. Later, I became the officer in charge of separation for all personnel in the Ferrying Division. I figured it would be a long time before I could get out of the service because I hadn't accumulated enough required points for separation, since I had no overseas duty. I received many calls from congressmen and other VIPs as to why so-and-so had not yet been released from the service. I had no problem handling this, and along the way I got to know the officers, via phone conversations, up and down the chain of command. After a few weeks, I noticed there were several letter requests for individuals to be released from the service to return to essential civilian work. My commanding officer was a Colonel Korth, and I told him about these letters and felt that I qualified to return to civilian life on the same basis. Colonel Korth agreed and told me he would endorse my own application. I was able to reach officers of the various commands by phone, and it didn't take long for me to get myself separated from the service.

On a cold, snowy December afternoon, I drove about fifty miles south to Wright Field, where I was mustered out of the service. The last question before being separated was, "Do you want to retain your reserve commission?" I replied, "No." Later, when our country was embroiled in the Korean War, those officers who accepted reserve commissions and didn't serve overseas in World War II were recalled for service in Korea. I, too, would have had to serve in the Korean War, had I accepted a reserve commission. It was good to get back to civilian life, and good to get back to Haggar.

CHAPTER 5

Haggar Corporation

The end of World War II marked one of the biggest economic growth spurts in this country's history. Millions of American soldiers came home and went to work. Our nation's factories were operating at maximum production levels. The housing market exploded. United by the patriotic issues of the war, Americans stepped forward, eager to achieve success.

Another significant factor of the day was the invention of a new medium called television. From the very start, television's popularity was overwhelming. Recognizing the ability to attract audiences in the millions, advertisers were eager to participate in the TV era.

Haggar Company grew right along with the rest of the nation. Starting in the mid-1930s, we identified ourselves for the first time by using the Haggar label in about 50% of our pants. Manufacturing facilities expanded. Our product line became more diversified. And finally, we benefited by the gigantic advancements in technology that enabled us to make better products from better fabrics, faster and more economically, and distribute them throughout the country and the world.

¤ ¤ ¤

For many years we ran our business, more or less, as a partnership, not paying too much attention to titles. However, as the company grew and we eventually evolved into a public corporation, more clarification was required. We established the positions of chairman of the board and chief executive officer. Prior to this time, the chairman of the board was recognized as the chief executive officer. The first to carry the title of chief executive officer was Joe Haggar, Jr., followed by Joe Haggar III.

Membership on the board of directors changed as our family and company grew. Initially, in 1927, Dad and Mother, along with Mother's brother, Harry Wasaff, sat on the board. When Joe and I were older, Dad reorganized the board once again: Dad as president; Mother as secretary/treasurer; and Joe and me.

In the early 1950s, and for many years thereafter, all the Haggar families lived in adjacent homes on Wedgwood Lane. Since we were the only board members at that time, it was often convenient to hold *unofficial* board meetings curbside. Whenever an issue arose, one of the three of us phoned the others and we met just a few paces from our respective front doors. Although we used to kid about this, many problems were solved on Wedgwood Lane.

In 1954 our board was as follows: J.M. Haggar, chairman of the board; Ed Haggar, president; Mrs. J.M. Haggar, vice president; Joe Haggar, Jr., secretary-treasurer.

In 1987: E. R. Haggar, chairman of the board; J.M. Haggar, Jr., president and CEO; E. R. Haggar, Jr., vice president and treasurer; J.M. Haggar III, vice president and secretary.

Before going public, we enlarged our board to include people other than Haggar family members: E. R. Haggar, chairman of the board; J.M. Haggar, Jr., president and CEO; E. R. Haggar, Jr., president of women's wear; J.M. Haggar III, president of men's wear; Jack Smith, president of men's wear manufacturing; Kevin Chisholm, director; Dick Heath, director; Norman Brinker, director.

Haggar became a publicly owned corporation in 1992. At that time, our board of directors consisted of Ed Haggar; Joe Haggar; Joe III; Frank Bracken; Ralph Beattie; Norman Brinker, head of Brinker International; Dick Heath, founder of Beauty Control; and Ray Evans, of Hallmark Cards.

As a private company from 1926 until the time we went public, in 1992, Haggar Corporation experienced only one loss year, in 1986.

¤ ¤ ¤

A few years after incorporating the business in 1927, Dad decided to split the ownership four ways. Mother and Dad owned 25% and the remaining 75% was equally divided between Joe, Rosemary, and me. This was considered a pretty radical move in the early 1930s. I still remember Mother and Dad discussing the issue before the actual transaction took place. "What if our kids turn out bad?" Mother asked Dad. Dad's reply, "Then we did a bad job raising them." From an estate and gift tax point of view, this was really a very wise move on Dad's part.

Tim Ferguson, an auditor with the public accounting firm of Prince, Harris and Company, audited our books for many years and eventually came to work for the company. Tim was a very practical man with a lot of good ideas. When we built the facility on Lemmon Avenue, it was Tim's idea that ownership of the building be divided among the four families. The company was charged a fair rental (whatever the going rate was in those days). Later on, the family purchased additional facilities and leased them to the company. Over the years, the company purchased some real estate for investment purposes. As the third generation of Haggars grew up and started their own careers and families, we felt it would be best, once again, to let the company own the buildings that were necessary for the operation of the business and let the Haggar family members own the raw land that had been owned by the company. In this way, the company could control its own destiny. As Jesus Christ said, "Render unto Caesar what is Caesar's and unto God what is God's."

¤ ¤ ¤

Selling the product has been an integral part of business, probably since the beginning of time. The basic rules of supply and demand — the essential core of economics — are facilitated by the salesman.

Dad set up the original sales programs and staff. In the late 1920s word got out that Jim Haggar was looking for salesmen to expand the company's sales and distribution. Initially, he sought experienced salesmen who had a following in certain territories. The first sales force numbered seven gentlemen. In their day, they were all good salesmen and helped build the company. At that time, Dad hired two brothers, Herbert and

Clarence Grunsfeld, of Los Angeles, to represent Haggar Company. Clarence was the ultimate "hot-shot" salesman, while Herbert—a big, burly guy—was as gentle as a lamb.

Clarence was quite a creative guy. By the mid-1930s, we were making 50,000 pairs of pants a week. Clarence suggested that we advertise this fact on billboards. We rented billboard space in Texas, New Mexico, and Oklahoma and prepared huge signs that read, "Haggar Pants... 50,000 pairs a week." Our earliest advertising.

Clarence came up with another idea. He created a little game called "1938 Keen Built Sweepstakes." Six numbered horses were printed on onionskin paper. The idea was to light the paper strip, and whatever horse burned the fastest won! The horses were named Price, Style, Fit, Fabric, Service, Patterns. The following message was printed on the bottom of the paper, "There are no handicaps in the Haggar Line. A Keen Built ticket always pays off." It was a clever idea, and we printed up thousands of these little games and distributed them to our customers, who in turn gave them to the consumers.

¤ ¤ ¤

Here's an interesting story about the old axiom *"It's not the amount, it's the principle that matters!"* In 1933, under the National Industrial Recovery Act (NIRA), Dad mistakenly declared the company's capital stock value equal to its par value of $120,000. Before the income tax return became due, however, Dad corrected his mistake by amending the declaration to reflect the actual value of $250,000. Guy Helvring, the commissioner of the Internal Revenue Service, rejected Dad's amendment as improper because the NIRA, according to the commissioner, did not allow any amendments. Over the course of the next seven years, our attorneys filed appeals to the U.S. Board of Tax Appeals and the U.S. Circuit Court of Appeals, but both failed.

Of course, Dad's legal fees far surpassed the paltry amount in question, but committed to the belief that truth and right would prevail, Dad convinced his attorneys to try his case before the U.S. Supreme Court. In the landmark ruling of *Haggar vs. Helvring,* the highest court in the country ruled in Dad's favor and severely criticized Mr. Helvring for his unreasonable, overtechnical interpretation of the statute.

Justice Stone, writing for a *unanimous* court in 1940, reversed the decisions of the lower courts and held that the capital stock tax return filed by Haggar in 1933, pursuant to Section 215 of the National Industrial Recovery Act of 1933, could be amended within the time required for filing income tax return.

¤ ¤ ¤

In the mid-1940s, J.C. Penney was still our largest customer, by far. Up until then, most transactions were handled directly by Dad. However, Dad began to encourage both Joe and me to establish direct contacts with the Penney management. Joe recalls a story that took place in 1946:

> In the early days, Ed and I accompanied Dad on his buying trips to New York. On this particular trip, we discovered a fabric—55% Dacron Polyester/45% Worsted Wool—that greatly interested Dad. Not only was it a good looking and durable fabric, but Dad quickly figured out that we could retail pants made from this fabric at $8.95. This price reflected a 38% mark up to the customer. I shared Dad's enthusiasm about the fabric and the high profit margin to our customers. On this same trip, Dad asked me to call on Mr. E.E. Cummings, who was the buyer of men's pants for J.C. Penney Department Stores, and make the pitch for these Dacron Polyester-Wool pants.
>
> Mr. Cummings was a very deliberate man; a smart buyer and a tough negotiator. I entered his office and found him sitting behind his huge desk, a cigarette in his mouth, which he always held between his teeth. I showed him swatches of the fabric and eagerly explained about the $8.95 retail price and the 38% mark up. Mr. Cummings took the swatches in hand. He carefully looked them over, then looked up at me and said, "Joe, we could sell a lot more of these pants at a retail price of $7.95." Following Dad's advice, I remained steadfast and argued for the $8.95 retail price. Finally, Mr. Cummings agreed. Penney's sold many, many pairs of these fine pants throughout the country.

◘ ◘ ◘

Haggar Company expanded their manufacturing facilities beyond the Dallas city limits beginning in 1936, the same year as the Texas Centennial, and continued opening new plants until the early 1990s.

In 1936 we chose the city of Greenville, located fifty miles east of Dallas, for several reasons. Greenville had a large population base from which to draw workers. Our biggest concern was finding a better class of help. Too much turnover killed production-line efficiency. Greenville was the first of many plants we opened. Primarily, it functioned as a sewing operation.

Located thirty-five miles south of Dallas, Waxahachie, Texas, was the site of our second factory. In addition to pants, this facility manufactured shirts. The Waxahachie plant opened in November 1938. Our next plant opened in McKinney in 1946.

Beginning in the late 1950s, four plants opened. The Temple plant opened in 1957, and then the Duncan plant in 1966. Our plant in Lawton opened in August 1967; the plant in Oklahoma City opened in June 1973.

Located 300 miles southeast of Dallas, the Rio Grande Valley is a vast area predominantly populated by Spanish-speaking people. Labor was plentiful in this area. The company opened several plants throughout the Rio Grande Valley, beginning in 1968 with our plant in Robstown. Many of our competitors accused us of locating there for cheap labor. However, it must be stated that we went down there *not* because labor was cheap, but rather because labor was *abundant*. Our wage scales were the same in the Rio Grande Valley as they were in any of our other plants—same benefits, vacations, holidays, and profit sharing.

Eventually we opened five plants in that area we referred to as "The Valley." Robstown opened in 1968; Edinburg opened in January 1969. The Brownsville plant, which manufactured men's sport coats as well as pants, opened in January 1973. We opened two plants in Weslaco. The cutting plant opened in June 1975, and the sewing plant opened in January 1986.

Two important similarities emerged throughout the Valley plants: First, these facilities employed the largest numbers of personnel. And second, they were our most efficient plants.

Dad always took the time to speak to and get acquainted with as many associates as possible. Speaking in Spanish, he told them of his early life in Mexico; stories about his poverty and his struggles to achieve early successes. Dad always thanked God and the Blessed Mother for all the guidance and help he received, especially in those early days in Mexico. (All of our facilities in the Rio Grande Valley had shrines and altars to Our Lady of Guadalupe.) Our associates in the Valley plants called Dad "El Patrone," which means father or chief.

The following is a complete listing of our plants and the year they opened. (Currently all our sewing operations are offshore.)

Dallas Plants—1928	Olney—1963	Weslaco Sewing—1975
Greenville—1936	Duncan-1966	LaRomana—1984
Waxahachie—1938	Lawton—1967	Leon—1984
McKinney—1946	Robstown—1968	Weslaco Cutting—1986
Corsicana—1955	Edinburg—1969	Higuey—1991
Temple—1957	Brownsville—1973	
Bowie—1961	Oklahoma City—1973	

¤ ¤ ¤

The National Highway Act was passed during the Eisenhower administration in the early 1950s. This concerted effort to improve and interlock our nation's highways was important to us because Haggar had facilities spread out over two states. We were dependent on trucking to move our products from place to place.

Initially, in the late 1940s, we started with a small fleet of trucks that transported raw materials from fabric mills to our manufacturing plants. We designated five southern cities as "free on board (F.O.B)" sites, which meant that we also transported freight, other than our own, when the trucks were empty. Doing so provided additional revenue. Retailers paid for transportation from the various F.O.B. points.

At its peak, our trucking fleet comprised twenty-one power trucks and fifty-five trailers. Each trailer was a rolling advertisement for Haggar Company. Over the years we've received many wonderful letters thanking our courteous drivers who stopped to help stranded motorists on the highways. With the advent of offshore production, we've reduced the number of trucks and trailers used by the company.

Joe recalls:

> As a boy of fifteen, it was always a great thrill for me to ride in the truck when we delivered cut parts to our sewing plant in Greenville, Texas. In those days, the trip took about one and a half hours each way, and I always had a great time riding along with the drivers. After graduation from Notre Dame, I became involved in the operation side of the business. During those early days, I used to drive between our five manufacturing plants... some were a four- or five-hour drive from Dallas. Finally, I convinced the company that an airplane would enable me to be more productive on the job. I was already a licensed pilot. It didn't take much of an argument to point out that my time could be used much more effectively at the plants, rather than driving in the car to reach the plants. The company agreed and purchased a Beechcraft Bonanza.

¤ ¤ ¤

The only job I ever had where I didn't work for the family was in the military during World War II. Most of the time I worked in administration and personnel. I learned a lot about organization, saw a lot of boondoggling, and enjoyed the positive results when there was the right mix of people, training, and jobs.

It was during this time that I first envisioned a new breed of salesmen for Haggar. I met a lot of sharp guys in the service: dynamic, well-educated men. I really wanted our product to be sold on its own merits, rather than on the personality of a particular salesman. Following the war, the company started a sales training program, where the salesman learned all about the product, starting with a swatch of fabric, through the manufacturing process and finally distribution.

College graduates with dynamic personalities and good personal presentations were the criteria we used in hiring our salesmen. The training program was not presented in a classroom format. Instead, the incoming salesmen toured our different manufacturing plants and studied how our clothing was put together. They also spent time in the shipping department, learning different models, fabrics, and styles. After six months, we put them out on the road with one of our seasoned salesmen. Eventually, the trainees went out on their own, in virgin territories.

The new salesmen that came aboard had larger territories. They educated the retailers about the Haggar product and updated inventory more often.

Our national advertising programs created nationwide distribution. Subsequently, the sales force was divided into two divisions—east and west—and within that structure, eight regions were established. Each region had its own regional sales manager. Today, Haggar maintains regional sales offices in New York, Chicago, and Los Angeles.

Our sales force is a well-organized, productive arm of Haggar Corporation. Until recently, we had two sales meetings each year: the first in May, when we previewed our spring and summer lines; and the second in November, when we showed our upcoming fall and winter lines. Our advertising people were on hand, as well, to explain different campaigns and strategies to the salespeople. Designers and people from the marketing department were also available to answer questions. In addition to learning about the new lines, our salespeople are asked to evaluate and offer their own comments and suggestions regarding the new items being presented. All of this input was incorporated into our forecasting program.

Some thirty years ago, we initiated a program called "Pre-Line," where we invited our biggest customers to view the line before it went into production. All of our key department store buyers, managers, and regional managers came to review and make suggestions regarding models, fabrics, and styles being shown. Our salespeople were also on hand. This was always a learning experience for all of us. Pre-Line also attracted a lot of corporate spying, so retail prices were never mentioned. Subsequently, our biggest competitors, Farah and Levi Strauss, also began a Pre-Line program. As always, they followed our lead!

In the last ten to twenty years, large retailers and department stores have experienced significant changes. For example, the great consolidation of retail store ownership and shopping malls marked the end of many independent retailers. Today, many retailing conglomerates have central buying. At one time, we had 165 sales associates. To keep abreast of the changing times and trends, our sales force was reorganized and greatly reduced. We have approximately thirty-four salespeople and about sixty retail marketing associates who work in conjunction with our retailers.

¤ ¤ ¤

THE BEGINNING OF HAGGAR NATIONAL ADVERTISING

Between 1938 and 1940, the company started advertising in trade journals, such as *Men's Wear* and *The Daily News Record*. Inspired by Cadillac's slogan "Cadillac — standard of the world," our ads featured "Haggar — the standard of America!" In 1939, a fellow named Morris Hite, from the Dallas-based advertising agency Tracy-Locke, called on Dad. My desk was just down the hall and Dad told Morris, "You better see Ed, because I don't know a thing about advertising!" Morris and I talked quite a bit that day about establishing the identity of Haggar nationwide.

"I'd like to use the advertising to build up our accounts with the Haggar name," I informed Mr. Hite.

"If that's what you want, then we'll do it!" Morris assured me.

And that was the beginning of a long and fruitful association between Haggar Company and Tracy-Locke.

Tracy-Locke was a regional agency, whose clients and demography were situated in Texas and throughout the Southwest. At the time we began this association, the agency's largest customers were Dr Pepper, Mrs. Baird's Bread, and Borden's Milk.

Our first foray into national advertising began in 1940 with a full-page color ad in *Life Magazine*. The cost was $10,000. It was a huge risk, since we were putting the cart before the horse, in that we didn't have national distribution at the time. But I felt that ad would introduce the Haggar name — and so it did. Our early national advertising program enabled our salesmen to establish new accounts across the country. *Our association with Tracy-Locke, along with the building of a new sales organization, was the second most important turning point in the success of our business.*

Our first full-page advertisement in *Life Magazine* introduced the Haggar Harmony Chart, which became a very popular merchandising tool. Printed with colored swatches and patterns, the chart mixed and matched different colored pants, shirts, and sport coats. Several years later, we published a small pamphlet entitled "Keeping Up With Your Trousers" that pointed out to the consumer exactly what made Haggar slacks better than any other brand. These pamphlets were included with the purchase of Haggar slacks.

Our advertising budget increased with our sales and distribution. Shortly after *Life,* we placed full-page color ads in other national magazines, including *The Saturday Evening Post, Esquire, Sports Illustrated, Look,* and *Colliers.*

Our ads featured many of the top professional athletes of the day wearing Haggar pants. From the world of major league baseball came endorsements from Nellie Fox, Mickey Mantle, Roger Maris, Phil Rizzuto, Eddie Mathews, and Robin Roberts. Professional football players Cloyse Box, Frank Gifford, Otto Graham, Bobby Lane, Don Meredith, Roger Staubach, Pat Summerall, and Doak Walker appeared in Haggar advertisements. Cloyse Box was a wide receiver and Bobby Lane a quarterback for the Detroit Lions. We ran several ads in *Sports Illustrated* that stated, "A winning combination... Lane to Box... Haggar pants and a sport coat." (At the time, we weren't manufacturing sport coats.)

Roger Staubach graduated from the Naval Academy in 1965 and began his stellar career with the Dallas Cowboys in 1969, after completing his tour of duty with the U.S. Navy. Jim Walsh, the chief lay-officer of Jesuit High School in Dallas, arranged a meeting for me with this awesome quarterback shortly after his arrival in Dallas. Roger avidly agreed to endorse Haggar slacks in magazine and television commercials, and he did so for many years, until his retirement from the Cowboys. Roger became a great personal friend of mine, as well as the other Haggars. Even though he's been off the gridiron for over twenty years, Roger continues to endorse Haggar slacks today, on a non-paying basis! I am honored to call him a friend.

Throughout the years, the most celebrated professional athletes in the world have endorsed our products. Here are a few stories about some of these remarkable men:

I first met Mickey Mantle in the late 1950s. At the time,

Mickey endorsed Haggar slacks for magazine advertisements. During the off-season, Mickey and his family lived in Dallas, and we played golf together from time to time.

The Dallas Cowboys' great superstar Don Meredith endorsed Haggar pants for many years. My daughter, Mary Alice, was just about the biggest Cowboys fan in Dallas, and her favorite player was Don Meredith. Don was very thoughtful and sent her some autographed photos and autographed footballs.

Sam Huff, a fine football player and a fine gentleman, was a linebacker for the New York Giants. During the off-season, Sam worked in the marketing department for J.P. Stevens, a large textile company. Haggar did a lot of business with J.P. Stevens, and I got to know Sam quite well. Whenever Sam's business travels brought him to Dallas, we always found time for a visit.

On one particular night, Sam joined us for dinner at the house. After dinner, I drove him back to his hotel. On the way, we passed St. Paul's Hospital. "Sam," I said, "my daughter is in that hospital being treated for asthma. She's a great football fan, and I know she would love to meet you. Do you mind stopping in for a few minutes?"

"Ed, I'd be delighted," Sam replied.

Sam and I entered her room together. "Mary Alice, do you know who this is?" I asked.

"Yeah... It's Sam Huff, and he creamed Don Meredith in the last game!" she scowled.

Sam walked closer to her bed and said, "Honey, I was only doing my job!"

The introduction of television changed the advertising industry altogether. Suddenly, Haggar was able to display their product to millions of people at a single moment.

Our first TV commercial was done in conjunction with the Emporium, a large department store based in San Francisco, and their sister-company, The Broadway, in Los Angeles. "If you put in a stock of Haggar pants, we'll show you how to advertise them on television," we offered. Filmed in black and white, the commercial began with a wide-angle shot of the store, then showed the Haggar pants collection, and ended with "Haggar slacks are available at the Emporium and at The Broadway." The ad campaign was successful. Both retailing chains sold a lot of Haggar slacks. Our first national network TV commercial featuring the "Haggar dancing pants" ran in the early 1950s.

Through Earl Stewart, Jr., who at the time was on the PGA tour and earlier was a golfing buddy and good friend of Joe's, we signed up Arnold Palmer, Dow Finsterwald, Doug Ford, Art Wall, Jr., Tommy Bolt, Tom Nieporte, and Bobby Nichols for our early television commercials. Arnold Palmer had won the Masters Tournament. The other three, at one time or another, had won the PGA Championship.

All of this was so new. These fellows were happy to contribute. As time marched forward and television ads became more commonplace, many professional athletes wanted us to put out products with their own names, rather than the Haggar label. A little after the Ben Hogan Company, which manufactured golf clubs, came into vogue, Ben called and inquired about manufacturing Ben Hogan Golf Slacks. We explained to Ben that we didn't have the funds to promote our Haggar name as well as a second label.

A few years later, Arnold Palmer asked us to manufacture a line of slacks using his name only. At the time, Arnold was signed up with us for a year's contract. As I had done earlier with Ben, I explained to Arnold that we couldn't support two names. Still under contract, Arnold told me about an offer he received from a small manufacturer in Florida called Sun State Slacks. I told him that we didn't want to lose him from our stable of sports celebrities; however, if this was a good deal, we would certainly be glad to let him out of his contract. He decided to try out the offer from Florida.

Years later, I was going through some family movies and discovered the original black and white television commercial with Arnold Palmer. I sent the film to Arnold with a note that read: "Dear Arnold—After being released from your Haggar Contract, you went on to great success with Sun State Slacks and other endeavors. All of your endorsements have been very successful. So Arnold, where are my residuals?" A few weeks later I ran into Arnold and Dow Finsterwald at the Bob Hope Classic. Again, I asked Arnold about my residuals. His answer was, "They're in the mail." I haven't gotten them yet!

Formula 5000 Road Racing was very popular with many

young kids during the mid-1960s. David Hobbs and Carl Hogan, two of the most famous race drivers of the day, acted as spokesmen for Haggar. Both of these champion drivers helped us in promoting our "Snug Duds "and "Mustang Pants," aimed at that age group.

In the mid-1970s, Lamar Hunt started the World Championship Tennis series. Haggar actively participated in this venture for four years, sponsoring the Haggar Scoreboard. All the great men's tennis superstars of the day, such as Arthur Ashe, Bjorn Borg, Rod Laver, Ille Nastase, John Newcombe, and Stan Smith, competed in this prestigious event. The winner of the series was awarded a solid gold tennis ball, valued at $25,000. For two successive years, Arthur Ashe received top honors. When we presented the second award to Arthur Ashe, I made a faux pas when I said, "Arthur, you now have two gold balls!"

Charlie Martin, our director of advertising, was very active in the tennis promotion, as well as many other events during his time with the company. Charlie was an excellent advertising man. He did a tremendous job and certainly contributed to the success of our company.

Haggar served as corporate sponsors for several major golf tournaments: the Bob Hope Classic (broadcast every year on NBC), the President Gerald Ford Invitational in Vail, Colorado, and the Byron Nelson Open in Dallas. Dad, Joe, and I played in many of these tournaments.

The Bob Hope Classic is played on four courses in the Palm Springs area. The first four days are devoted to pro-am play, and the pros battle it out the last day. NBC always televised the tournament. Because of Bob, the tournament has always drawn the best pros and an interesting array of celebrities.

Pairing for the pro-am is done by draw. One time, I was paired with Glen Campbell and Arnold Palmer. Walking down the fairway between Glen and Arnold, I was surprised to learn later that announcer Bruce Devlin said, "And here comes Mr. Slacks himself, Ed Haggar." I wasn't hitting the ball worth a darn that day. The last four holes were televised. By the grace of God, I was on camera a couple of times and made excellent shots both times.

Our advertising program really stepped up with the introduction of double-knit pants in 1970. At that time, a one-minute commercial on network television during prime-time hours cost about $25,000 per ad. A lot of people saw our ads on national TV. We advertised about sixteen times per week on such popular shows as *Sugar Foot and Bronco, Twelve O'Clock High, Naked City, Monday Night at the Movies,* and *Big Valley.* Later on, we advertised during Super Bowl games and many of the national PGA golf tournaments, as well as several major league baseball games.

We spent a lot of money on advertising and did so consistently. None of our competitors advertised on this scale until Levi's introduced their Dockers line in 1986. Some of our competitors ran ads on a national level from time to time. However, most advertising was sporadic and certainly on a lesser scale of production and saturation. Our advertising was effective because we were consistent, year after year.

In those days, the tax rates, including excess profits, climbed as high as 90%. It was my idea to spend the money advertising and let Uncle Sam pay for the bulk of it.

Recently, Super Dave Osborne was featured in two very successful television commercials for our "Wrinkle Free" pants. In the first, he is seen going through an automated car wash wearing our slacks. The second ad shows Dave crashing into a bridge.

¤ ¤ ¤

Closely associated with sales and advertising, merchandising is the finishing touch that draws the customer's eye to our product.

Popular conversational topics in the late 1930s dealt with "leisure time" or "slack time." The phrase "slack time" intrigued Morris Hite and me, and that's when we first coined the word "slacks" to describe men's trousers. This term became an industry standard.

Years ago, men's pants were stacked on large display tables. Whenever there was a sale, people sorted through those stacks, looking for color, size, style, etc. By the end of the day, the table looked like a big bowl of spaghetti. There was no rhyme or reason to the jumbled pants. Some poor clerk spent hours rearranging and restacking the pants.

It was our idea that the consumer should be able to find our pants in the correct sizes, etc., as easily as a housewife found what she needed in the supermarket. Then we came up with the idea of putting our pants on small, disposable hangers. The Batts Hanger Company of Michigan created a small, inexpensive, plastic hanger with clips at each end, which enabled our pants to be neatly hung on display racks. These hangers really provided easier accessibility for the customers. For several years thereafter we shipped our pants on the hangers. Hanging pants were a big success. In fact, within the retail industry, the display hangers were always referred to as "Haggar Hangers." That little hanger helped revolutionize the way pants were displayed.

Contests and games are sure-fire merchandising tools. Men's apparel and football—a match made in heaven. We started with a small brochure entitled "How to Get More Fun Out of Watching Football" by Doak Walker, which was given away with each pair of pants we sold. Several years later, we started a game called "Pinpoint the Pigskin." Our store displays featured photographs from different professional football games. Hidden somewhere in the photo was a football. Whoever found the exact location of the football, or came closest, won the contest. Game tickets and transportation and accommodations were always the prizes of choice. We also sponsored many contests in connection with the pro-bowl games, which were extremely successful promotions for us.

We always listened—especially to our customers. Over the years we heard a great many suggestions for merchandising our products. Most were successful; a few were not. However, we kept an open ear and an open mind and realized that by no means did we have all the answers.

¤ ¤ ¤

Before World War II, our tabulating was done by hand: coordinating the orders from our sales force; lot numbers of our various models, etc. At the time, we used a system that utilized IBM-type punch cards that were skewered and manually sorted. Known as the McBee System, it was much faster than tabulation by hand, but still much slower than electronic tabulation. During the war, I had the opportunity to observe IBM tabulators working many different functions. When I was mustered out of the service, we contacted IBM and installed a system at Haggar Company. Those early tabulating machines evolved into computers of every sort and function.

All big operating changes pose problems at the beginning; it's just human nature. We were actively training our personnel to operate the machines and handle the punch cards used in the system. Still, there were glitches and setbacks that caused some minor problems and lots of frustration. Somebody told us about a fellow named Roland Ferguson, who worked for Texas Power and Light Company. Fergie had a penchant for getting the optimal results from these tabulating systems. After several conversations I learned two things about Fergie: First, he really was an ace on this equipment; and second, he wasn't too happy with his job at Texas Power and Light Company. Fortunately for us, Fergie joined Haggar Company and supervised our data processing.

Roland Ferguson was a man of many talents, in and outside the office. Some of our associates got together and formed a softball team. I played first base, mainly because, so to speak, we owned the ball and bat. We were delighted to find that Fergie was one of the best softball pitchers in the state. Later on, we were accused by some leading Dallas businessmen of hiring Fergie simply to advance our softball team.

¤ ¤ ¤

The Haggar Foundation was started on July 6, 1950. Mother and Dad always had a saying, "If you take out of the pot, you've got to put back into the pot!" Starting in the early 1930s, during the Great Depression, Dad took us down to the poor sections of West Dallas at Christmastime to help him distribute $5 and $10 gold pieces to the needy people there. (This was before the U.S. got off the gold standard.) The tradition was really the genesis of the Haggar Foundation. Mother and Dad continued to do charitable work and make charitable donations all their lives.

A certain percentage of the company's profits were automatically transferred into the Haggar Foundation each year. The good part about a foundation is that money can be accumulated, so grants can be made every year regardless of the profitability of an individual or a company.

Originally, the Haggar Foundation was set up pretty much like a corporation, with officers and a board of directors. Dad was the first president of the foundation. Rosemary served as executive director for many years. Later, I became president. The directors and officers met quarterly to discuss investments and review requests for the foundation's funds.

The Haggar Foundation supports educational and training programs for the disadvantaged and helps the disabled and those in need of health care from our city. We have always been a major contributor to the United Fund Drive. And we've made significant contributions to the cultural enhancement of our city. Over the years, we've contributed to every hospital campaign in Dallas: Methodist, Baylor, Presbyterian, and St. Paul's. The Haggar Foundation also made sizable contributions to the University of Dallas and Southern Methodist University. In addition, the foundation set up a scholarship fund for the children of our associates. The University of North Texas oversees the screening program, so there is no favoritism.

Our policy of gifting was mostly confined to Dallas, our headquarters, and the communities where we had facilities. In addition, the Haggar Foundation also contributed to the University of Notre Dame, St. Mary's College, St. Jude's Children's Research Hospital in Memphis, and the City of Hope Hospital in Los Angeles, where Dad received the Golden Torch Award. Other notable gifts were to the Philadelphia College of Textiles and Science, Metropolitan Museum of Fine Arts, SMU Tennis Complex, SMU School of Music Scholarship Program, Haggar Hall and scholarship programs at the University of Dallas, and Dallas Baptist College.

As the third generation of Haggars came of age, new ideas were added to the mix. We agreed to split the Haggar Foundation into four individual foundations: the Ed Haggar Family Foundation; the Rosemary Haggar Vaughan Foundation; the Joe Haggar Family Foundation; and the Haggar Corporation Foundation. The Haggar Corporation Foundation continues the ongoing projects such as the scholarship program. Contributions from the different family foundations are left up to the discretion of the different family members. The effects and good work of all the foundations remain beneficial and far-reaching.

¤ ¤ ¤

The Haggar Profit Sharing Fund was started December 1, 1953. We were allowed to share profits with our associates annually. The amount of sharing depended on the profitability of our business. After a six-month eligibility, each associate became a member of the plan and shared a portion of the profits. The amount was dependent on the individual's annual earnings. An account, similar to a regular savings bank account, was established for each participant in the fund. Income enhancement from investments and profits added to an account each year. The longer an individual stayed in the plan, the more money accumulated in his account.

Joe recalls the origins of our profit-sharing program:

> One reason we were always successful was that we had a great team of people who had very positive attitudes, and with whom we had a very positive and solid relationship. We worked hard at making certain that all management and supervisory personnel were trained in how to listen, lead and motivate the people under them in a positive manner. Our concept was, "Always maintain the confidence of the people working under you, and they will help you accomplish any task." In order to make sure this really worked, we wanted to share with our associates the profits of the operation of the business. In the 1950s we established a very fine profit-sharing program in which every associate in the organization participated. At the end of each year they were rewarded with a percentage of the profits, based on their income. This was then put into a deferred profit-sharing program. When our associates retired from the company, they took with them considerable sums from the profit-sharing program.
>
> At the end of each year, we determined our profits and a certain share of that profit went back to those managers, supervisors and department heads in the form of a cash payment. This was a great incentive, because it showed that working together really paid off.
>
> We always believed that if we shared the success with all of our associates, it would help us become a more profitable and a better organization... and it did.

¤ ¤ ¤

In the early 1950s we discovered a 65% polyester and a 35% rayon linen that looked as good as Irish linen. We merchandised them as Shanghai Weave. We featured two models—plain front and new pleated model with an attached half belt made from the same fabric—advertised as "The Sarasota Model." This went over very big with golfers expecially. In the fall we followed up with forecast flannels—65% polyester and 35% rayon—which had the look and feel of wool flannel, two great winners.

In the mid '50s we introduced Pimalon (65% polyester and 35% Pima Cotton) and Capetown Tropicals (65% polyester and 35% rayon). These were offered with pre-finished bottoms—instant slacks. The buyer could find his exact waist and inseam without waiting for alterations. This really exploded the pants business; all our competitors followed us. Now all our slacks are sold pre-finished.

¤ ¤ ¤

Here is a brief summary of events that preceded the union strike in 1955. In 1940, Haggar Company left the Santa Fe Building and moved to our new facility on Lemmon Avenue. The move represented a giant step forward for the company; we truly had room to grow. The move enabled us to double our sewing facility, from 300 to 600 operators.

When word got out that we were doubling the number of our sewing operators, some union members infiltrated the ranks of our new employees. Perhaps we were remiss in not thoroughly screening the new operators, because we had no prior experience with the unions. In any event, the union caused a lot of dissension among the new employees by telling them that failure to join the union would result in lower wages and poor working conditions. Well, there was just no truth in these accusations, and our older employees knew it. But the union played on the vulnerability of the new workers.

In 1941 push came to shove, and an election was held for union representation at the Dallas Pants Company. The final vote was very close. Our long-term employees were against union representation. However, the vote to admit the union was victorious by a small margin. From that point on, we were legally obligated to negotiate with the union. Eventually, we had contracts with the union in the following, separately incorporated plants: Dallas Pants Company, Greenville Pants Manufacturing Company, Waxahachie Garment Company, McKinney Pants Manufacturing Company, and Corsicana Company.

Bargaining with the union in good faith, it was always our policy to have the best working conditions, fairest treatment, and best benefits and wages in the industry. The main thing the union wanted, however, was a closed shop—and we weren't about to force our employees to join the union.

It should also be noted here that all of our manufacturing divisions were separately incorporated. Each individual facility served as a contractor for Haggar. Our Dallas facility on Lemmon Avenue was originally incorporated as the Dallas Pants Company. The Waxahachie facility was the Waxahachie Garment Company, etc. By doing this, we put each of our manufacturing facilities in lower tax brackets. Otherwise, if these facilities were part of Haggar Corporation, we would have been spending most of our profits on taxes. Also, in case of a union organizational drive, each facility would have to be organized separately. As a result, we plowed back the savings into the business.

In 1955 the union tried to force us into a closed shop, *"or else!"* We *wouldn't agree*. At that point, the union called a strike. It was early winter and we offered coffee and doughnuts to the strikers in the picket line. In the early 1950s, we hired Fritz Lyne, a respected labor attorney, to advise us. Several weeks after the strike was declared, Mr. Lyne suggested that we hire new workers to replace those who walked out. Eventually, we filled nearly every position at all our facilities, enabling us to continue manufacturing. Because we operated out of several different locations, the union was never able to completely shut us down. However, they caused a lot of damage. About 40-60% of our operators went out on strike, and we were forced to use contractors to supplement some production. Union members marched in picket lines in front of our facilities. They threatened our customers and ordered them to stop buying Haggar merchandise.

Well-organized picket lines marched in front of department stores, verbally abusing shoppers who crossed the lines. A great many of the department stores had alteration departments that were unionized. The stores did not want their tailors to walk out. In some instances, we used neutral labels to assuage the fears of customers and clerks. During this whole debacle, I spent most of my time on the telephone, or on the road, reinstating orders. In my personal opinion, that strike was the lowest point in the history of our company.

About a year later, the union leaders called us and told us they were ready to settle the strike. "What strike? As far as we're concerned, the strike is settled," we replied. Since that time there have been few efforts to unionize our facilities.

¤ ¤ ¤

November 22, 1963 — a day Dallas citizens of my generation will always remember. Schools declared it a holiday and closed for the day, allowing children the opportunity to view President and Mrs. Kennedy as they drove through Dallas.

All of the Haggars and their children had the opportunity to see the presidential envoy close-up. Our plant on Lemmon Avenue was one mile south of Love Field, where *Air Force One* landed. President and Mrs. Kennedy and Governor John Connally and his wife, Nellie, rode in the first open-top car. The car left the airport and slowed down in front of our plant. Perhaps Governor Connally leaned toward the president and said, "The Haggars are good friends of mine," as the car passed by. All of us were thrilled to see President Kennedy and Jackie.

The president was scheduled to address a group of business leaders and prominent citizens at the Trade Center. We drove over in two cars. I drove the first car: Mother and Dad, Joe and Isabell, and Patty. Rosemary and Eddie Vaughan followed in the second car. There by invitation, we still battled traffic detours all the way to Market Center. I drove directly to the front of Market Center to let Mother and Dad out of the car. Pulling out of the area in search of a parking space, I turned on the radio and heard the shocking news. President Kennedy had been shot! President Kennedy assassinated! The whole world viewed this horror in Dallas on television and grieved. The television networks played and replayed film clips from those horrifying moments. Mother and Dad were seen quite often in the footage.

¤ ¤ ¤

In the late 1960s a new merchandising team came into being at the Penney Company and the head merchant wanted Haggar to be a contractor. Penney would buy the piece goods, choose the patterns, style the line, and pay a small contracting fee. Penney's, one of our earliest and best customers, was certainly responsible for our company's early growth. However, we refused the offer for contract work because it would have been, at best, a very low profit or break-even deal. As a result, we didn't do business with the Penney Company again until the mid-1980s. We parted as good friends and stayed that way until we started selling them again with the Haggar label.

Several years before, we had many discussions with Barger Tygart, who was one of Penney's top merchandisers. We told Barger that we certainly wanted to sell to Penney's, but with the Haggar label. We were worried, however, that our other department store accounts would object. I told Barger, "Time cures everything. The way you folks are building your stores and reputation, you will soon be as good as, or better than many of the department stores we are doing business with now." And that's exactly what happened.

Eventually, we did agree to sell our merchandise to Penney's, this time with the Haggar label. We did receive complaints from several of our customers, but in time, most of the opposition ceased.

¤ ¤ ¤

Sorting through seventy-five years of memories... I always remember Dad saying, "Make a good product and sell it at a fair price." And Dad truly practiced what he preached.

Retail sales evolved and changed drastically from the time Dad started the business in 1926. By the late 1960s, the number of large department store chains increased, which increased competition in the retailing industry. Huge shopping centers sprung up all over the country, giving consumers a wider variety of stores in convenient, accessible locations. And finally, high-volume, discount merchants opened stores that offered brand-name items at prices lower than traditional department stores.

At Haggar Company, we were beating our brains out to try to give the consumer a good value. We offered our product at the same price, across the board. But some merchants were selling our pants for $12, while others were advertising and selling the same pants for $9.95. In order to make sure that the consumer got good value and the retailer a fair profit, Haggar instituted the practice of "pre-pricing" our merchandise. In other words, each pair of pants, or each item we manufactured, left our factories with tickets attached that listed the "suggested retail price." The whole industry followed our lead.

¤ ¤ ¤

In the late 1960s the Justice Department accused us of price fixing, which is a criminal offense. Our definition of price fixing is as follows: When a manufacturer gets together with his competitors and says, "This is a new and great product. Let's don't give it away. Let's charge the same price!" That *is* price fixing.

At the time, we were tagging our products with suggested retail sales prices. We were accused by the Justice Department of threatening a retailer. For example, if "Retailer A" was adhering to the suggested retail price of $12.95 and "Retailer B" was selling the same item at $11.95, the threat to "Retailer B" would be: "If you don't adhere to our retail policies, we will quit selling to you!" We never treated our retailers in this manner.

We had to hire a so-called "Philadelphia lawyer." He was truly an expert and coached us regarding any possible future testimony and the manner in which we submitted our records. We knew the company wasn't guilty. After fifteen months, our records were returned and the Justice Department cleared us of any alleged wrongdoing.

Subsequently, the fifty chairmen of the National Alliance of Businessmen (I was the Dallas chairman) were recruited to help Mr. Nixon with his campaign for re-election in 1971. I was asked to chair the campaign for the Dallas-Fort Worth area. Since Haggar Company was under the watchful eye of the Department of Justice, I declined President Nixon's request. I did not want to embarrass the president or call attention to our company's situation. The Justice Department's investigation was fortuitous in one way. Had I accepted President Nixon's offer to serve on the re-election committee, I would have worked under Maurice Stans, who was very involved in the Watergate affair.

¤ ¤ ¤

The introduction of double-knit fabrics in 1970 was a sure-fire, major home run for Haggar Company. Dad's genius for selecting this unique fabric put us miles ahead of our competitors. We were the "firstest with the mostest."

One day Dad called me into his office. On his desk was a swatch of a new double-knit fabric. As he spoke, Dad's hands were busy crumbling, crushing, and patting this unique material. The thing I remember most distinctly that day was the hideous color of the fabric... sort of a coral-orange hue.

"What do you think?" Dad asked.

"It's definitely a ladies' wear fabric," I replied.

"Forget the color... This is a miracle fabric. It's practically indestructible, yet it's soft against the skin. It's washable and dryable. Imagine taking a pair of pants directly from the dryer... putting them on... pressed and ready to wear! Housewives across the country will buy these for their husbands, just because they are so easy to care for...." Dad's excitement was contagious. "Ed, I'm going to the mills and order this wonderful stuff in every suitable color and pattern. We're going to revolutionize the men's pants business." And that's exactly what happened.

What is a double-knit fabric? The *American Heritage Dictionary of the English Language* defines double-knit as follows: "A jersey-like fabric knitted on a machine with two sets of needles, so that a double thickness of fabric is produced in which the two sides of the fabric are interlocked."

Milliken, J.P. Stevens, and Texfi manufactured most of the double-knit fabrics we purchased. While some mills produced a heavy, coarse material, described as "16-cut," we always insisted on the best fabrics knit from the best yarns. The finer yarns produced a knitted fabric known as "22-24 cut," which is what we used for our dress pants.

Dad *sold* me and the rest of us on double-knits. I said, "Let's really go big-time and advertise and market this product." First we started with strong representation in trade journals; advertising in *The Daily News Record* and *Men's Wear Magazine,* as well as advertisements in national magazines and strong national TV advertising. Also, a strong co-op plan and excellent point of sales material at the retail level. People asked us why we promoted double-knits. They didn't realize at the time that it was the only fabric that the retailer and consumer wanted.

One particular TV ad really sold the product for us. The ad was filmed in Acapulco, Mexico. Known worldwide for high diving off jagged cliffs, we hired one of the local diving champions to dive off the highest cliff, wearing a pair of Haggar double-knit pants. In the next shot, this fellow gets out of the water, his pants, though wet, remain perfectly pressed.

A little aside: A very good friend of Dad's, Fred Bantz, who was the general merchandise manager at J.C. Penney Company, called Dad and told him that the son of the famous golf professional at Baltasrol, John Farrell, was applying for the job of head professional at Brook Hollow Golf Club in Dallas. He asked if Dad could help the young man. Dad asked me if I knew the president of Brook Hollow, and I did. He was a good friend named Arch Owens. So I talked to Arch about Johnny Farrell's son. Arch confided in me that the club had just made the decision to hire another pro for the job, although Johnny's son was one of the top three contenders. At just about the same time, my good friend from Dallas, Bobby Russell, made a career move to New York City. Bobby joined, and eventually became president of, Baltasrol, one of the premier golf clubs in the States. On my first visit to Baltasrol, Bobby introduced me to Johnny Farrell. After Johnny found out that I interceded on behalf of his son at Brook Hollow, I was always welcomed at the club. On a couple of occasions, Johnny helped me with my short game, which has always been lacking.

The Duke of Windsor spent part of his summers at Baltasrol. Johnny Farrell gave him many lessons. During one particular visit to New York, Bobby invited me to play golf with another guest and himself. I arrived at the club and immediately recognized the Duke of Windsor. "This is Ed Haggar, of Haggar

Slacks," Johnny Farrell told the Duke. Well, I had never met an ex-king before and I didn't know whether to genuflect or shake his hand! His Royal Highness extended his hand toward me, and I shook it. "Oh yes," he said in the most charming English accent, "I remember that chap diving off the cliff in double-knit pants." I don't know if the House of Windsor wore double-knits, but it was a nice compliment and showed the success of our advertising campaign.

Another time I was playing with Bobby in a golf tournament, and I flubbed (chili-dipped) a sand-wedge shot. Bobby was quite funny and made the remark: "Even the teacher of kings can't help him!"

¤ ¤ ¤

Existing customers and new accounts from every corner of the country wanted Haggar double-knit pants for their customers. After filling the pipeline, we realized that people really liked this product and it looked like it was going to be around for a while. After a great deal of discussion, Joe, Dad, and I decided that we would put double-knits on a Service Plan (which meant that the retailer would put in a stock of the goods, and that we would replenish the stock every two weeks). We hadn't put anything on a Service Plan since the days of our khakis in the late 1930s. As the volume of our sales increased, our overhead lowered and we were able to sell this fine product at the lowest prices, which made them even more attractive to the customers. When we first introduced double-knit pants on the market in 1970, our suggested retail price was $20. As the price of the fabric came down, because so much was on the market, we sold them at a suggested retail price of $16.

Following our lead, polyester double-knits became the rage in the men's wear industry. Hickey Freeman, Hart-Shaffner and Marx, all the best suit makers, brought out stylish men's apparel made from double-knit fabrics. J-Mar Ruby and all of our competitors saturated the market with double-knit pants. But the key word to remember here is *followed*. We introduced the product, and the rest of the market followed our lead.

Farah, one of our major competitors, was the last in the industry to bring out a line of double-knit pants. By this time, it seemed there was almost a glut on the market. Some manufacturers were using poorly knit inferior fabrics for their product, which caused pilling and unraveling. Early on, Farah referred to this period as the "Ill-Fated Double-Knit Era." Well, it was ill-fated because they came out so late—after so much was already on the market—and they were forced to take a big bunch of markdowns.

But it was inevitable that double-knits would eventually go out of vogue. Woven polyester fabrics were introduced to the market. Unlike many of the poorer double-knits, these fabrics were almost indestructible and wrinkle-resistant. While our competitors were dumping inferior double-knits, we jumped on the woven polyesters and kept the lead in this category until the market was saturated.

¤ ¤ ¤

Data processing continues its evolution, always improving and becoming more sophisticated. Joe remembers:

> In the late 1970s our group from Data Processing attended some meetings with representatives from textile mills, apparel manufacturers, and retailers. The topic of discussion was point-of-sale markings on tickets. At the time, several methods were being used and no one could agree on a single, correct method. Returning to Dallas, our people in this department concluded that the most effective point-of-sale marking was done by using bar codes. The bar-code method was already being used quite extensively in the grocery industry and it had proved to be a very good system for catching point-of-sales information. Following this data enabled us to keep up with pertinent sales information, replenishment of stock, and inventory build-up. Hence, we began putting bar codes on all our tickets.
>
> In order to get the entire industry to buy into this program, we organized a committee that included Roger Milliken, of Deering Milliken Company; Jack Shewmaker of Wal-Mart Stores; and myself. This group represented the fabric manufacturer, the apparel maker, and the retailer. Our objective was to show the industry how this point-of-sale information

fed back to the manufacturer and let them plan production based on sales at the retail level. The system also allowed the manufacturer to fill orders and more readily supply the retailer, so that their in-stock position would always be very good. It took a lot of meetings to get these three entities in the apparel cycle to buy off. Eventually, everyone concluded that the bar-code system was the best, and they, too, adopted the system. We at Haggar had a leading position in this procedure. We pioneered the method. Eventually, we were able to convince the rest of the industry to follow our lead. As a result, our business increased tremendously because we could fill orders quicker and more efficiently than our competition. Therefore, the retailer didn't have to carry as much inventory and didn't lose sales because an item was not in stock.

In 1981 our company implemented the drive to use UPC-OCR bar coding on garments that launched Electronic Data Interchange (EDI) in the apparel industry. Haggar was the first apparel company to do so. This eventually became known as our Haggar Order Transmission (H.O.T.) program.

¤ ¤ ¤

Joe recalls our first investigation of offshore manufacturing:

By the mid-1950s, some products manufactured offshore, primarily from Japan, were beginning to show up in the U.S. Dad and I took a trip to the Orient to evaluate what was happening and whether we needed to get into offshore production. After visiting Japan, Hong Kong, and other countries in that part of the world, we concluded that we could still compete because we had developed many automated pieces of equipment, through our Research and Development Department, which enabled us to be more productive and more efficient. Because of the excellent productivity of our associates, we were able to keep our costs down and kept the manufacturing in the United States.

Oxxford manufactured the finest men's suits at the time. The products were completely hand-made and were really beautiful. On that same trip to Japan, Dad and I discovered a company that was making a good knock-off of Oxxford Suits. After examining the Japanese product, Dad and I thought it a good idea to style slacks in the Oxxford method, but machine made. We purchased special sewing machines that produced a garment that had a hand-tailored look. We called the line Haggar Imperials, and it was an extremely successful venture, launched in 1961.

Eddie and I traveled to Japan and met with several potential licensees to represent us in Japan and the Far East. In 1974 we signed with Toyoba (of Japan), one of the largest trading companies in the world. Our decision to go with Toyoba marked the beginning of our world-licensing program.

Haggar Corporation has licensing agreements in Mexico, Canada, Japan, India, Australia, New Zealand, Indonesia, South Africa, and Great Britain. In addition to men's pants, Haggar Outer Wear, Haggar Ties, Haggar Dress Shirts, Haggar Hosiery, Haggar Footwear, and Haggar Eyewear are now available to consumers worldwide.

Reed St. James is a Haggar-owned subsidiary that distributes such diverse products as pants, sport coats, and coats for suit separates to mass merchants such as Wal-Mart. Clay Huston, one of our fine regional sales managers, originally had the idea to license Arrow shirts and other manufacturers to make goods under the Reed St. James name. I didn't think Arrow would be interested in a new name, but they were. As a result we licensed many fine apparel companies to make Reed St. James products, such as Host Pajamas, Jockey, Wembley Ties, and a host of others. These additional products such as sport shirts, dress shirts, ties, belts, hosiery, underwear, and some outerwear are produced under our supervision and quality standards.

Looking back on the events that dictated our move offshore, we realized that our world evolved into one global marketplace. Small nations, some that didn't exist twenty or thirty years ago, borrowed huge sums from world banks to jump-start their economies. Really, there are very few manufacturing or technological secrets in today's world, especially in the apparel manufacturing business. First-time sewing machine operators learn on computerized, highly developed machinery, which enables them to do so much more. Circumstances are such that, with money, every nation is capable of sophisticated manufacturing. Competition is fierce among the emerging nations as they enter the global marketplace.

Today, 85% of our manufacturing is done offshore. In 1984 we purchased an already established women's wear plant, La Romana, in the Dominican Republic. Later, starting from the ground up, we built a plant in central Mexico, in the town of Leon. The United States government introduced a bill called the 807 Program, which enabled us to purchase the fabrics and trimmings in this country, cut them here, and then ship them to our offshore facilities for sewing and finishing. So, some of our labor stayed here.

As more of our product line was being manufactured offshore, we began closing our facilities at home. The oldest plants were the first to be closed. Fortunately, many of our people had accumulated significant funds from the Haggar Profit Sharing Program, so they were able to start retirement with a sizable nest egg.

When Dad started the business, some seventy-five years ago, he considered every aspect of manufacturing and marketing. Today there are individuals in the corporate system whose duties and jobs are probably beyond Dad's imagination. Haggar employs an individual in charge of what we call "sourcing." He and his staff negotiate contracts for manufacturing and materials all over the world. Haggar also has a corps of inspectors who travel to the different plants we have contracted to do our manufacturing, to make sure the work is done to our specifications. This ensures that our quality remains consistent.

¤ ¤ ¤

Many products have been added and deleted from our basic production since Dad started the company in 1926. Styles change, men's needs change, and the fabrics that we offer change. No history of Haggar Company would be complete without mentioning some of the products we manufactured. Here is a summary of our additional products, beginning in 1938 with Slack Suits (Dad's own concept and design) and continuing into tomorrow with the introduction of our newest innovations, Micromatics and Micro Khakis.

In 1938 Dad had the idea to manufacture ready-to-wear matching pants and shirts that he called "Slack Suits." My idea was to sell them packaged in a box. One of the first things I ever purchased in a big way after joining the company were the boxes used to package the slack suits. The boxes, manufactured by the Interstate Folding Box Company, were constructed of a fairly heavy cardboard covered with a sort of woody veneer paper. The lid had a large cellophane window to display the colors and patterns of these suits. Slack Suits were very, very popular in the late 1930s, and we sold tons of them. I remember Dad's initial buy was 1,000,000 yards of fabric manufactured by the Celanese Corporation of America, called Celanese Sharkskin. It was used in all types of apparel, especially women's wear. Later, we manufactured Leisure Suits that sold in tremendous quantities. Haggar was always a company for big-volume items.

Pre-cuffed, finished slacks hit the market with a big, successful bang in the 1950s. Two fabrics provided us with real bonanzas: PIMALON, a blend of 35% fine pima cotton and 65% polyester, and Cape Town Tropicals, a blend of 65% polyester and 35% rayon, sold millions of pants for us. The pre-finished slacks were packaged in an attractive plastic wrapper that highlighted the name and performance of these fine fabrics.

In the early 1960s, we were approached by an organization that had an idea they wanted us to go with. Basically, what they envisioned was a "beltless" pair of pants with a wide elastic waistband, half of which was hidden, and the other half exposed. It was called "Sans a Belt" (French for "without a belt"). It really was a fine idea, but we didn't like the elastic showing on the outside of the trousers. Also, to make it a viable product, we would have had to pour a lot of money into a separate advertising campaign, which we were reluctant to do because of our already ongoing Haggar ads. In any event, we turned down the offer. The Hoosier Manufacturing Company of Michigan City, Indiana (one of our J.C. Penney competitors) went with the idea and called the product "Jay Mar Ruby—Sansabelt." They spent a lot of money advertising the product and were very successful.

Later on, we came up with the idea of pants with a wide elastic waistband, called "Haggar Expandomatic." Unlike the Sansabelt, our waistband was completely hidden. That style became a very famous item in the pants business, and we sold a lot of slacks. We still have a lot of old-timers calling for the product!

The introduction of double-knits in 1970 was a bonanza for the company. In the late 1970s, Haggar produced a completely washable suit. We advertised the product on television with several clever ads. The most popular showed a man, dressed in the washable suit, going through a washing machine spin cycle.

We began manufacturing sport coats in 1976 and later men's Custom Fit Suits. The concept of Custom Fit Suits was also a Haggar innovation. The sizing of suits is generally determined by a man's chest measurement. However, men who wear a size 46 suit, for example, may differ on their waist sizes. Haggar Custom Fit Suits enabled gentlemen to purchase jackets and pants separately, by size, which eliminated the need for tailoring the pants.

The introduction of Wrinkle Frees in 1992 was a real home run!

¤ ¤ ¤

After so many years in the men's pants business, it was only natural that Dad always looked closely at the pants men were wearing — on the street, in business meetings, at sporting events. Wherever he was, Dad studied the styles and fabrics of men's pants. Sometimes his stares became obvious. "It's a good thing we don't make ladies' pants," Mother warned him, "because you'd be in big trouble all the time!"

In general, women bought a lot of clothes for their husbands. They were familiar with Haggar slacks. Many women asked the sales clerks, "Why doesn't Haggar make pants for us?"

The continuing demands for women's apparel was very appealing. Haggar entered the ladies' apparel market in 1983. By this time the Haggar name was so well established with consumers nationwide, we decided to retain the Haggar name for our women's clothes as well. However, we did establish a separate ladies' wear division. Initially, we started out making women's pants only. We used a lot of the same fabrics as in our men's wear lines, but hired different designers and increased the number of basic styles and fabrics. We soon learned the vast differences between the ladies' and men's wear markets and hired a completely different sales staff for this division. Subsequently, we added blouses and some women's coats, but 90% of our line was women's pants.

Our ladies' products sold well throughout the country, but our profitability was low. At this time, most women's clothing was manufactured offshore. Emerging nations competed for contract work, offering low wages and good quality workmanship. All of our clothes were manufactured in the States. So even though we were well represented in clothing and department stores throughout the country, and the clothes sold well, the higher cost of domestic manufacturing kept our profits down.

My oldest son, Eddie, who headed the ladies' division, had been working for the company for several years. Starting out in production, Eddie learned all the ins and outs of manufacturing. He showed a great talent for getting things done on time and efficiently. Subsequently, we decided to sell the ladies' wear division and license the name. Eddie stepped forward and wanted to buy the division. There was some concern among the board members, but eventually we agreed to sell Eddie the business, as well as the building that warehoused the product.

¤ ¤ ¤

Here are the events leading up to our going public in 1992. In the early 1960s, I was asked to join the Young Presidents Organization (YPO). As the name implies, this prestigious group is made up of American corporate presidents under the age of fifty. They are an active group, socially, and in all matters of business.

At that time, "going public" (forming a publicly owned corporation) was the latest and greatest craze among YPO members. If it was a decent company with value and potential (what YPO members called a company with "coming attractions"), going public enabled a company to expand by raising large sums of capital. In addition, a public company had the advantage of issuing secondary issues, which provided more capital.

Well, the YPO piqued my curiosity and I spoke with my friend Bobby Stewart, who at the time was chairman and CEO of the First National Bank in Dallas. "Ed, there are only two firms to talk to about this... Goldman Sachs and Merrill Lynch." Gus Levy from Goldman Sachs in New York City gave us sufficient information about the process and its outcome. We talked to both firms and decided, at that point, there was no reason for us to go public. Even though we were a large and successful corporation, the business was still family owned. We kept putting back earnings that enabled us to expand, and we really didn't need any additional capital. Going public also meant that we would be responsible to pay dividends to our shareholders. As a privately owned corporation, we paid small dividends to family members and some valued associates, allowing us to plow money back into the business.

Several years later we did a recapitalization of the company. At that time the senior Haggars took preferred stock in the company and gave away the common stock to our children. Aware that the value of the common stock would grow, passing it on to our children eliminated some inheritance and estate taxes. As our children grew up and started families of their own, the common stock began shifting around to third- and fourth-generation Haggars.

We made the decision to go public in 1992, not because capital was needed for expansion but because we felt that going public put an immediate value on our stock.

We employed both firms of Goldman Sachs and Merrill Lynch to administrate the change. Accountants and analysts from these firms studied our assets, past performance, and future earning projections, as well as world market trends in our particular business. Putting all the facts and figures into the mix, they came up with an initial public offering price of $16.50 per share. Haggar Corporation trades on the National Association of Security Dealer's Exchange, commonly known as NASDAQ. The company has about 8.5 million shares of stock, of which 4.5 million are owned by the public.

Prior to going public, we knew that Joe was going to retire as CEO. At that time, we felt it would benefit the company to look outside for Joe's replacement. However, we wanted to consider Joe III a candidate, and I also wanted Eddie to be a candidate. Since Eddie had already purchased the Women's Wear Division, he decided to stick with that business. After an exhausting search and a great deal of interviews, we decided Joe III was more qualified than any of the other outside candidates. The board of directors elected Joe III chairman and chief executive officer, which kept the leadership in the Haggar family.

Joe, Jr., recalls:

> In the late 1930s our executive management level instituted a stock-option plan, in which they were able to buy stock in the company on an option basis at book value. When they retired, or left the company, for whatever reason, the stock was bought back by the company at the current book value price. People who exercised their option to purchase stock showed extensive gains. When we went public, there were a number whose stock was converted to public shares, and they also did very well.

Joe III was at the helm at the time of our public incorporation:

> One of many correct decisions the second generation of Haggar's (Ed Sr., Joe, Jr., Rosemary) made was taking the company public. In family-owned companies, one of the key issues is *orderly* transfer of wealth and ownership once you get to the third and fourth generations. Recognizing this universal challenge that all family businesses face, the Haggar family studied the issues and decided the best way to handle this situation, in our case, was letting the public own part of the company and offer family members a chance to turn their paper into money.
>
> From my perspective, this was a good decision. The company didn't need the money (although it has been nice investing cash), but in 1992 we were in a position where only two family members of the third generation of Haggars worked in the company and eleven worked outside the company or didn't work at all. Once this happened, we thought it was wise to let everyone make their own decisions on his or her personal wealth.
>
> When we finished the IPO (initial public offering), there were millions of dollars that transferred from pieces of paper to family members, in the form of cash. Now everyone can take their own financial direction, based on their need and personal thought process.

Obviously, it is a lot different being a public company vs. a private company. The one question I was asked when we first went public was, "Do you like being public?" I answered it six years ago, and my answer will *never* change: "When business is good, I love being public. When business is not good, I hate being public!"

Just like all companies that have been in business nearly seventy-five years, I have seen both sides of this answer.

¤ ¤ ¤

From synthetics to wrinkle-free cotton, Joe remembers the history of our product lines:

Haggar was the pioneer of all types of wrinkle-free, no-press slacks. I remember the very first product we made. It was a synthetic blend of polyester and rayon in a seersucker weave, which we called Flitewate. We manufactured this with a web-like fabric for pocketing. It was light and pliable. Ed demonstrated the product at our sales meeting, by rolling up a pair and stuffing them into his pocket, then pulling them out to show the salesmen that there were no wrinkles.

The earliest textile lab was housed in my home! Using our washer and dryer, we evaluated the properties of the fabrics, by examining them under the lights that hung over our pool table, after several cycles in the washer and dryer.

Another fabric we developed was a blend of polyester and orlon. Through a special technique of high pressure and high temperature and extended time in the pressing machine, we were able to impart a wrinkle-free characteristic in this product and it worked quite well.

The next fabric we introduced was a synthetic blend of polyester and rayon. This fabric required a certain treatment at the mill and a new pressing technique at our plants. The finished slacks were run through a large baking oven. We soon discovered the pants had a tendency to sag in the oven, and we developed a special hanger that allowed the pants to go through the oven and receive the treatment without sagging. We titled the product "Forever Press," and it was extremely successful.

The most successful product we developed was the 100%

cotton, wrinkle-free slacks. Through a combination of mill finishes and a procedure we used in the manufacturing operations, we molecularly changed the cotton fiber so it had a memory, like polyester, and would resist wrinkles. This method became very popular throughout the apparel industry. In fact, I don't know of any cotton fabrics in the slacks category that do not contain this treatment today.

In the late 1960s Levi Strauss introduced their Stay Prest line—100% cotton pants. Apparently, Levi Strauss didn't do all the research necessary before putting their pants on the market. Initially, the pants performed beautifully, but after washing, the material deteriorated. The pants were taken off the market and the company lost a lot of money.

Responding to Levi's "Stay-Prest" fabric, Haggar produced one of our most notable television commercials for our "Forever Pressed" slacks. The ad began with a wide-angle view of a man driving a big, industrial steamroller. Sitting at the steering wheel, he addressed the camera: "Der's gonna be wrinkles on wrinkles in doze pants!" The next shot focused attention on a pair of Haggar Forever Pressed Slacks, about to be rolled-over by this megalithic machine. The last sequence showed the driver on the ground, examining the pants. Finding no wrinkles, he asked the camera, "Whad did you say de name of dem slacks was?"

Levi Strauss introduced a casual style, cotton pant called Dockers in 1986. The pants were extremely soft, but not wrinkle-free. Dockers invested millions in an advertising campaign before the pants actually appeared in the stores. Just prior to the introduction of Dockers, Haggar introduced Prestige—100% cotton wrinkle-free pants. While the hand was good, it was still not soft enough. Stressing softness, Dockers were extremely successful. Subsequently, we introduced several other styles that were fuller cut, 100% cotton: Haggar Casuals, C-Zone, and Haggar EZ's.

While the Haggar Textile Lab was busy experimenting and refining the process, the marketing and merchandising departments were busy conjuring up an acceptable name for the product. The team finally decided on the term "Wrinkle Free," which really says it all.

At the time we introduced our "EZ's" cotton pants to the market, Frank Bracken's team came up with the idea of printing the size on a sticky label that was affixed to the pants at the fold line. Finding the right size was as easy as finding your favorite cereal in the supermarket.

Frank Bracken recalls two very important merchandising innovations:

> We developed our EZ product line in 1987 to compete with Levi Dockers. At that time, virtually all pants were displayed on hangers whether they were dress pants or casuals. Hoping to easily distinguish between dress pants and casuals, Dockers provided many retail customers with display tables for their casual pants. Haggar followed suit and offered display tables to those customers who purchased our complete EZ line. As had been the case since the mid-1930s, the pants on the display tables were soon haphazardly strewn about, because it was nearly impossible to decipher sizes without unfolding the pants, in order to read the inner labels.
>
> I remember many brainstorming sessions about what we could possibly do to improve this situation. We came up with many ideas, but none seemed to work. Finally, basically out of thin air, our team came up with the idea that we could put an adhesive strip around the fold of the pant with the waist and inseam listed on the strip. It took us virtually no time working with one of our suppliers to come up with a workable version of a size strip, and at that point we also started the patent process.
>
> There were many lessons learned here, not the least of which was the resistance we received from our salespeople and retailers to the new idea. Both salesmen and customers commented that the size strip looked like a stripe down the side on the pant. Well, this is all history now because that size strip is being used on hundreds of millions of garments throughout the country and throughout the world.
>
> Wrinkle Free's were introduced to the market in late 1992. We took our fiscal budget that year (approximately $5.5 million) and spent the entire amount during the fall of 1992 with our Super Dave advertising campaign. Up until this time, we had shipped less than 300,000 pairs of Wrinkle Frees. Well,

this advertising campaign launched one of the biggest successes in the history of Haggar Company. During the fall of 1992, we booked over a million and a half pairs for the balance of fiscal 1993.

We chose Delta Mills as our partner when we developed Wrinkle Free cotton. As Delta started producing millions of yards of fabric, they lost control of their quality, and tensile and tear problems began to show up.

One of the most effective teams ever put together at Haggar was the Wrinkle Free Task Force. I organized this team to oversee and fix the tensile and tear problems and to maintain our quality as we continued to chase this business. The team was made up of fifteen members from every discipline throughout the company that touched Wrinkle Free in any way and was represented from textile lab, to cutting, to production control, to manufacturing, all the way through sales. Against some pretty heavy odds, this team performed exceptionally well. To this date, it is still talked about as one of the outstanding examples of what a team of Haggar people can do when they are confronted with a big problem and by working together, how they beat the problems.

In my opinion, the introduction of Wrinkle Frees was a very strong turning point in our business, as significant as double knits had been twenty-five years earlier. We had tried to get into the casuals business for years, never with much success. However, everything came together for Wrinkle Frees. It was a well-coordinated effort with a great marketing program for an excellent and fine performing product. As soon as we introduced Wrinkle Frees to the market, we were in the casuals business in a big way.

Shortly after the initial public offering of Haggar stock was put on the market at $16.50 per share, the company announced we had developed a totally wrinkle-free process and would soon start marketing our 100% cotton, wrinkle-free pants. The price of our stock soared. Within fifteen months, March 15, 1994, the price peaked at $40.50 per share. We certainly didn't have a monopoly on the process and didn't claim to have a monopoly. Apparel companies and fabric mills all over the world were developing their own processes. But again, just like the double-knits, we were first to come to market with the finished product and a tremendous marketing program.

Our pioneering work in wrinkle-free fabric continues with the introduction of two new micro fiber products: Micromatics, a special fabric of 100% polyester and Micro Khakis, 60% polyester and 40% cotton. Both fabrics have a great hand and are washable, dryable, and wrinkle-free.

¤ ¤ ¤

The plant on Lemmon Avenue remained the central hub of activity for more than fifty years. Several new additions to the Lemmon Avenue facility were added on periodically. Eventually, we had more than 500,000 square feet under one roof. As state-of-the-art technologies advanced, we found ourselves requiring newer and more updated computerized facilities. Haggar purchased land in Fossil Creek (in the Fort Worth area) for our Customer Service Center and began building a new, more modern facility.

May 1995. The new facility was nearing completion. Plans were being made to transfer most of the activities and personnel from Lemmon Avenue to the Service Center building in December. In the meantime, work proceeded as usual (daytime and nighttime shifts). May had been a month of record rainfall. High winds and heavy rains pounded the entire city of Dallas. At 9:00 P.M. on May 5, during a torrential downpour and windstorm, the roof over the central area of the plant collapsed, killing two and injuring twenty associates. Haggar Company had been in business for more than seventy years with no serious accidents or injuries to any of our associates. Loss of life was the greatest catastrophe we faced. Circumstances were similar to the Santa Fe Building fire: we were unable to ship merchandise and lost a lot of business. It was an act of God, but the ironies between the collapse of the roof and the Santa Fe Building fire are overwhelming. Both occurred just a few months before planned moves to new facilities.

¤ ¤ ¤

Haggar Corporation corporate offices remain at 6113 Lemmon Avenue. As our manufacturing locations spread throughout the world, we found it necessary to come up with new ways of keeping track of what was being made and where. In 1996 we opened the Haggar Customer Service Center in Fort Worth. This building is both the central receiving point and distribution point for all our products. A maze of computers directs our business now.

¤ ¤ ¤

Our basic product, men's pants, hasn't really changed that much since Dad started the company seventy-five years ago. The two biggest changes are the way we make the product and how the product is sold and marketed.

In essence, retailing (selling goods directly to consumers) is still pretty much the same as when Dad envisioned starting up his own business so many years ago. But as our lifestyles change, where and how we go about buying the product seems to be an ever-changing process.

Consumers, to a great extent, seem to be drawn to factory-owned outlet stores. There are about 350 factory outlet malls in the country. Our company created the "Haggar Clothing Company Stores" in 1996. This is really our first venture into retailing our own merchandise. There are about 150 excellent malls throughout the country, and we plan, within the next three to four years, to have 100 or so Haggar stores in these particular malls. Other new methods of retailing under investigation are catalogue sales and cyber-sales (over the Internet).

¤ ¤ ¤

Before leaving the subject of marketing, we should discuss Ely Callaway. Ely and I are members of the Eldorado Country Club in Indian Wells, California. A few years ago we met on the golf course. "Ely, I think we've known each other for almost forty-eight years," I recalled.

Ely replied, "Ed, we've known each other for fifty-five years. We first met when you were handling government contracts and I was contracting officer for the Quarter Master Division."

Ely Callaway's career has been extremely diversified and successful. Dad, Joe, and I enjoyed a long and fruitful business relationship with Ely when he was head honcho of Burlington Mills, and before that, Deering Milliken.

What's the secret of Ely's success? Marketing! Ely Callaway is one of the best marketeers in the business. That's a pretty powerful statement, but it takes a good marketeer to know one. The key to success is that you have got to have a good product that represents value. And that product has to be advertised, marketed, and merchandised. Today it means the product has to be advertised on television with interesting commercials; tied in with displays at the store level and good retail co-op advertising. Haggar Wrinkle Frees were an excellent product and we marketed them to the hilt, as we did with double-knits and Haggar Black Label. Several years ago, Ely started manufacturing "Callaway Golf Clubs." The star of the line was the "Big Bertha." In a sense, the Big Bertha woods and irons were not new to the market. Ping, another manufacturer, introduced clubs that were very similar. However, Ping didn't know how to market the product. The end result is that most golfers know all about Big Bertha, while very few know about similar Ping products. Marketing a *good* product is the name of the game.

One day at Eldorado, Patty and I met up with Ely in the clubhouse. "Ely, where's my Big Bertha?" asked Patty. Ely looked at Patty, winked his eye and said, "Patty, I'm going to send you a club, but I'm not sending one to Big Ed."

"I can't accept it, Ely," I said, "I'm tied up with Cobra for another year and a half!" That stopped him cold!

¤ ¤ ¤

A few words about our official name. When Dad started the business in 1926, he called the endeavor "Haggar Company." The evolution of our company, from making men's dress pants to manufacturer of coats, shirts, sport coats, and custom-fit suits, necessitated another change of name. In the mid-1980s, we changed the name to Haggar Apparel Company. The advertising wizards advised us that today's younger generation felt comfortable with the more recognizable term "Clothing." So today, we are officially known as "Haggar Clothing Company." When we went public in 1992, our corporate name was changed to Haggar Corporation.

CHAPTER 6
Haggar Corporation (Postscript)

The fiftieth anniversary of Haggar Corporation was celebrated in 1976. Dad wrote the following remarks for the corporate *Annual Report* that year:

> Now, I don't want anybody to think that I made this business all by myself. While I gave it a good start and built it up in the early days, my sons have made many lasting contributions to our company; first Ed, who's now Chairman of the Board and looks after our merchandising and marketing; then Joe Jr., who's President and really stays on top of the operations and manufacturing of our products.
>
> When Ed first joined me in the business, he knew we made quality products at fair prices. But he was concerned that we were not building a name for ourselves, because all our goods were sold unbranded to chain stores and scattered accounts. So in 1938, he started our national advertising and building of a national sales organization to represent our national brand. We've really come a long way since then. We now have the strongest and best-known name in the industry.
>
> Then in 1946, it was Joe's idea for us to have the most cost-efficient manufacturing and cost systems in the industry. By working to reduce waste, he made the company more efficient and cut costs. He also established our Research and Development

Program, plus our Management Incentive Plans. Those management incentives are a big part of what made our company great.

Dad always believed that his greatest asset was the people who worked for the company and made the business go. Time and time again, he stressed that a plant could be damaged by fire or tornado, but that it could always be rebuilt. The hardest loss was losing people, for they could never be replaced.

"Value" — giving the consumer the best product at the best price — along with Dad's idea of a "One Price Policy" were certainly driving forces at Haggar Company.

In the very earliest days of the company, and while still on the road selling the product himself, Dad used to conduct business with a store-owner from Brownwood, Texas, by the name of Shorty Bunyan. A Harvard graduate, Shorty stood just a hair under five feet tall.

Shorty owned a general store in Brownwood. Even though Shorty had hired a sales assistant to wait on the trade, the little man always managed to become involved in each and every transaction, with or without help from his assistant.

While the consumer might have appreciated this amiable trait, it drove Dad crazy. Whatever sales that could have been transacted within a matter of minutes were prolonged by hours, stopping each time Shorty waited on the customers himself.

By isolating Shorty, Dad had hoped to wrap up his business quickly and be on his way. On this particular day, he was waiting for Shorty on the doorstep and announced: "Shorty, I've got something to show you, but I don't want anybody else to see it. Let's go to the back of the store." The plan was unfurling without a hitch, until a cowhand from a nearby ranch walked into the store and stole Shorty's attention.

The cowhand stopped at a table near the back of the store and held up a blue chambray shirt. "Shorty, how much for this one?"

"Eighty-five cents," Shorty replied. The customer placed the shirt back on the table and headed for the front of the store.

"Come on back, Mr. Potter," Shorty called out. "You can have it for seventy-five cents." The fellow didn't answer and continued walking toward the front of the store. Potter stepped outside, spat out his wad of chewing tobacco, and returned to the store just as Bunyan pushed his way past Dad and yelled out to the customer, "You can have it for sixty-five cents."

Potter grinned and said, "I'll take it, Shorty."

Dad turned to Shorty and said, "It's a good thing this store isn't ten feet longer, or you would have given him the shirt!"

Then and there, Dad realized that unless the price of a garment was firm, somebody was going to get the short end of the stick.

¤ ¤ ¤

Dad's real love for the business was merchandising. He also loved buying the fabric and styling the products. Dad always had the habit of bouncing his ideas off others. He usually selected one particular person whose input he valued most at the time. Those of us close to Dad always referred to that person as Dad's "Alter-Ego." Starting with his brother-in-law, Harry Wasaff, in the 1920s and 1930s, Dad depended on different people at different times to exchange ideas and dialogue. Over the years Clarence Grunsfeld, Jake Henson, Archie Fowler, and Sylvan Landau all bore the mantle of Dad's "Alter-Ego."

For many years Dad always had the final say on what styles and how many pieces were included in our line each year. He worked out his own formula—and he was always right on. "You have to have balance," was Dad's motto. We always allowed the salesmen to contribute their input as far as what they needed at our sales meetings. However, we had 165 salesmen, and each had his own ideas. Of course, if we accommodated even a small percentage of the requests, our line would have been too big. At one meeting I presented the salesmen with Aesop's fable regarding The Man, the Boy, and the Donkey:

> A man and his son were going with their donkey to market. As they were walking along, a countryman passed them and said, "You fools, what is a donkey for, but to ride on." So the man put the boy on the donkey and they went on their way. Soon they passed a group of men and one said, "See that lazy youngster, he lets his father walk while he rides." So the man ordered his boy off and got on himself. But they hadn't gone very far when

they passed two women, one of whom said, "Shame on that lazy lout, to let his poor little son trudge along."

Well, the man didn't know what to do, but at last he took his boy up before him on the donkey. By this time, they had come to the town and the passersby began to jeer at them. The men said, "Aren't you ashamed of yourself for overloading that poor donkey with yourself and your hulking son?"

The moral of the story: "Try to please everyone and you please no one."

¤ ¤ ¤

To paraphrase William Shakespeare, from his play "As You Like It": "All the world's a stage/ And all the men and women merely players/ They have their exits and their entrances/ And one man in his time plays many parts..." In our day, each of us played many parts for the company.

Under Dad's watchful eye, Joe and I began working in the business as young boys. As we matured and developed our skills and talents, he encouraged each of us to make our own contributions to the company. Dad was blessed with longevity, and the three of us worked as a partnership for many, many years.

An aside: Following Joe's graduation from Notre Dame, Dad, Joe, and I went to the New York market together. It was a forty-hour train ride from Dallas to New York. We always stayed at the Hotel New Yorker, which was a new hotel in those days. An older Irish gent manned the door. Whenever he saw the three of us enter the hotel, he always opened the door and said, "Well, as I live and breathe, here comes the Father, the Son, and the Holy Ghost!"

¤ ¤ ¤

In the company Joe was nicknamed "Mr. Make-Em" and I was known as "Mr. Sell-Em." Joe recalls:

> Ed always liked to oversell, knowing there would be cancellations and returned goods. This really bothered me. I didn't want to sell a lot more product than we could make. Ed told me, 'Joe, there are two types of ulcers you could have. If you

6113 Lemmon Avenue, Dallas, Texas. Our corporate headquarters and customer service facility, just before completion in 1940.

Members of the sales force and administrative team in front of the Haggar Building. The photo was taken in the late 1940s.

Aerial view of our corporate headquarters on Lemmon Avenue.

Haggar Customer Service Center, Fort Worth, Texas.

An early Haggar promotion.

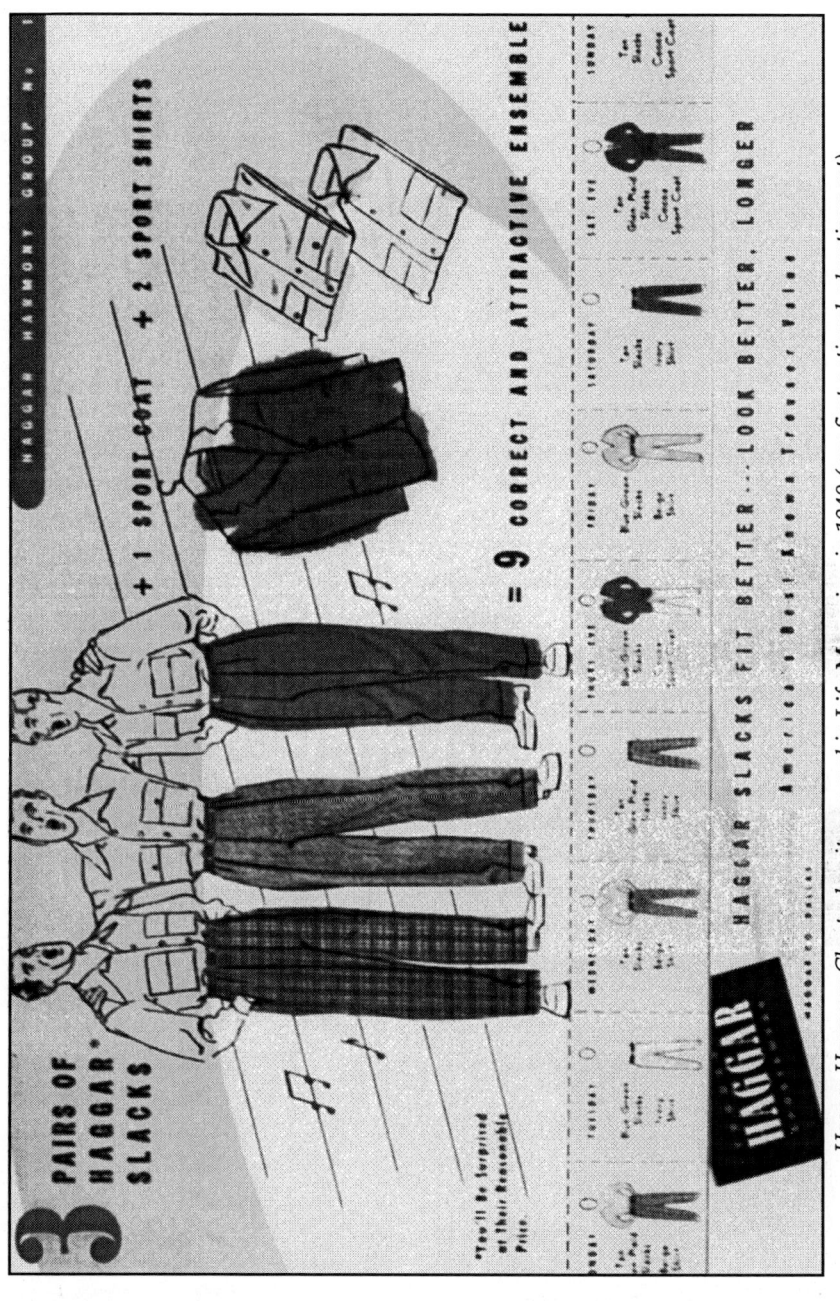

Haggar Harmony Chart ad as it appeared in Life Magazine in 1940 (*our first national advertisement*).

HOW TO GET MORE FUN OUT OF WATCHING FOOTBALL

by Doak Walker

HAGGAR Slacks

The Haggar Solid Gold Tennis Ball...

Ms Cathy Stratemeyer,
"The Golden Girl of Tennis"

Johnny Carson dropped the ball — literally! — but no damage was done as approximately eight million people saw the world's most unique sports trophy — the Haggar solid gold tennis ball.

Arthur Ashe, winner of both the 1975 and this year's Haggar Slacks Scoreboard, brought along the 13 pound, 24 karat, $35,000 ball when he visited with Johnny Carson, Orson Welles and "Lonesome" George Gobel on the March 25th Tonight Show.

The Carson appearance has been only one of many television stops for the Haggar trophy this year. Since January, Cathy Stratemeyer has been a Haggar spokesperson and has taken the gold ball to over a dozen U.S. cities on the World Championship Tennis Tour. The gold ball has appeared on both commercial and public broadcast television, as well as Canadian network T.V.

Cathy was given the unofficial title of "The Golden Girl of Tennis," and has been interviewed on three nationally syndicated radio programs and 40 local radio shows. She appeared with the gold ball on approximately 30 TV shows, and Haggar has been mentioned in local newspapers in every city visited.

Cathy's job may sound glamorous, but it is also hard work carrying around a pocket-sized fortune. Armed guards must accompany Cathy and the gold ball to and from all destinations, and the ball is stored in a bank vault overnight. Cathy says, "I've never really been afraid, but I always breathe more easily at night when the ball is locked up safely in the bank vault."

The 1976 World Championship Tennis Finals were held in Dallas May 3-16, and Cathy gave her solid-gold responsibility back to Ed Haggar to present to this year's Haggar Scoreboard winner. Will she miss it?

"Well," says Cathy, "it's a great way to meet people."

Excerpts from two national television ads. Top: for double-knit slacks. Bottom: for Haggar Forever Pressed.

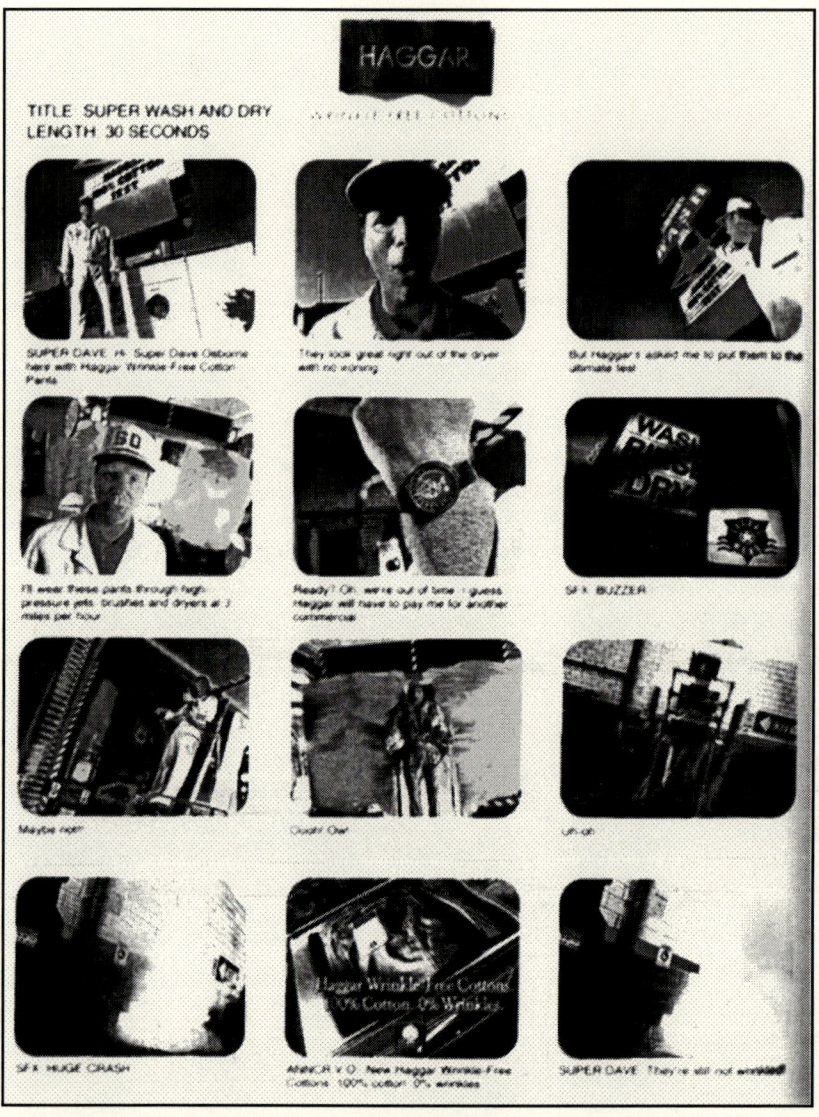

Television storyboard for commercial that kicked off Haggar's fabulous 100% cotton Wrinkle Free pants.

Storyboard for second "Crazy Dave Osborne" commercial for Haggar Wrinkle Frees.

Ad campaign for Haggar Black Label.

don't sell all your production, those ulcers really hurt. If you oversell, the ulcers hurt... but only a little bit!'

Starting in his early teens, Joe spent his summers working from one end of the plant to the other. He also made several road trips with some of our salesmen, although he never had his own territory.

Our plants in Dallas, Greenville, Waxahachie, and McKinney were operating full-steam-ahead when Joe joined the company. Earlier on, we hired Gordon Armstrong, from the Rose Clothing Company, a fine manufacturer of contract clothing, to oversee our facilities. Gordon's expertise was manufacturing and quality control. Initially, Joe spent time working under Gordon, learning the manufacturing end of the business and honing his own skills. Within a short time, Joe became an expert in manufacturing in his own right.

Under Joe's guidance, each plant was organized into different units. There was a manager and an assistant manager at each plant. The plants were organized into different zones, depending on their geographical location. For example, the plants in the Rio Grande Valley were located in the Southern Zone. Dallas and its environs comprised the Central Zone, and the Oklahoma plants and North Texas made up the Northern Zone. The plant managers reported to the zone managers, and the zone managers reported to Joe. About 90% of the plant managers and zone managers worked their way up through the ranks.

Joe also centralized and organized our cost accounting and budgeting. As an incentive to keep manufacturing levels high, he organized different contests between the plants. Monetary prizes were given for Production Line of the Year, Plant of the Year, and Zone of the Year.

Joe was responsible for several manufacturing innovations introduced during the time he ran this part of the business. One of them was the computer-aided design equipment, which actually simulates a weaving machine and can design a pattern almost instantaneously. Waiting for a mill to make a woven sample can take two to three weeks. This equipment can simulate a woven pattern on a machine and instantly transmit it, electronically, to any place in the world, such as China or the Philippines, where we source a lot of our products.

Instead of cutting around each pattern individually, the Gerber Cutting Machine is a computerized die that speeds up the entire cutting process. Accuracy is also improved using this equipment.

A computerized pressing process, introduced by Joe, sped up the pressing time and the quality of the final-press.

Joe and his team also instituted the Haggar Order Transmission system, or H.O.T., which he promoted very strongly. This is a computerized network program that enables retailers to reorder inventory instantly. As a matter of fact, Joe first introduced the system worldwide on *CNN Headline News*. H.O.T. has been a major contributor to our growth and success.

¤ ¤ ¤

Beginning in those early days when I was out on the road in East Texas, Dad directed my attention toward the sales force. He was hoping for a more dynamic and structured unit. Taking a broader overview, I reorganized the sales force into different geographical areas for more effective distribution, initiated training and sales programs, and structured a more efficient sales management system.

In 1940 our full-page ad in *Life Magazine* introduced the Haggar name and Haggar products to the entire country. This ad marked the beginning of a major turning point in our company's history. Well, the Haggar name became a household word. We advertised on national television, sponsored sporting events, and placed ads in many national publications.

In my opinion, there were five turning points that contributed to our success. The first was getting a listing with J.C. Penney, as discussed in Chapter 4. The second real turning point was when we began to wean ourselves away from private label, and started building the name "Haggar." The third turning point was building a Haggar national sales organization. Our fourth and fifth turning points were double-knits and Wrinkle Frees.

¤ ¤ ¤

Joe Haggar, III, or "Joe Three" as he is affectionately called, began his career under the watchful eye of his grandfather, father, and Uncle Ed, unloading trucks in the Piece Goods Department.

After graduation from Jesuit College Preparatory in 1969, Joe III attended the University of Notre Dame and graduated with a degree in business administration.

Joe III joined the company full time in 1973, working in Data Processing, Production Control, Manufacturing and Sales. He later trained in the Dallas corporate headquarters and the Bowie and Greenville manufacturing facilities.

In 1976 Joe III was named Dallas Service Center manager, responsible for shipping operations. He joined the merchandising staff in 1977 as national brands manager, and in 1978 was named vice president, directing the three Haggar brands. He was promoted to executive vice president of merchandising and sales of Haggar Men's Wear in 1981, before being named president of the Men's Wear Division in 1985. In April 1991 he was named president and CEO. And in 1994 he was named chairman and CEO, his current position.

Joe III is a member of the Young Presidents Organization and the Salesmanship Club of Dallas. He is on the boards of the Salesmanship Club, Presbyterian Healthcare Foundation, Notre Dame Business Council, and Texas Commerce Bank. Joe III and his wife, Jayne Frederick Haggar, have three daughters; Jennifer, Joanne, and Jessica.

¤ ¤ ¤

Frank Bracken was named president and CEO of Haggar Clothing Company on July 20, 1994. Frank is the first non-family member in the company's history to assume this responsibility. He joined the company in 1963 as a management trainee and progressed through the positions of sales associate, regional sales manager, vice president, national sales manager, and vice president of sales and merchandising. In 1988 all marketing, sales, and manufacturing functions were added to his responsibility, and he was named senior vice president of marketing and manufacturing. In 1991 the company consolidated all of the non-Haggar labels, including Private Label and Reed St. James, under the Horizon Group. Frank was named executive vice president. In addition, Frank inaugurated the Retail Marketing Associates Program to improve Haggar's visual sales at the retail level and merchandising with key retailers. Frank Bracken and his team are responsible for the product development and breakthrough advertising campaign that introduced "Wrinkle Free" cotton, which really revolutionized the pants business. With the advent of casual slacks that were once again stacked on display tables, Frank developed sticky labels that were placed on the crease of the trousers, which easily identified size and style.

¤ ¤ ¤

As a kid, my son Eddie worked at different jobs throughout the plant. After graduating from Notre Dame, Eddie came back to the company, where he spent most of his time in the manufacturing end of the business. I'd say between Joe, Joe III, and myself, Eddie accumulated more experience running many different aspects of production work. He is also a great manager. Eventually, he managed our facilities in Corsicana and Temple. During those years, his plants placed at the top of the list for productivity.

Eddie recalled an incident involving a hook-and-eye machine and an employee named Sarah:

> During the time I was plant manager at Corsicana Company, we made several changes in our manufacturing procedures. Small groups of people were organized into prep units. Each member of a prep unit had a specific task to perform. If one person failed to keep up with the others in the unit, they slowed down the whole unit's production, and the unit failed to earn money.
>
> An associate named Sarah, who had been at Corsicana for several years, always had a hard time making her production quotas. Sarah fell way behind when she was moved to a special prep unit of six people, where she operated a hook-and-eye machine.
>
> Following company policy, I spoke with Sarah on several occasions, and encouraged her to do better. These discussions did not solve our problems. As plant manager, I was then required to issue a written letter to her, stating the problem and warning her that if she failed to meet her production quota, she would be replaced.

On this particular day, I called Sarah into my office. "Sarah, by not performing, you're holding back the whole unit. I've written all this down for you," I said, and handed her the letter. Sarah looked at me and said, "So you're telling me, Eddie, that you're going to give me a letter?" I replied, "Yes, I am, it's only fair to the group." Sarah threw the letter on my desk. On her way out she said, "Well, if you think you're going to give me a letter, you can take that old hook-and-eye machine and stick it up your ass!"

As a rule, we taped all such conversations between managers and associates to maintain consistency between plants. After this incident with Sarah, I sent the tape to my boss, Ted Sullins, who was the head of manufacturing. Ted used these tapes as a means to monitor the work throughout all our manufacturing facilities. The next day I got a call from Ted. "Eddie," Ted started out, "I just want to know if you got a receipt for that hook-and-eye machine!"

There were lots and lots of stories from my factory days. On several occasions, I drove people with severed thumbs to hospitals. It was a taste of the real world!

Eddie, along with some of our other key people, really pushed hard for offshore production. Unfortunately, the elder Haggars stayed too long with their own personal feelings and were late using offshore production. Through Eddie's influence, we diversified into ladies' wear and expanded our men's line by adding more casual sportswear such as coats and suit separates. Another time, the stock price of our competitor, Farah, fell to $4 per share. Eddie suggested that the company purchase Farah and use the name for our discount market. Subsequently, we created Reed St. James for this purpose. Eddie was also instrumental in creating an internal-external inventory management system utilizing bar code technology.

When Joe, Jr., served on the City Council, Eddie pretty well filled in where necessary for Joe in the manufacturing and administrative end of the business and made many major contributions to the company.

¤ ¤ ¤

More than anyone else in the family, my son Jimmy inherited many of Dad's styling traits and expertise. He is a fine designer and has an uncanny ability to predict future trends in the apparel business.

After attending Texas Tech, Jimmy began his full-time career at Haggar as a sales rep in East Texas and later worked in merchandising.

Jimmy drove me to the airport one day when I was on my way to New York. We talked about business and I said, "Jimmy, we're going to have to come up with some new items. People don't want polyesters anymore." He said, "Dad, when you get back, I want to show you something." When I got back, Jimmy showed me his designs. In essence, these were casual, cotton pants. All of these events took place long before Levi Strauss introduced Dockers to the market. Had we followed Jimmy's suggestion, we could have beaten Dockers to market by at least six months.

In my opinion, we missed being first to market with Jimmy's idea because we were more focused on dress pants. Initially, we didn't have the confidence to put big money into an advertising campaign for this type of pants. We applied for the C-Zone trademark in late 1985, and it was finally approved in August 1986. But in 1986, Levi Strauss introduced their Dockers line with an extensive and remarkable advertising program and a tremendous shop concept for the retailer.

Jimmy had done some research and read about a tailor named Edmund Magrath. In his day, Magrath was quite an innovator of fine men's apparel. Jimmy approached the company and wanted to create a higher-priced line of men's clothing made from better fabrics. (The name was later changed to E. Magrath.) The company agreed and began showing a line of E. Magrath coats and pants. The line sold fairly well, but it really didn't fit in with the company's other products because the production runs were too small. Jimmy's thought, later, was to make these products offshore, and he asked if we would spin off the name of E. Magrath to him, which we did. Jimmy created an upscale line of men's golf attire, and he has enjoyed great success with this business. E. Magrath products have been very popular with the fine Green Grass Golf Shops.

¤ ¤ ¤

Prior to graduation from Southern Methodist University, my youngest son, John, worked summers in the shipping department and in the accounting office. Later, he joined the Haggar Sales Training Program. After his training, he was assigned to a territory in the Los Angeles and Southern California Territory as a sales associate for trade accounts (independent merchants). He was then promoted to a larger territory in the Denver area, where he serviced department stores and trade accounts. Unfortunately, John got caught up in the merger and consolidation era in the mid-1990s, and like the bulk of our sales organization, he lost his job. He could have had a similar job in another territory, but John knew the same thing would probably happen a year or two later, so he declined this offer. John was also offered a position at our Dallas headquarters, but he felt it was like starting over. He chose not to stay with the company. Currently he is in the investment business in Colorado.

¤ ¤ ¤

Sylvan Landau, executive vice president for merchandising and marketing, began his career as a packer and driver for Clarence Grunsfeld. Sylvan made many contributions to the company, especially in the areas of sales and merchandising.

Hal Tehan, executive vice president for administration: Negotiations for insurance, freight rates, and buying of all items other than fabrics and trimmings came under this office. Hal was such a good negotiator and trader that we nicknamed him "Sam Tehan."

Ted Sullins, executive vice president for manufacturing, was an excellent manager and manufacturer. He came up through the ranks as a manufacturing trainee, sewing line manager, plant manager and, eventually, executive vice president for manufacturing. Over the years, Ted contributed many successful ideas regarding manufacturing to our company.

After Ted retired, Jack Smith became president of menswear manufacturing. Jack came up through the manufacturing end of the business and always did a great job for our company.

Greg Baloyan, vice president for sales and service, followed Beryl Tansil. Greg was a loyal and dedicated manager.

¤ ¤ ¤

It is well worth noting the achievements of the talented and dedicated men and women of Haggar Corporation who added so much to our success. Many who dedicated more than twenty-five years of loyal service to our company remain employed by Haggar, while others have since retired or passed away.

The following list honors our associates for their contribution to Haggar Corporation. An asterisk (*) indicates service over twenty-five years but exact number of years not available:

Adame, Paula	25	Barrios, Minerva	25
Alegria, Esperanza	*	Battle, Ottlean	*
Alexander, John	*	Bearding, Mazell	*
Alexander, John D.	25	Bench, Mildred	*
Allen, Darlene	37	Bennett, Wally	51
Allen, Evelyn	36	Benthall, Jerry	35
Alvarado, Imelda	27	Bernal, Jesusita	*
Alvarado, Julia	25	Biggerstaff, James	*
Alvarado, Lydia	26	Blair, Danny	*
Alverson, Peggy	*	Blair, Florence	28
Anderson, Cora	28	Blair, Gloria	*
Anderson, Kaye	25	Bloyed, Sandra	*
Anes, Carmen	28	Bond, Barbara	33
Anzaldua, Marta	25	Boor, Jane	*
Arce, Georgia	28	Booth, Phil	25
Armstrong, George	*	Boswell, Barbara	*
Armstrong, Norma	*	Bracken, Frank	37
Askins, Edna	*	Bray, Hugh	31
Bailey, Clayton	26	Bryant, Leon	25
Baldinelli, John	27	Burk, Wanda	32
Baldwin, Gwayne	38	Burns, Eula Mae	*
Ball, Ima	29	Burns, Marthel	28
Baloyan, Greg	38	Butler, Mary Ann	*
Bannon, Mark	44	Campbell, Dolores	30
Barker, Avon	35	Camplis, Lura	*
Barrera, Flor	25	Cano, Margarita	35

Haggar Corporation (Postscript) 129

Cantrell, Frances	33	Dunning, Albert	*
Carr, R.N.	*	Eddins, Ruth	*
Carreon, Elva	28	Eschelar, Mary	*
Carter, Pat	*	Escobar, Juanita	28
Cassas, Aurora	27	Escobedo, Maria	26
Castillo, Maria	*	Esparza, Elisa	26
Cavazos, Angie	25	Evans, Vada	*
Champion, Shirley	25	Farias, Margarita	25
Chaney, Margie	*	Ferguson, J.R.	36
Chapman, Grace	*	Ferris, E.J.	28
Chapman, Minnie	*	Finney, Gloria	25
Chaves, Elisa	25	Fisher, Elaine	*
Chavez, Reyes	25	Fisher, Ron	32
Chisholm, Kevin	26	Flores, Margarita	27
Cisneros, Elma	28	Flores, Teresa	25
Cisneros, Victoria	*	Floro, Craig	*
Clausey, Kevin	27	Fortenberry, Robin	*
Connell, Virginia	*	Fowler, Archie	28
Contreras, Sara	28	Fox, Joan	37
Copeland, Nadyne	27	Fox, Michelle	25
Cornelison, Jerry	31	Franco, Idalia	25
Coronado, Criselda	*	Freeman, Rachel	*
Couch, Wilma	*	French, Don	*
Cox, Dennis	27	Garces, Josefa	25
Crockett, Emma	25	Garces, Piedad	25
Dailey, David	*	Garcia, Augustina	26
Daniel, Gil	25	Garcia, Blanca	26
Davis, Lily	*	Garcia, Elidia	29
DeAngeles, Jack	25	Garcia, Lucila	26
Degardo, Owanna	*	Garner, Joe	32
DeLaCruz, Ofelia	*	Garza, Arcelia	27
DeLaRosa, Delfina	25	Garza, Dolores	28
Demmerle, Ted	32	Garza, Ernestina	28
Denig, Jim	28	Gathings, Beth	*
Diaz, Maria	25	Gipson, Bettye	26
Dickins, Bob	*	Gomez, Elena	29
Donahue, C.J.	*	Gomez, Maona	*
Dubberley, John	27	Gomez, Ramona	29
Duncan, Ola	*	Gomez, Raquel	*

Gonzales, Ernestina	25	Ingram, Rex	26
Gonzales, Gloria	*	Isham, Betty	*
Gonzales, Irma	*	Jackson, Edward	29
Goodstein, Arthur	34	Jacobson, Lester	*
Goughler, Angelita	*	Jameson, B.J.	26
Graham, Mike	28	Jauregui, Alicia	*
Gray, James	35	Johnson, Dorothy	*
Green, Mike	25	Johnson, Lucy	*
Green, Tyoka	34	Jones, Edna	*
Grunsfeld, Clarence	37	Joyner, Bobby	25
Grunsfeld, Herbert	35	Just, Jim	*
Haggar, E.R.	59	Keeney, Leslie	29
Haggar, J.M., Jr.	50	Keys, Olivia	*
Haggar, J.M., Sr.	62	Kilroy, Thomas	29
Haggar, J.M. III	29	Kimmell, Dale	36
Haliburton, Barbara	25	Kirby, John	26
Hanson, Johnny	*	Klapholtz, Sandy	35
Harper, Jeanette	*	Krohn, Karl	26
Harrington, Donna	*	Laimo, Robert	25
Harris, Dave	48	Landau, Sylvan	38
Hederi, Kay	26	Lara, Gabina	*
Heffernan, John	31	Leek, Effie	37
Henson, Jake	*	Liggin, Roberta	28
Herman, Jim	26	Lightfoot, Leora	*
Hernandez, Enedina	25	Long, Olena	*
Hernandez, Eva	*	Longoria, Julie	*
Hernandez, Evelia	*	Lopez, Belgica	*
Hernandez, Socorro	25	Lopez, Guadalupe	*
Hickman, Milton	26	Lopez, Hilda	*
Hodges, Dorothy	*	Lopez, Pedro	*
Holly, Norma Jean	*	Lowery, Edna Mae	*
Hoskins, Lois	*	Lucus, Mildred	*
Huckabee, David	*	Lynch, Malvern	*
Hudson, Jerry	*	Maldonado, Evelia	26
Hughes, Dorothy	33	Maldonado, Irma	*
Hughes, Lena	*	Maples, Florence	*
Hunt, Bobby	27	Marin, Elia	*
Hurston, Chuck	27	Markham, Tim	25
Huston, Clay	37	Martinez, Antonia	*

Martinez, Ascencion	26	Paul, Ola Fay	*
Martinez, Edimensia	29	Pena, Carmen	29
Martinez, Elena	*	Peralez, Archie	29
Martinez, Gloria	25	Perez, Irene	*
Martinez, Leopalda	*	Perez, Sigfredo	30
Mascorro, Gloria	27	Phillips, Lynn	28
Matthews, B.A.	*	Porter, Mary	*
McCamey, Linda	*	Qualls, Bob	25
McCarter, Jerry	33	Quezada, Herminia	*
McSherry, George	*	Quintanilla, Oralia	*
Mercado, Hector	*	Raibly, Jo	29
Michael, George	27	Ramos, Irene	*
Michael, Lenore	*	Reddine, Christine	*
Minor, Clara	26	Reece, Judy	*
Moffett, Esta	*	Reyes, Filomena	25
Molina, George	*	Reyes, Mary	*
Moore, Elaine	27	Richardson, Dorothy	*
Moore, Margie	36	Ritchey, Angel	31
Moore, Refus	*	Rivers, Shirley	27
Moore, Sylvia	*	Robinson, Rea	40
Morris, Edna	28	Rodriguez, Amelia	*
Moser, Jewel	*	Rodriguez, Manuel	*
Moses, Fred	30	Rodriguez, Orlando	*
Moses, Veoma	*	Rodriguez, Reyes	29
Mullins, Barbara	*	Rogers, Brenda	28
Mullins, Eloise	28	Rook, Bill	30
Mullins, Mary	30	Saba, Louis	43
Munoz, Argelia	*	Salas, Emma	*
Nash, Lela	*	Salazar, Francisca	*
Neie, Phyllis	25	Salter, Henry	34
Norwood, Rich	25	Salter, Liz	35
O'Brien, John	30	Santos, Consuelo	*
Oneal, Pearl	*	Shanks, Susie	*
Ortega, Teresa	25	Shelton, Rex	*
Ortiz, Mary	27	Shields, Cleola	28
Oviedo, Nelia	26	Siebler, Bob	31
Owens, Deborah	26	Siegel, Carl	33
Palosota, Jimmy	28	Sifuentes, Idalia	*
Patry, Bill	33	Simmons, Howard	28

Name	Years	Name	Years
Smith, Jack	42	Tullbane, Delia	*
Smith, Jamie	*	Turner, Loyce	*
Smith, Louise	35	Turner, Margie	25
Smith, Nora	*	Urbina, Janie	25
Soffen, Fred	29	VanDyken, Eugene	25
Soto, Nancy	*	Vecchio, Mary	*
Spencer, Jr., Norman	*	Veliz, Virginia	*
Stafford, Sue	37	Venable, George	*
Standler, Yvonne	*	Verzcruz, Mary	*
Stanley, Opal	*	Vierling, Ed	*
Stovall, Carolyn	*	Vogel, Harry	26
Stovall, Mary	25	Wallace, Mary	30
Stovall, Mary Ruth	41	Walls, Annette	29
Stuart, Melba	31	Warren, Neva	37
Sullins, Ted	32	Wasaff, Alex, Jr.	36
Sullivan, Estelena	26	Wasaff, Alex, Sr.	37
Sweatt, Bettie Young	25	Wasaff, Jimmy	36
Sykora, Theresa	*	Webb, Irma	*
Tansil, Beryl	26	Weeks, Marie	*
Teate, James	29	White, Robert L.	37
Tehan, Hal	32	Whitlow, Victor	25
Thomas, H.H.	39	Wielman, Lannie	*
Thompson, James	26	Wiley, Annie	30
Thompson, Ola	*	Williams, Stella	*
Thrash, Linda	25	Williams, Virginia	*
Tijerina, Natalie	26	Williams, W. Smith	30
Torres, Maria	*	Williamson, Nelda	*
Toumbs, Pearl	*	Yochum, Ariementa	53
Toumbs, Sam	*	Zamora, Abelia	*
Tracy, Bill	31	Zuniga, Odillia	*

We've collected a lot of employee records over the past seventy-five years. Unfortunately, a few have been lost in the shuffle of moving from office to office. Some of the oldest records are no longer available to us. Apologies are in order if names or exact number of years do not appear on this list.

CHAPTER 7
Presidents We've Known

Dad, Joe, and I have been most privileged to maintain friendships with several American presidents. Visiting the White House, one is constantly reminded of the phenomenal emotional and physical strength each of these men possesses and the enormous responsibilities encumbered governing the most powerful country in the world.

¤ ¤ ¤

Dad solidified his friendship with President Lyndon Johnson during a grand Texas-style barbecue at the LBJ Ranch in 1963. Their friendship continued for many years. Joe was also privileged to share this friendship and remembers this story:

> I went down to the ranch on another occasion and took my daughter, Lydia, and son, Joe, with me. LBJ was oblivious to anybody in the room. He began to try on some pants, and asked his secretary, Jewel, to get certain slacks from his closet, because he wanted me to see the fit. I asked Lydia to step outside the room while this was going on. Lyndon was busy trying on pants and putting them back on hangers, etc. When he was finished, I asked the President if he would mind taking some pictures with my children, and he agreed. I called Lydia back in the room. She and Joe III were posing for a snapshot when LBJ suddenly remembered something he wanted to show me about another pair of pants. He asked Jewel to bring him a certain pair of pants... and LBJ just dropped his pants

134 "Big Ed" and the Haggar Family

and started changing into the other pair. Lydia was still in the room. She quickly became flustered and left on her own. It was an unforgettable incident.

¤ ¤ ¤

The year was 1970. Embroiled in a sales meeting, I was certainly surprised when my secretary walked into the room and announced, "Mr. Haggar, the White House is calling!"

"Mr. Haggar," the voice on the other end of the telephone began, "President Nixon would like to appoint you as one of the fifty City Chairmen to the National Alliance of Businessmen. Pat Haggerty, president of Texas Instruments, is vacating this post. You have been nominated as his successor!" Now, to be honest, I wasn't too sure what this job was all about.

I called Pat Haggerty. "Ed, you ought to accept this position. As chairman from Dallas-Fort Worth, you would be helping people right here, as well as helping the country, by getting people off the welfare rolls and onto the payrolls."

Following Pat's advice, I accepted the presidential nomination and remained chairman for the next five years. Working with other business leaders from the community, we established many diversified job-training programs. Our intent was to help people improve their skills, so they weren't relegated to low-paying jobs. Basic training began by teaching our trainees how to set an alarm clock! During my term, I am pleased to state, more than 5,000 people completed training programs and found jobs.

Shortly after accepting the chairmanship, I received the following letter from President Nixon:

THE WHITE HOUSE
WASHINGTON

February 16, 1970

Dear Mr. Haggar:

I appreciate your agreement to serve as Metro Chairman of the National Alliance of Businessmen in Dallas, Texas.

The task you have undertaken is not an easy one, but the

Alliance has made impressive progress during the past year and I am confident that greater advances can be made in the year ahead. Your willingness, and the willingness of other businessmen like you, provides the leadership required to solve the problems of hard-core unemployment. It is the critical element of the success of the program. It is vitally important that we work to alleviate the distress of people who are able to work if given an understanding opportunity, and I firmly believe that service in the crucial effort is in our country's best interests.

>With my best wishes,
>Sincerely,
>Richard Nixon

I enjoyed two White House visits during President Nixon's terms of office. The first was a black-tie, stag party for the fifty chairmen. Each of our names was printed on a small card and placed in a punch bowl. Each guest drew a name and table assignment. President Nixon joined us for dinner. It was really a thrill. The following year we were invited to the White House, this time for a cocktail party. Former Texas governor John Connally had recently been appointed secretary of the treasury and stood beside President Nixon in the receiving line. I flew up to Washington with Clyde Skeen, regional chairman of the NAB and president of LTV. There was a lot of handshaking and back patting when the Texas delegation came face to face. Standing in the middle of the to-do, President Nixon remarked, "Hey, we've got too many Texans here tonight!"

¤ ¤ ¤

Gerald Ford became the thirty-eighth president of the United States in August 1974. I first met Mr. Ford when he was campaigning on behalf of Dallas candidate Jim Collins. Later on, Dad and Joe befriended him as well.

While serving as vice president, Mr. Ford invited me to join him at Preston Trail. You couldn't believe the Secret Service! They were everywhere. My golf bag was inspected before I joined the vice president on the first tee. No one was allowed to play in front of us or behind us. At first, I thought all the men riding around

136 "Big Ed" and the Haggar Family

the course in golf carts were spectators, wanting a closer view of Mr. Ford. They were, of course, Secret Service agents.

The following telegram was sent at the time Gerald Ford assumed the presidency:

WU Infomaster
Haggar Co Dal
ZCZC 02 Dallas, TX August 9, 1974
PMS The Honorable Gerald Ford
President
The White House
Washington, D.C.

Dear Mr. President:
Congratulations on becoming president of these great United States. I'm sad that President Nixon had to resign, but glad that the reins of government have been put in your capable hands. Your positive approach in dealing with people and problems can keep America the great country that it is. Because of your fairness and interest in running America for everyone, my suggested name for your administration is "The All America Team."
Dad and Joe join me in expressing our good wishes to you for a most successful administration.

      Warmest regards,
      Ed Haggar
      Haggar Co Dal

A few days later, I received the following letter from President Ford:

THE WHITE HOUSE
WASHINGTON

September 2, 1974

Dear Ed:

Many, many thanks for your nice telegram of congratulations and good wishes.

Yes, the circumstances under which I became the President were sad: but we must look to the future and try to solve some of the difficulties our country is facing. With God's help and the confidence and support of fine friends such as you throughout the country, I will do my very best and perhaps as you suggest we can make this Administration "The All America Team."

Please express my gratitude to your dad and Joe and extend to them my very best wishes.

Thank you again and warmest personal regards.

Sincerely,
Gerald Ford

¤ ¤ ¤

Shortly after President Ford assumed office, he granted a full pardon to President Nixon. This action caused quite a bit of controversy. I sent some editorials from the Dallas newspapers to President Ford and received the following letter:

THE WHITE HOUSE
WASHINGTON

November 6, 1974

Dear Ed:

First, let me apologize for the long delay in responding to your very thoughtful letter. Because of the heavy demands of recent weeks, I haven't been able to give your letter the prompt personal attention I would have liked.

As you expected, I was pleased indeed to have Felix McKnight's editorial comments on my pardon of former President Nixon. This was a difficult decision to make, but one which I am convinced was clearly in the national interest.

What particularly strikes me, in the editorial and also in

your own comments, is the spirit of understanding and goodwill they reflect. If we can again find these qualities in ourselves and if we can renew our confidence in our institutions, then we will certainly succeed in our efforts to build a better future for the American people and for people everywhere.

With warmest personal regards and appreciation for your thoughtfulness.

     Sincerely
     Gerald Ford

¤ ¤ ¤

During his term in office, President Ford invited Patty and me to two White House State Dinners. The first honored visiting English Prime Minister Harold Macmillan. A few months later, we attended another State Dinner for President Tolbert of Liberia. Two years after that dinner, in 1980, President Tolbert was assassinated in his own country.

¤ ¤ ¤

The year was 1978. President Ford had finished serving his term in the White House. I found out that the president had agreed to play in the Bing Crosby Classic at Pebble Beach, California. It was at this time that Preston Trail Golf Club and the Salesmanship Club of Dallas joined forces to sponsor a new major tournament in Dallas. Byron Nelson, professional golfer and much loved celebrity, added his endorsement, and so began "The Byron Nelson Tournament." I called President Ford and said, "I see where you played in the Bing Crosby Tournament in Pebble Beach. Will you come down here and play in the Bryon Nelson Tournament?"

"If it fits my schedule, I'll be glad to do it," replied President Ford.

And he played in the Bryon Nelson for the next ten years. During that period, I was always teamed with President Ford, Bob Hope, and the defending champion.

President Ford was our houseguest for five of the years he played in the Dallas-based tournament. Located seven miles south of Preston Trail, our house on Wedgewood Lane sat on one and a half acres of beautifully landscaped gardens. When

President Ford was at the house, the Secret Service patrolled every square inch of ground. They set up their headquarters in our garage. Before each visit, my sister-in-law, Isabell, always remarked how safe she felt when all the Secret Servicemen were patrolling our neighborhood.

Prior to President Ford's first visit, the Secret Service arrived at the house a day or two early to set up. Patty was as scared as she could be. "Relax," I told her, "President Ford is a real down-to-earth guy. He's like an old shoe." The president and his entourage arrived on schedule. Early the next morning, he joined us for breakfast. Mary, our cook, prepared some grits, and the president had second helpings. All of us sat around the breakfast table for quite some time. Patty sure relaxed after that. Subsequently, the tournament was moved to another course, farther away, and it was more convenient for President Ford to stay at a hotel closer to the golf course.

Joe's affiliation with St. Jude's Hospital provided still another opportunity for Joe and President Ford to tee off. Joe recalls:

> I was responsible for influencing President Ford to play in the St. Judes/FEDEX Tournament. We've been sponsors of that tournament for years, supplying pants and shirts. As a result, I was always included in the group that played with last year's champion and President Ford. I was playing with him the day he made his famous hole-in-one at the St. Jude's Tournament. It was a very exciting occasion. That same day, PGA pro Al Geiberger shot a 59, which was the lowest score in any PGA tournament.

President Ford started his own tournament, "The Jerry Ford Invitational Tournament," in Vail, Colorado. Haggar Corporation was one of the first corporate sponsors and continued to be involved for twenty years. (The tournament was discontinued after twenty years.) Between Joe and me, we never missed playing in a single tournament.

Integrity, courage, and honesty... Betty Ford publicly admitted her problem of alcohol addiction and overcame it. Recently, I was watching Larry King interview President Ford on his national television program. I was reminded of the following story. Twenty-five years ago, President Ford told the nation that his wife was hospitalized at the San Diego Naval Hospital. Bob Barrett, who would have been President Ford's chief of staff had Ford been elected for a second term, called with an urgent request. "Ed, the president was scheduled to leave for Virginia tonight, where he was to deliver an important speech. However, he's going straight to San Diego to be with Betty. Henry Kissinger is in Dallas this evening and I've already asked him to speak for President Ford tomorrow morning in Virginia, but I need your help in procuring a private plane to get him to Virginia tonight." I made arrangements for Dr. Kissinger to board a private airplane in Dallas bound for Virginia. After her hospitalization in San Diego, Mrs. Ford established the Betty Ford Clinic in Rancho Mirage, California, helping others with their own struggles to overcome alcohol and drug addiction.

President Ford was a big fan of Haggar products and wore a lot of them before, during, and after his stay in the White House. In fact, they're still his favorites.

We are deeply honored that President Ford graciously added his comments to this volume of memoirs:

> In 1962, I was a member of the House of Representatives and one of the leaders who was getting higher and higher in the echelon. I was asked to come to Dallas and make a fund raising speech for Jim Collins, the Republican candidate for Congress. Jim was one of our very first Republicans from Texas to get elected. I met Ed Haggar for the first time at that fund-raising event.
>
> After that initial meeting, I got to know Ed's brother, Joe and their father, who was the patriarch of that fine family. I should like to say that my friendships with Ed and Joe and their father expanded well beyond political fundraisers.
>
> When I started my own golf tournament in Vail, we invited people from all over the country. The Haggars were corporate sponsors for many years.
>
> There is something very impressive about the Haggar family. They are closely knit. They believe in doing things in the community and they are very generous in their support of charitable organizations. The Haggars, in my opinion, are a classy family.

¤ ¤ ¤

I was first introduced to President George Bush in 1965, when he was campaigning for the Senate against Lloyd Bentsen. At the time we met, Fred Zeder was George's state finance chairman. Subsequently, I became finance chairman for the Dallas area.

During the Ford administration, George Bush served as ambassador to China. Later, he headed the Central Intelligence Agency. Bobby Stewart, chief executive officer of First National Bank, appointed Mr. Bush to the bank's board of directors. As a fellow board member, I saw Mr. Bush at several meetings. Most of our time was devoted to discussing issues on the agenda. When it was time for small talk and minutiae, Mr. Bush and the rest of the board members always talked about tennis. Several of the board members were avid players, including Governor Clements, Ed Cox, and Trammel Crow. It never dawned on me to ask him if he played golf!

Following our first meeting, I sent Mr. Bush some Haggar slacks. I continued sending him various items from the Haggar line: pants, sport coats, and suits. After being elected to the presidency, he continued wearing our products, but always insisted on paying for them. In fact, for three or four years in a row, the president sent each of his sons something from the Haggar line as Christmas gifts, which he always paid for.

When George Bush served as vice president, I attended a fundraiser in Houston. An entourage of reporters and television cameramen preceded President Reagan and Vice President Bush. Passing by my table, on the way from the podium, Vice President Bush paused, opened his coat to reveal the label, and said, "Here it is, Ed... a Haggar suit, and I'm wearing it!"

Shortly after he was elected, the president invited Patty and me to a State Dinner at the White House. King Hussein of Jordan and his American-born wife, Queen Noor, were the honored guests. Dad was a friend of the queen's father, Mr. Halaby, who was Lebanese. The king and queen stood beside President Bush in the reception line. When introduced to King Hussein, I shook his hand and said in Arabic, *"Uh la wi shala al United States,"* which means "Welcome to the United States."

"Ed, stop showing off and move on," the president kidded me.

After drinks and dinner, we were entertained in the East Room of the White House. It was a remarkable evening.

November 13, 1989. I arrived in Washington, D.C., scheduled to address a Sorin Society meeting in Baltimore in midafternoon. My evening plans included visiting with some of our Haggar customers in Washington. I called the White House, hoping to pass along greetings to President Bush, via his secretary, Patty Presock. "I bet he'd like to see you," Patty told me. A few minutes later I answered my hotel-room phone. "The president would like you to join him at 6:30 for cocktails in the private living quarters," Patty informed me. Approaching the president of the United States on any occasion is an event filled with protocol and details. Patty told me which entrance and elevator to use. Waiting to greet me with a big bear hug when I stepped off the elevator, President Bush escorted me to his living quarters.

Three large television sets were tuned to three different international news programs. This was during the Persian Gulf crisis with Saddam Hussein. Early the next morning the Bushes were leaving for a trip to Saudi Arabia to visit the American troops. I greeted Barbara Bush and was introduced to the other man in the room, President Bush's counselor. All of us watched in horror as Saddam threatened our troops and the people of the Middle East. I leaned forward and whispered in the president's ear, *"Hatic dean em ibin shalmute!"*

"What does that mean?" asked the president.

"It's Arabic and means 'He's a goddamn son of a bitch!'" I replied.

The president shook with laughter... a much-needed respite at such troubled times.

"Ed, Barbara and I get on our knees every night and pray that this guy will shape up and get out," President Bush confided to me. Burdened with the enormous stress and responsibilities of leading this country to war in the Middle East, President Bush kept his wits and cool demeanor. He asked about Patty and the rest of the family. When I informed him it was Patty's birthday, the president placed a call to her. Patty was not home. I looked at my wristwatch and noticed it was nearly 7:00. "Mr. President, I'm here in town to meet with some of our Haggar customers, and I'm afraid that I am running late." President Bush walked over to his desk, took a personal notecard, and asked for the names of my guests. "I'm sorry Ed is late. It's my fault, please forgive him. George Bush." Ink still drying on the card, I left the White House. As promised, the president called Patty later that evening and told her all about my White House visit. It was a visit with a most remarkable man at a most remarkable time in history.

During both his presidential campaigns and his term in office, I was an unsolicited advisor to President Bush. We exchanged letters and ideas. Here is a brief sampling:

E. R. Haggar
6113 LEMMON AVENUE
DALLAS, TEXAS

February 18, 1988

Dear Mr. Vice President:

Congratulations on your great New Hampshire victory. A real comeback, and I know you got the "Big Mo" back on the track—but we just can't be satisfied with success, as you know.

I'm attaching some ideas that I'm sure you, and your staff and advisors have already thought of; however, in case your folks have missed something, these ideas may be of some help.

I think the American people are interested in the issues and your vision of what you see for the country and how you can get these executed...

Good luck for the balance of the campaign and with my warmest regards I am, Sincerely...

(The following viewpoints were included in the above letter.)

My Vision for America is:

An educated America—I want every American to reach the high school level and to finish at this level. It is my dream to have every individual who finishes high school, and wants to work to achieve success, have a college education.

Incentive and morality start at an early age in the home. Unfortunately, today, we have many children who are fatherless. This includes whites, Hispanics, and blacks. We must instill morality and incentive in these disadvantaged children, through the parents; through public television; through the public sector. We need to teach our children there is a God. That God has blessed this country and God-fearing people made it what it is.

We need an arm, such as Operation Headstart, to get young children off on the right foot, morally and educationally. I propose to do this through the private sector. Let me explain. The National Alliance of Businessmen educated disadvantaged men and women of all races, enabling them to get better jobs. This early education program could be something additional for the NAB—or another private sector organization.

A drug free society (100% may be a pipe-dream, but 60-80% improvement over the next four years is an achievable goal).

We all believe in welfare and must help our fellow man. However, those who are able must help themselves, unless we want to continue to perpetuate [first-, second- and third-generation families] now on welfare. The welfare program, in my opinion, is feeding the drug, alcohol and other abuse-type habits.

In order to maintain the peace, we must—and will—have a strong defense program. A lot of our defense spending goes toward defending other countries in the world. Countries like Germany and Japan must pay for their share—and we plan to ask them to do just this.

We need a fair trade policy to eliminate dumping. We must be able to bid and get contracts on large projects in foreign countries (i.e., the new large airport in Japan). We have to help the rest of the world make a living. But we don't have to give them the whole store. Possibly, quotas are needed when certain levels of our country's production are swamped by imports from certain countries.

We need a strategic policy regarding oil. I'm against the import tax. However, that doesn't mean I'm against the oil industry. I'm for it. And we must, for defense purposes, have access to all the oil we need at fair and equitable prices, so heating oil, gasoline and other oil products do not go through the ceiling, as they did four or five years ago.

We should work closer with Canada, Mexico and Venezuela, all of whom are in our backyard. We should have oil depletion back at 20 to 27-½% for all segments of the industry. Depletion will not add to the price of oil; it will create more production and business for the oil industry, thereby more individual and federal income taxes.

It takes money to reach these goals we need and must have. Yet it is absolutely necessary to have a balanced budget. We can do this by eliminating waste and unnecessary programs; continue to boost our economy so we do not have to raise taxes. *Lastly, to help balance the budget and to keep it balanced, we need and must have, a line-item veto.*

These are visions that I will fulfill. I have the will and leadership ability to get the job done. I know the Congress well. I was a member of Congress. I've been involved in helping President Reagan get his Congressional bills through Congress. I know most of the Congress on both sides of the aisle. It is a selling job. Most congressmen, regardless of political affiliation, want to do what is right for America. In addition to knowing Democrats and Republicans, I've worked hard campaigning for many Republicans, helping them get elected or re-elected. So, I've got a lot of chits out and if a program makes sense for the American people, I can get it through Congress. I'm reminded of one of Aesop's fables: The Council of Mice—For many months, the mice in a basement were constantly harassed by a large cat. At a meeting, one of the younger mice proposed, "Let's put a bell around the cat, and when the cat approaches, the bell will ring, sounding an alarm." The head of the mice clan retorted, "That's a wonderful idea—but, pray tell me, who will bell the cat?" *The moral of the story is "To propose is one thing—to execute is another." I can and will execute!!!*

The president's reply:

146 "Big Ed" and the Haggar Family

VICE PRESIDENT OF THE UNITED STATES
ABOARD AIR FORCE TWO

February 22, 1988 (en route to South Carolina)
Mr. Ed Haggar
6113 Lemmon Avenue
Dallas, Texas 75209

Dear Ed:
Thanks for your great letter and the suggestions on "vision." Some of your themes I've sounded, and this week I will be coming out with a major statement on the oil industry. Forgive me if some of your ideas crop up as my own.

¤ ¤ ¤

E. R. Haggar
6113 LEMMON AVENUE
DALLAS, TEXAS

November 19, 1990

Dear Mr. President and Barbara:
Thanks so much for asking me for cocktails and to visit with you and Barbara in your private residence—it was a real thrill, an honor and most flattering. I had called Patty Presock, just to say hello and figured if I was lucky, I might get to say hello over the phone. You can't believe the reaction of my dinner partners when they received your note—they couldn't believe it and were ecstatic.

Patty and I have been following your trip to Europe and it looks like everything is falling into place for you and our country.

You are in our prayers, and I know you and Barbara will end up with a most successful trip, highlighted by your visit with our troops in the Saudi desert.

God bless you both—take care of yourselves. Patty joins me in sending you our very best regards and prayers.

¤ ¤ ¤

GEORGE BUSH
WASHINGTON
October 25, 1992
(Onboard Air Force One)

Dear Ed,

George passed along to me your wonderful letter of October 20, and I appreciate the suggestions.

You are right when you say that my export message should be tied to jobs for Americans and I am trying to do just that. I am sure you know I agree with you on the question of those ridiculous lawsuits and the cost they impose on society, with special emphasis on health care costs.

I am encouraged by today's national polls and remain confident that I am going to win despite the ugliest press I have ever seen.

[Note: When the president begins his letter, "George passed along to me..." he is referring to his son, George W., who served as campaign manager for his father.]

¤ ¤ ¤

E. R. Haggar
6113 LEMMON AVENUE
DALLAS, TEXAS

November 4, 1992

Dear Mr. President:

With the reins of government, for the past four years, in your most capable hands, you've blazed a trail that history will never forget. You have ended the Cold War and have paved the trail creating new world markets and jobs for the near future and for many years to come, positioning America to win the world-wide economic war. Under your leadership, you've made America the envy of the world.

Your talk last night was most gracious—just what Americans and the world would expect from President George Bush.

Glad you plan to spend more time with your grandchildren. Now you will have time for more hunting and golfing (you should consider playing in some tournaments like the Bob Hope and Byron Nelson Classics). Mainly, I hope you will stay involved as a private citizen, using your many years of experience in government to continue to promote good government for our great nation.

We love you; we're proud of you.

¤ ¤ ¤

The President

November 11, 1992

Dear Patty and Ed,

Barbara and I are deeply grateful for your message about the election. Now that all is said and done, we especially appreciate our true friends who never gave up the battle. I have no rancor in my heart at all.

It was a tough campaign, but we are thankful for so many blessings—among them our family and loyal, wonderful friends like you.

Barbara joins me in sending best wishes.

¤ ¤ ¤

GEORGE BUSH

January 1, 1994

Dear Ed,

I was voted 'best dressed' in our Ford Van yesterday. That's because I was clad in some of those great pairs of Haggar slacks. I tried other products and they are the best.

This is my *1st* letter of 1994. That it goes to a good friend gives me joy.

¤ ¤ ¤

The George Bush Presidential Library in College Station was officially dedicated in April 1998. My grandson, Garrett Turner, and I flew down with my good friend Bob Wright on Bob's airplane. There were nearly 20,000 invited guests. George's son Jeb served as master of ceremonies, and Governor George W. made a fine speech. Walking through the library, I recognized a photograph taken at Walter Annenberg's estate in Rancho Mirage, California, in December 1997. Standing together were President Ford and President Bush. Bob French, a personal friend of President Bush, was the third man in the foursome, and I was the fourth that particular day.

President Bush walked by. He was completely surrounded by a throng of press members, Secret Service agents, and guests. I asked, "Mr. President, how come Bob French and I were left out of the photo?" Suddenly, the president was swept up amid the crowd and pushed on. My question remained unanswered.

We are deeply honored that President Bush sent the following comments regarding our many years of friendship for this volume of memoirs:

> January 27, 1998
>
> Ever since I have known Ed, I have considered him a loyal trustworthy friend, a man of great warmth.
>
> I first met Ed through our mutual friend, Fred Zeder. Fred was on the City Council in Dallas and was also running my Senate campaign in Dallas. Fred Zeder signed up Ed Haggar to work on the finance committee. From that day on, Ed has been a wonderfully loyal supporter of mine.
>
> Over the years, I depended on Ed as a kind of unofficial advisor. He would take the pulse of the people from time to time and send me helpful advice. That advice continued right up through my being President of the United States.
>
> I should also note that I had great respect for Ed's father and, of course, his brother, Joe. The Haggars represent the best in strong families. They have been a real inspiration to Barbara and me and, as a matter of fact, to all the Bushes. Their family love is exemplary, and they all live lives of service to others. What a wonderful thing.
>
> My impressions of Ed are varied. But I think of him as a highly successful man, a man of great loyalties and a decent, honorable man.
>
> I love playing golf with Ed. He is fierce and friendly on the links great fun to tee it up with.

¤ ¤ ¤

The presidential election of 2000 was the most highly contested race in this nation's history. For thirty days following the election, citizens of the world focused on counts and recounts in Florida. The total votes cast between Vice President Al Gore and Texas Governor George W. Bush were just about dead even. The electoral college cast the final affirming votes in Governor Bush's favor in mid-December.

I was honored and pleased to serve as an *unsolicited advisor* to President George W. throughout his term as governor of Texas and his campaign for the presidency.

The following letter was sent to the White House on January 27, 2001, along with my notes and observations on the Baby First Program and different educational programs in which I have been involved.

> E. R. Haggar
> 6113 LEMMON AVENUE
> DALLAS, TEXAS

January 27, 2001

President George W. Bush
The White House
Washington, D.C. 20500

Dear Mr. President:

I congratulated you as Mr. President Elect after the election but the above salutation sounds much better. You have handled all the unanticipated problems during the election, vote recounts and your final win masterfully. Your inaugural address was excellent; concise and reassuring to the vast majority of Americans—those who voted for or against you.

With your leadership and ability to get along with legislators of different political views, I predict you will accomplish more than any other United States President in the early years of their presidency. Again, heartiest congratulations to you and Laura (she will be an "out of this world" first lady).

I am enclosing a paper about early education starting right after birth. This may have some merit as part of your education program. I sent the memo to you on September 14, 2000 through Joseph I. O'Neil III.

All our love and best to you and Laura.
Ed & Patty Haggar

¤ ¤ ¤

President George W. responded to my letter just four days later:

THE WHITE HOUSE
WASHINGTON

January 31, 2001

Mr. and Mrs. E. R. Haggar
6113 Lemmon Avenue
Dallas, TX 75209

Dear Patty and Ed:

Thank you so much for your kind words. I do hope we will be able to accomplish much through bringing the Nation together. We have had a promising start.

Thank you also for the education paper. We do hope business leaders will play a critical role in accomplishing our goals in education. Laura and I feel strongly about making real progress in this vital area.

You are great friends.
Sincerely,

[signature: George W. Bush]
all my very best

At our 75th Anniversary Celebration in the San Diego area we had two video greetings from former presidents Gerald R. Ford and George H. Bush. We didn't have enough time to get a similar video from George W. because of his travel schedule, but we received a beautiful color photograph and a nice congratulatory message read off camera.

CHAPTER 8

Work, Directorships, and Other Business Interests

Dallas was a very pretty, clean, metropolitan city in the early 1960s. Three banks — First National, Mercantile, and Republic — fought like cats and dogs for the majority share of business in town. However, when it came to matters of the city's growth and integrity, the banks worked together for the common good.

Beginning in the early 1980s, events unfolded which rocked the real estate markets in Dallas and sent the city into a tailspin. Here's an example: In the mid-1950s, Dad bought some real estate in Carrollton, Texas, for about $500 per acre. The price of raw land kept escalating. Dad wanted to sell the land on two or three occasions, but Joe and I urged him to hold on to it. To make a long story short, Dad ultimately sold the land for a ton of money. By this time, the land value was so over-inflated, it was uncanny! Very shortly after that, the real estate market went to hell!

In 1964, Bobby Stewart, the CEO of First National, invited me to join the board of directors. As time went by, our bank, as well as several of the others, had many, many real estate loans — some very good, others not so good. After the above incident in Carrollton, I called Bobby Stewart and said, "Things are going to really burst. It's ridiculous the way real estate prices are going up, especially when there are no plans to build." I told him that the bank had to get out of some of these loans. We did, but not enough. Subsequently, real estate really crashed.

Under the leadership of Bill McCord, the Dallas Gas Company acquired other oil-related businesses, exploration companies, and engineering companies, and reorganized under the name of Enserch. Bill McCord was quite a colorful and well-respected civic leader in Dallas. He invited me to join the board of directors for Enserch. "Bill, I don't know anything about engineering, or what your company does," I told him. His reply, "Ed, you're a businessman and we need your business experience." During my tenure, I served on the Audit Committee and the Conflict of Interest Committee. Being such a diversified organization, there were always conflicts of interest!

Some of our board meetings were conducted at different sites around the world, wherever Enserch was engaged in business. At the time, I coined the phrase, "Join the Enserch board and see the world with Bill McCord!"

The first overseas board meeting I attended was in South Africa. At the time, Enserch was building an oil rig in the Indian Ocean, near Durban, a major industrial city on the eastern coast of South Africa. After inspecting and touring the rig, we flew to Johannesburg for our board meeting. At the conclusion, several of us went on a photographic safari. We traveled by bus through such diverse countryside. I was amazed at all the agriculture—orchards and fields of cotton, wheat, corn, alfalfa, bananas, coconuts, and pineapples. Beyond the cultivated country, lions, elephants and antelopes roamed the boundless plains.

Our next international board meeting found us in Sydney, Australia. Enserch owned a company called Solis Engineering and Diving Company, which built huge diving bells. Following our meeting in Sydney, we were flown by helicopter to a big oil platform in the Tasman Sea, between Tasmania and southern Australia. I joined several of my fellow board members and dove nearly 700 feet in a diving bell. On retelling the story stateside, people were amazed. "Did you really do that?... Wasn't it scary?" Actually, it wasn't much different from riding in an elevator. The bells are outfitted with double oxygen systems and double phone systems. Huge windows in the diving bell revealed all sorts of sea life. It was magnificent!

Enserch owned several oil leases in the Gulf of Mexico. We had a meeting in New Orleans, after which, we enjoyed a sumptuous dinner at Antoine's. The next day we were ferried out to the platform in two helicopters. We had lunch with the crewmembers on the platform. The food served was equal to that of Antoine's. Food was an important perk to the men stationed in the middle of the Gulf. Many of the workers stayed on because of the excellent food.

One of the two helicopters that brought us out to the platform developed mechanical troubles just before taking off. In order to get everyone back safely, one helicopter made two trips. I was assigned to the second flight. While waiting for the helicopter to return, I played Ping-Pong with several of the crewmembers.

Another board meeting found us in Anchorage, Alaska. We were flown to an oil platform in Prudhoe Bay, near the North Pole. Enserch was building a series of oil platforms right off the shore. It was a gorgeous day; there was no wind. We really didn't need the heavy coats and gear provided for us until the helicopter's rotor blades started spinning, in preparation for our departure. We stayed at the Crazy Horse Hotel and enjoyed sunshine nearly twenty-four hours a day, for three days.

I used to kid some of my friends in the oil business, calling them "Oil Typhoons!" But kidding or not, I did two things in the oil industry that few of my friends in the oil business have ever done. Some may have spent time on oil platforms, in such remote places as Prudhoe Bay. But few, if any, dove into the Tasman Sea inside a diving bell! No one has done both. I served on the Enserch board from 1981 through 1988.

When I was about to retire from the board, the chairman of the Nominations Committee happened to catch Joe on CNN when he was talking about the Haggar H.O.T. program. He was really infatuated with Joe and asked me, "Is that your brother?" I said, "He sure is." To which he replied, "We've got to have him on the board. Would you ask him?" I answered, "I won't ask him now because he just got off the City Council and he really wants to get back to work. But I will ask him in six months." In any event, Joe did become a member—and a good member— of that corporation's board of directors.

I was asked to head the first annual fund drive for the University of Dallas. Subsequently, I became a member of the board of trustees of this fine school. Throughout the years, I've enjoyed working with the school's founders and trustees: Eugene Constantine, Edward Maher, Sr., Pat Haggerty, Eric Jonnson, Louis Maher, and Tom Unis. The last few years have been especially enjoyable working with Monsignor Milam Joseph, president of the university, and James M. Moroney, chairman of the board.

Representing the University of Dallas, Jim Moroney, Neil O'Brien, and I called on one of Dallas's most generous philanthropists and civic leaders, Ralph Rogers, for a contribution to the school. Ralph graciously agreed to our request. After the business at hand, Ralph spoke to us about a project he initiated called Preschool Educational Programs. Ralph said, "It is up to us, responsible parents, care-givers, day-care providers and teachers to educate young children." I replied, "I'm interested in helping if you think we can also find a way to teach these children right from wrong at a very early age."

Later on, this program expanded further to assist expectant mothers with pre-natal care. The program was called "Baby First" and helped young mothers nurture and show love to their newborn children. All this loving care helps develop the child's brain, of which 90% is developed by three years and is fully developed at age four or five. The program is now called "First Impressions" and is being promoted by public television station KERA, Dallas-Fort Worth. It is my hope that additional public television stations in Texas and throughout the nation will join us.

Ralph Rogers passed away recently. He was truly the patron saint of this program. His sons, Bob and Dick, are following in their father's footsteps. I became enamored with this endeavor, and it is the intention of our Ed Haggar Family Foundation to continue supporting this fine program.

A listing of civic affiliations, board of director memberships, awards and honors for Dad, Joe, Joe III, Frank Bracken, and myself is included at the end of this book.

¤ ¤ ¤

Dallas has been our hometown for seventy-seven years. The city has survived phenomenal growth spurts and strangling economic depressions. Haggar Corporation has been, since its very beginning, a major contributor to the growth and solidarity of the city. The company has always had very strong ties with Dallas, and vice versa. Dad, Joe, and I have all been active participants in city and civic affairs. We experienced, firsthand, enormous changes within the city.

Founded in 1937, the Dallas Citizens Council was made up of chief executive officers from companies in the Dallas area. The group provided good leadership and guidance and helped make Dallas a better city. For years, many critics referred to it as "The Oligarchy." As the city changed and diversified, so did the Dallas Citizens Council. At various times, Dad, Joe, and I were members of this influential organization.

During my tenure on the Dallas Citizens Council, I was asked to sit on the executive Tri-Racial Committee. As the name implies, the committee's focus was on the diverse ethnic and racial communities in the city. If there were problems brewing, this committee solved the problems before they got out of hand. The committee consisted of two blacks, two Anglos, and two Hispanics. Bob Cullum, Reverend Sam Wright, and Masio Smith were fellow members. We met every other month in the offices of the Dallas Gas Company. Meetings were informal; no minutes were recorded.

The Dallas Gas Company was located in the central perimeter of the city. We always tried to end our meetings by 4:30, to avoid getting stuck in traffic. The Dallas chief of police was our guest at one particular meeting. At the time, I was driving a brand new Cadillac Eldorado. The odometer showed less than 400 miles. On this day, I pulled into the lot and told the attendant, "I want to beat the traffic. Please have the car up front and ready to go by 4:30." I returned to the parking lot after the meeting, looked high and low, and couldn't find the car. A different attendant was on duty. "It's a brand new gold Eldorado, almost a buckskin color," I explained. He smiled at me and said, "Well, if you had a brand new Eldorado, that mother ain't here now!" How ironic... my car was stolen as I sat in an office with the Dallas police chief, just a few yards from the parking lot! The car was found a day later, completely stripped.

¤ ¤ ¤

Dedicated to revitalizing the ancient spirit of thanksgiving, the Center for World Thanksgiving at Thanksgiving Square is a worldwide resource set in the heart of Dallas. The unique Chapel of Thanksgiving, with its distinctive spiral tower and stained-glass Glory Window, attracts visitors from around the world. Set amid soaring skyscrapers, the Center's peaceful courtyard, fountains, and gardens provide a serene setting for personal reflection, international gatherings, and weddings alike.

Thanksgiving Square was the vision of Peter Stewart, a wonderful and tenacious man, who campaigned among Dallas civic and business leaders for funds to purchase the land. Honoring our mother, Rose Mary Wasaff Haggar—who loved and was inspired by beauty—the Haggar family made a sizable contribution.

Construction began in 1975 and was completed in 1976. The original board of directors consisted of four members representing Catholicism, Protestantism, and Judaism. The original Catholic director, Joseph Neuhoff, passed away before construction was completed, and I was honored by the invitation to replace him on the board of directors. Julius Schepps, a very fine Jewish civic leader, was a fellow director. He was funny and smart as hell. Shortly after we began serving on the board of Thanksgiving Square, Julius facetiously put me up for membership in the Columbian Club, a Jewish golf club in Dallas. The membership committee, much to the chagrin of Julius, blackballed me. When asked why, they replied, "We do have gentiles in this club. But they have to look like gentiles!"

¤ ¤ ¤

During my lifetime, I've been honored with several awards. In 1980 I received the Humanitarian Award from the National Jewish Hospital in Denver, Colorado. This extraordinary institution specializes in the research and treatment of respiratory problems. There are several asthmatics in our family, and that's how I learned about the hospital. I was able to lend my skills as a fundraiser and sponsored several functions in Dallas and throughout the Southwest to benefit the hospital.

A little aside: I was invited to Denver to tour the hospital before the award ceremony and meet some of the key personnel. David Florence, a hospital trustee, accompanied me on the trip to Denver. He dropped me off in front of the Braniff terminal and drove away to park the car. The Braniff stewardess was just about ready to close the jet-way to our plane when I arrived at the gate. David had to walk over from the parking lot and was nowhere in sight. I had to do something to delay the departure. I managed to stall the flight by stumbling and faking a knee injury. Limping and bent over in pain, I delayed the process long enough for David to make his way to the gate.

I remembered a story about Knute Rockne, when he found himself in a similar situation at the Notre Dame vs. Army game. Knowing he could not arrive at a certain activity on time, Coach Rockne faked an injury. Immediately, someone called an ambulance. When the ambulance arrived, Coach Rockne admitted his injury was only faked, but asked to be transported to the site in the ambulance, thus enabling him to get there on time.

We arrived in Denver on time. After the meeting at the hospital, I joined our Denver regional sales manager, Tom Kilroy, and played in a golf tournament at the Broadmoor and returned to Dallas the following day. Had I missed that plane, our entire day in Colorado would have been fouled up!

The University of Notre Dame honored me with the Sorin Award in 1988. This award is bestowed upon an alumnus who has performed a high degree of service to the university and to his community. I began my acceptance speech by alluding to the days of student unrest in the late 1960s and a remark Father Hesburgh had made to the student body: "I'll give you fifteen minutes to meditate and shape up... or you're out of here!" I continued with my speech, "Well, they shaped up... and in less than fifteen minutes! Father Hesburgh and Father Ned Joyce (executive vice president) gave Notre Dame thirty-five years of truly excellent leadership. Father Edward 'Monk' Malloy, our current president, and Father William Beauchamp (vice president) have done a brilliant job of moving 'Our Lady's' University forward. As you know, Father Malloy was an outstanding varsity basketball player for Notre Dame. So now we have 'Fifteen Minute Hesburgh' and 'Slam Dunk Monk!'"

In 1991, I received the Herbert Hoover Award for Boys and Girls Clubs of America. President Bush was a previous recipient. Again, my efforts were mainly geared to sponsoring several regional and national fundraising drives to benefit different clubs. President Hoover started the Boys Club of America nearly 100 years ago. At the time I served on the board, the big issue before us was combining the Girls Clubs of America with the Boys Clubs! It's a worthwhile endeavor. Instead of being on the streets after school, inner-city children can spend time with their peers playing organized sports and participating in other social groups.

¤ ¤ ¤

Dad got burned on a real estate investment just about the time I was born. At that time, he vowed never to get into the real estate market again. And for the most part, he stayed pretty true to his word. However, Mother, Joe, and I always liked real estate as an investment tool. The family bought some tracts in Carrollton, Texas, north on Preston Road, by Lake Hubbard and several other tracts. Eventually, we put these properties in a real estate investment partnership that we named the Jezzeen Partnership, after Dad's birthplace in Lebanon. Although it's an equal partnership, Joe is the head of this operation. He manages the partnership on our behalf and has done a great job.

¤ ¤ ¤

Son of Lebanese immigrants, entertainer Danny Thomas became famous across the country in the 1950s through his television show *Make Room for Daddy*. Danny was a close friend of our family, especially Joe. In addition to his on-stage charm, Danny had a good head for business and a great heart for charity. He dedicated much of his time supporting St. Jude's Children Hospital in Memphis, Tennessee.

Danny put together a small group of investors and started the Miami Dolphins football franchise. At that time, he offered a very small percentage of ownership to Joe. In turn, Joe asked me if I wanted a part of the team as well. Both of us eagerly accepted Danny's offer. Joe's name appears often in the book *Miami Dolphins*. A lot of people assumed we were major owners. We had, what I called, a "rooting interest." However, we did share in the glory. Joe and I each received a magnificent Super Bowl Ring after each of Miami's two Super Bowl victories.

Joe recalls:

During my student days at Notre Dame, I met my father in Chicago, when he visited the city to call on customers. On one occasion, one of Dad's customers invited us to accompany him to see a young, Lebanese nightclub entertainer named Danny Thomas. After the show, our host invited Danny to join us at our table. We discussed many things that night. It marked the beginning of a very special friendship. Later on, Danny founded St. Jude's Children's Research Hospital. He asked me to join the board of trustees, which I did. And I've been a member ever since. During my early tenure on the board, Joe Robbie, another Lebanese friend of Danny's, and Danny decided to get into the professional football business and they asked Ed and me to join them.

At the time, I was very friendly with Lamar Hunt, who, earlier, had founded the American Football League. For whatever reason, the National Football League would not accept the Miami Dolphins franchise. I approached Lamar and told him about our failed negotiations with the NFL. Subsequently, the Dolphins became a distinguished team in the American Football League.

Miami Coach Don Shula is one of the finest persons I ever met. He led the Dolphins to two consecutive Super Bowl victories in 1971 and 1972. The Dolphins won every game they played during the 1971 season, in addition to winning the Super Bowl. No other team in football history has ever held that record. Had it not been for the formation of another franchise team, who robbed us of five of our finest players, I'm confident the Dolphins would have won the Super Bowl three years in a row.

CHAPTER 9

My Wonderful Family, Special Friends, and Favorite Pastime

In the spring of 1940, one of my buddies from Notre Dame, Jack Shortall, arranged a blind date for me with a beautiful Irish girl from Kansas City, Missouri, named Patricia Ann Daley. My life has never been the same since that fateful evening some sixty-one years ago!

Patty's maternal family hailed from Covington, Kentucky. Her grandmother came from a prominent Southern family. "She was a real Southern Belle," Patty told me. Her grandparents, Edward Everett and Minnie Bell Stevens Pugh, moved to Kansas City and raised a family of four children—two boys and two girls. Patty's mother was named Alice Marie Pugh. Alice's brother, Ed Pugh, practiced law in Kansas City.

James Joseph Daley was born in the town of Canna, in County Cork, Ireland. Patty's paternal grandmother, Kathryn Daley, brought her young family over from Ireland after her husband was killed in a farm accident. She settled in Kansas City, among immigrants she had known in the old country. Patty's dad was a great athlete and sports fan. As a young man, he played on a semi-pro baseball team in Kansas City. After marrying Alice, Jim Daley took up selling as his career in Hutchinson, Kansas, where their only child, Patty, was born. He sold everything from candy and cookies to automotive parts. Later, they returned to Kansas City.

Patty graduated from Southwest High School in the middle of the Great Depression. After high school, she attended Kansas City Junior College. Times were tough. Patty worked for her uncle, Ed Pugh, as a legal stenographer for minimum wage— two bits an hour!

Patty was a career girl when I met her in 1940. Here are some of her recollections about her career with Braniff Airways:

> After two and a half years, I was just bored to death in Uncle Ed's law office. In 1939, I received a letter from a girlfriend in Marshall, Missouri, telling me about her job interview with a new commercial airline called Braniff. She urged me to come down to Dallas, the headquarters of Braniff, and apply for a job.
>
> I had never been on an airplane before. The idea of working for an airline company absolutely thrilled me to death. I asked Mother if she thought I was crazy, wanting to pursue this kind of career, and she told me to go to Dallas and interview for the job. In Dallas, I was interviewed and hired on the spot. I was 22 years old. Trans World Airlines was Braniff's only competition in 1939. The girls who became stewardesses for TWA were required to have degrees in nursing. At the time, Braniff flight destinations were mainly in Texas; Brownsville, Austin, San Antonio, Houston and Dallas. The airline also flew to Wichita, Kansas City and Chicago. A great many of the passengers spoke only Spanish and Tom Braniff wanted his stewardesses to speak the language well enough to address the needs and questions of the passengers.
>
> My dear friend, Mary Lou Moran, came down to Dallas shortly after I got the job, and she too became a stewardess for Braniff. We shared a rented room in Dallas. The rent was $7 per week, split between the two of us. In addition to three months of training, where we learned how to complete a ticket manifest, prepare food and deal with passengers, we also took an immersion course in Spanish.
>
> At the time, Braniff was headquartered in a yellow stucco building at Love Air Field. We had only one uniform: a gray

My Wonderful Family, Special Friends, and Favorite Pastime   163

wool skirt, worn with a starched white cotton blouse and a pleated navy blue cummerbund, over which we wore a gray woolen bolero jacket and a little gray hat. I was sure comfortable in the winter months, but come summer... it was hotter than the dickens!

The first planes we flew seated 10 passengers, a pilot, co-pilot and me. Shortly after that, Braniff started flying DC-2s which were quite a bit larger. There were no memorable flights that stick out in my mind today, but I do remember warming a lot of baby bottles.

It was such a new field. The girls were all friendly. It was like one big sorority. Mary Lou left behind a boyfriend in Kansas City who was always pestering her to come home and marry him. She was really reluctant about giving up her career. But she finally decided to return to Kansas City. At the time, I was very homesick. I really hadn't met too many people in Dallas and dreaded the idea of being alone after Mary Lou left. Her last words to me were, "Just wait, you'll meet somebody!"

At the time we met, I was twenty-four and Patty, twenty-two. I met a lot of planes at Love Air Field after our first date. We enjoyed playing golf, or going to a driving range and then out to dinner. We enjoyed spending time together and still do, after fifty-eight years of marriage.

Patty remembers our first date:

Daddy left the Luce Weils Biscuit Company and was looking for a new job in the automotive industry. Mother decided they needed a complete change of scenery. She suggested they drive down to Dallas, rent a little apartment and look after me.

My girlfriend arranged a blind date with Ed. When I opened the door and saw him standing there, my first thought was that he was the biggest man I ever laid eyes on. Later on, I told my girlfriend Mary Lou, "I know they grow them big in Texas, but this is ridiculous!"

Ed had just returned from a golfing holiday before our first date. He drove up in a red Buick convertible. He was well tanned and had the whitest teeth I had ever seen.

A few dates later, Ed took Mother and Daddy and me out to a lovely dinner at the Baker Hotel. After we got home and Ed left, Daddy said to me, "Do you know anything about this young man?" "He seems awfully nice," I replied. "Well, I don't know," Daddy said, "He looks like Mafia to me!"

Years went by before I finally told Ed that story. He nearly died!

We dated for a little over two years and were married on August 22, 1942—which was also my mother and dad's wedding anniversary—at the Sacred Heart Cathedral in Dallas. Doris Johnson Hewins was Patty's matron of honor. Also attending the wedding were Ramona Myers Thornton and Emma Barn-Hill Smith, who also worked with Patty at Braniff. My high-school buddy, Bill Lalla, was the best man. Following the ceremony, Patty and I left on a two-week honeymoon. We spent our first week of married life at the Broadmoor Golf Resort, near Colorado Springs, and the second week at Grand Lake, Colorado.

A few years earlier, Joe and I spent a golfing holiday at the Broadmoor. When Joe and I crossed the Continental Divide, we had our golf clubs with us. We stopped the car, teed up balls, and hit the longest drives we had ever seen.

The Broadmoor remains a favorite family getaway even today. There's some lore regarding the founding of this colorful place. It seems a young gold-miner named Penrose struck pay dirt in Colorado. Out to find a good dinner, he was refused admission to the Antlers Hotel and Restaurant because he wasn't dressed in a tie and proper suit of clothes. Penrose was so infuriated at being refused service, he bought nearby property and built the Broadmoor—the grandest and most imposing hotel in that corner of Colorado. Years later, Penrose bought the Antlers and made it part of his empire. In subsequent years, three very fine golf courses were added, along with other residential buildings, a magnificent ice rink, and rodeo stadium.

Patty and I settled in a little apartment at 4444 Fairway Drive, Apartment 18, in Dallas. I went back to work and Patty watched the mailbox every day, waiting for my draft notice. Patty moved in with Mother and Dad when I left for the service.

My Wonderful Family, Special Friends, and Favorite Pastime

She joined me in Wendover, Utah, where we lived in a little hotel on the Nevada-Utah state line. Patty found a volunteer job with the Red Cross on base. From there I was transferred to Nashville, Tennessee, where our first child, Patty Jo, was born.

¤ ¤ ¤

MY BELOVED CHILDREN

Patty Jo

Our oldest child, Patty Jo, was born on July 14, 1945 — Bastille Day. Patty Jo got off to a bumpy start; she was not getting enough nourishment. But when that problem was corrected, Patty Jo's true personality came shining through. She has always been a good, happy, well-adjusted child.

Patty Jo always had her best times at parties. Little girls' birthday parties... sweet-sixteen parties... graduation parties. Whatever the occasion, she just loved celebrating happy moments with her friends. In fact, to this day, we call her "Party Jo." Patty likes to tell everyone, "Patty Jo is just like her Daddy. She makes friends with everybody and keeps her friends throughout her life."

Patty Jo attended Ursuline Academy in Dallas. During her junior year, Patty and I took Patty Jo and her two girlfriends, Patty Caolo and Barbara Neuhoff, to visit some colleges in California. We started at San Francisco University, then on to Santa Clara and finally Stanford. After seeing the Stanford campus, the girls didn't want to see any more schools — that was the place for them! But in the final scenario, and with no coaching or encouragement from me, Patty Jo and her friends ended up at St. Mary's — Notre Dame's sister school — in South Bend, Indiana.

Following graduation, Patty Jo and her girlfriend, Pat Crouere-Denechoud, moved to New Orleans. Both were teachers at the Ursuline Academy. After a year, Patty Jo returned to Dallas and continued her teaching career at St. Rita's Grammar School. Subsequently, she worked for Lehman Brothers. Eventually, she focused her interests on real estate, and worked for Henry Miller and Company in Dallas.

Of course, as soon as she moved back to Dallas, Patty Jo started partying again with her friends. At one of these parties, she met a young man named John Turner. Patty Jo and John were married on December 27, 1978. Their son, Garrett Edmond Turner, was born in 1979.

In his junior year of high school, Garrett auditioned for a school play and won the leading role. Acting comes naturally to him. Garrett just lit up the stage in that first play, and in all the others he's performed in since that time. Garrett began his freshman year at Notre Dame in the fall of 1998. I am pleased and proud that he chose Notre Dame.

Eddie

Our second child, Ed, Jr., was born October 29, 1946. A natural athlete, Eddie's special talents were most evident on the track. While attending Jesuit Academy, Eddie for a while had the second best record in the state for the 220.

As a little boy, Eddie was always fascinated with cars. He built a lot of model cars. Later on, he built a small racing car that he actually raced once or twice. In his high school days, Eddie found an old Ford Model-A, which he fixed up and drove around town. When Eddie went off to college, the car was passed down to his younger brother Jimmy.

After graduating from Jesuit, Eddie set off for Notre Dame. On his third day at school, Eddie called his mother. There was a lot of small talk about his impressions of the campus, and classes, etc. Finally, he said, "Mom, my roommate, Steve Grace (one of Peter Grace's, head of Grace Corporation, many children), is the messiest kid I've ever seen. I really don't think I can live through another week with him!" To make a long story short, Eddie and Steve are still the closest friends today. Eddie graduated from Notre Dame with a degree in business administration.

Eddie met his wife, Ann Rogers, through a group of friends from Dallas. But the most amazing coincidence was that Ann worked in the Haggar Textile Labs at the time! Eddie and Ann were married July 3, 1971. Ann had a four-year-old daughter, Devon, from a previous marriage. After their marriage, Eddie adopted Devon. Devon is a joyful, free-spirited girl. She is happily married to a handsome chap named Aaron King. Last year, Devon and Aaron presented us with our first great-grandchild,

Maxwell Edmond King. Patty describes him as "just a little square bundle of joy!"

Eddie and Ann's daughter, Daley Christie Haggar, was born in 1976, and named after her two grandmothers (maiden names, that is). Daley is an extremely intelligent and talented young woman. While attending the Hockaday School in Dallas, Daley got a summer job at the *Dallas Morning News,* which is one of the premiere newspapers in the country. She wrote five editorials, three of which featured her photo and her own byline.

I asked her if she wanted to attend Notre Dame. "Not really. I want to go to Oxford," she replied. Patty and I took Daley and her cousin Melissa to England to tour Oxford. Daley met with several professors and administrators and took an in-depth guided tour of the campus. Most of the buildings are ancient, by our standards. The students reside in tiny little rooms called "cells." "The rooms smelled like the inside of a gerbil cage!" she told us after the tour.

Graduating from Hockaday with highest honors, she delighted her class with an imaginative and entertaining baccalaureate address. Daley began her distinguished academic career at Harvard. She was named the first woman editor of the university's 135-year-old literary magazine, *The Harvard Advocate.* After graduating magna cum laude, Daley returned to Oxford for a year to study Renaissance Literature and then moved to Hollywood, California, where she is developing her career as a screenwriter.

Jimmy

James Joseph Haggar (Jimmy) was born February 16, 1950, our third child. Jimmy was a free-spirited little boy right from the start. He was, and remains, a true maverick. All his life, Jimmy has had a great love of the outdoors. He loves to hunt and fish. In his high school days, he was a track runner and played football. Today, he is an excellent golfer, fisherman, and hunter.

Jimmy began his schooling at Christ the King. His teacher called Patty one day with a true story that happened in the classroom. While explaining a certain math problem, the teacher looked away from the blackboard and noticed a faraway look on

Jimmy's face. "Jimmy, what are you thinking about?" she asked. Jimmy continued staring off into space. "Jimmy, you're not thinking!" she said. A few seconds later, he replied, "Yes I am, Sister. I'm thinking about fishing!" Paul Crum, a popular *Dallas Morning News* columnist, heard about this and published the story, and the whole city of Dallas knew about it the next day.

We had a little creek that meandered behind our house. One time, Jimmy went down there with a bucket and filled it with four or five water moccasins, which he brought home to his baby sister, Mary Alice. All the kids liked to play in the attic. There was a little cupola up there, and at one time or another, all the kids used to go up there and smoke cigarettes. Jimmy was Culprit Number One.

Always a maverick, Jimmy was a constant source of new ideas for product lines, styling, and merchandising. One day he came to me and said, "If Grandpa Haggar started a business by making pants, I can start my own business, making shirts!" So, Jimmy left Haggar in 1975 and went into the shirt business. He called the line "Lee James," named for his wife and himself. It was a successful venture. However, Jimmy's capital was limited. From time to time, he had to borrow money when interest rates were running 20-22%. At those rates, Houdini would have had trouble showing a profit! As a result, Jimmy liquidated the business.

During his third year at Texas Tech, Jimmy fell in love with a wonderful girl named Lee Davidson, from Tyler, Texas. They were married on June 20, 1970, while still in school.

Jimmy and Lee have three wonderful children: Michael, Marc, and Melissa. We call them "The Three M's." Michael, like his dad, has a great knack for style and design. Marc is all business. After graduating from Texas Tech and surveying business opportunities, he joined E. Magrath. Melissa loves the outdoors and is a great runner. A few summers ago, Melissa completed the National Outdoor Leadership School. Basically, she was turned out in the wilderness and survived on her own wits and imagination. She's a beautiful young lady and a tough kid, because of the above schooling, and can handle almost anything. We are proud of her.

Patty's maternal grandparents: Minnie Belle Stevens Pugh and Edward Everett Pugh.

Patty at age three.

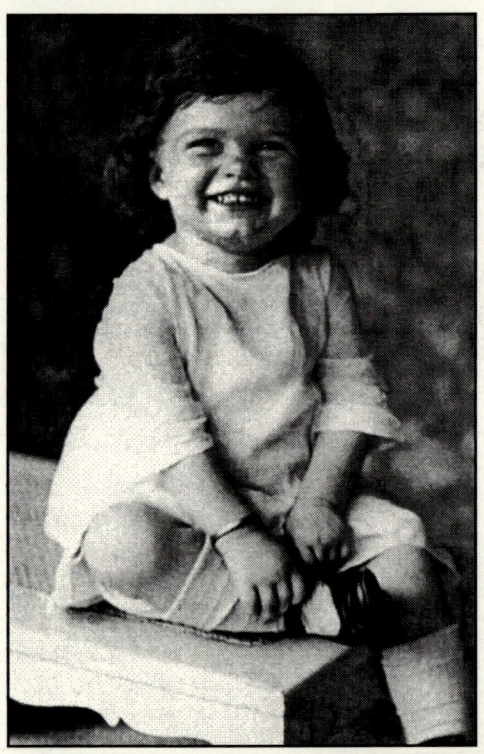

Patty

Patty appeared in this Braniff Airway ad.

Patty at the time of our marriage.

Honeymooning in Colorado.

With Patty's parents, Patty Jo, and Eddie.

L-R: Mary Alice, Eddie, Patty, Patty Jo, Jimmy, John Daley, and Michael.

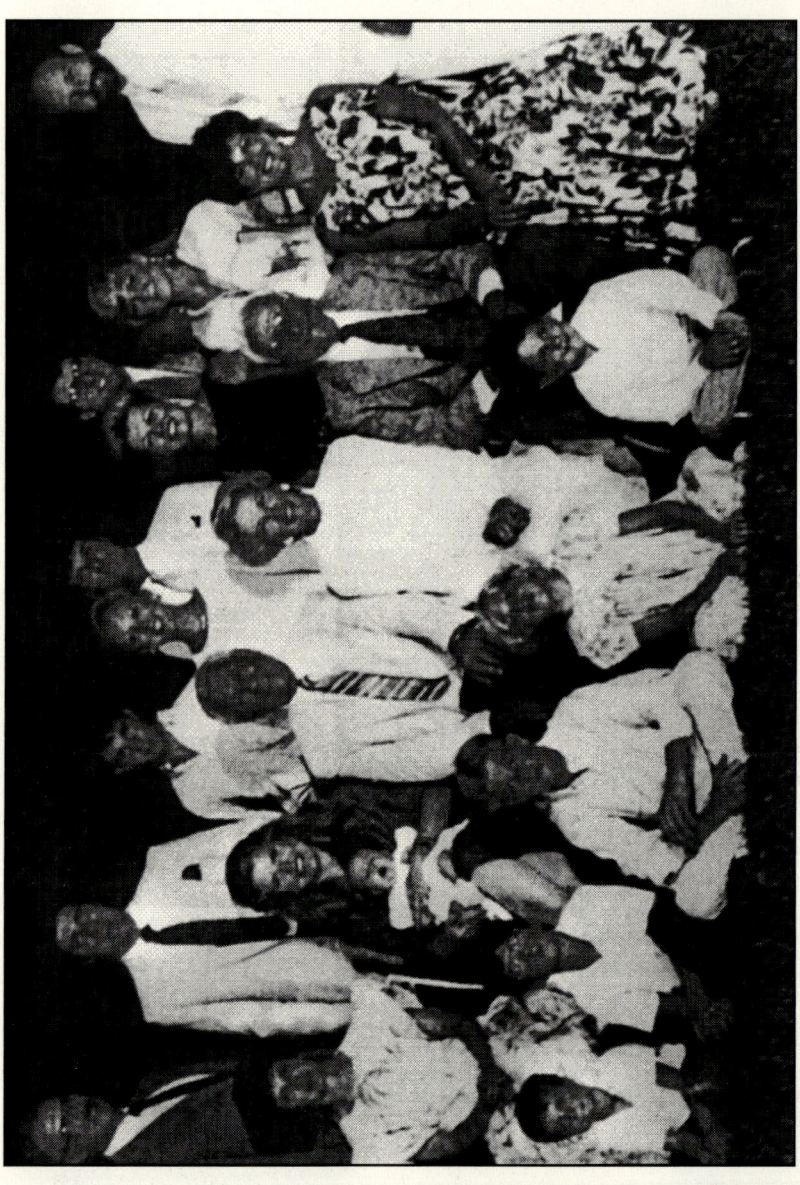

Top row, L-R: Terry Stedillie, John Daley, Michael and Lee Haggar, Jimmy and Ann Haggar, Eddie, Devon, John Turner. Middle row, L-R: Mary Alice, Dianna Haggar and Shaina, E.R.H., Patty, Grandpa Haggar, Patty Jo Turner. Bottom row, L-R: Steven and Anthony Stedillie, Marc and Melissa Haggar, Garett Turner.

Ed and Patty Haggar

The Ed Haggar Family wishes for you and yours

a most blessed Christmas and a new year filled with

God's choicest blessings.

Ed & Patty

*Ed Haggar at Eldorado Country Club,
Indian Wells, California. April 1999.*

Mary Alice

Our fourth child, Mary Alice, was born May 8, 1951. Plagued with asthma from infancy, Mary Alice was always a frail little girl. A great deal of her youth was spent in and out of the hospital, fighting for her breath.

Like her brothers and sisters before her, Mary Alice began her schooling at Christ the King and then attended Ursuline Academy for a brief time. Through caring teachers and concerned doctors, we learned of a small boarding school, not too far from Colorado Springs, Colorado, called St. Scholastica. The doctors felt the altitude and dry air might help her asthma. Well, Mary Alice and Colorado were absolutely made for each other.

Here's another football story about Mary Alice: After moving to Colorado, Mary Alice became an ardent Denver Broncos fan—and she still is. Mary Alice was always very friendly with Mary Noel Murchison, whose father and uncle owned the Dallas Cowboys. Well, Mary Alice came home from Colorado on a school vacation and Mary Noel invited her to a Cowboys vs. Broncos game. Arriving at the owner's box, Mary Alice shocked all those present by wearing a bright orange suit in honor of her newly beloved Denver Broncos, known as "The Orange Crush."

Mary Alice married a wonderful fellow named Terry Stedillie. They were married on November 27, 1976. Originally from South Dakota, Terry and his family have always been in the ranching and farming business.

Mary Alice and Terry have two fine boys, Anthony and Steven. At twenty-five, Anthony has a great propensity for foreign language, especially French. In order to encourage Anthony, Terry and Mary Alice hosted a French foreign exchange, after which time Anthony spent a summer with a family in France. Steven, age twenty-one, is an outstanding athlete. He loves baseball and is strong, fast, and extremely competitive. He excels in every sporting endeavor and is an excellent student, as is Anthony.

For many years, Mary Alice, Terry, and the boys lived in Sedalia, Colorado. Terry grazed and maintained his cattle on leased land. Recently, they purchased a ranch in Deer Trail, Colorado, which is about thirty miles east of Castle Rock.

They've just completed their home. It's a beautiful spot. You can see Pike's Peak from their property. Mary Alice still suffers from asthma, though her general health is much better. She's a wonderful wife and mother and a very happy rancher.

Michael

Our fifth child, Michael, was born May 25, 1954. At a very early age, Michael revealed two things about himself. He was an extremely bright little boy and very sweet and good-natured.

At age eleven, Michael got his first newspaper route. He was riding home on his bicycle one day when a crazy bum stopped him and grabbed his bike by the handlebars. "Give me your shoes!" the guy demanded. Michael was frightened. He took off his shoes, handed them to the man, and pedaled home in his stocking feet. When Mike got home, Patty noticed he was wearing only socks and demanded to know what happened.

February 4, 1965. The most traumatic event that ever happened to our family was when we lost Michael. Michael served Mass for the first time at Christ the King Church. I drove him home after the 7:30 Mass. At the time, Michael was recovering from a virus of some sort, which was complicated by asthma. When we got home, Michael complained of not feeling well. Patty decided to keep him home from school and sent him up to bed. Mike aspirated in his sleep and became unconscious. Jimmy tried to resuscitate him, but it was too late. He was rushed to the hospital, where he passed away.

A few weeks after Michael's death, we were watching the evening television news. The newscast ran a story about an eccentric man whom the police discovered living in an apartment full of stolen shoes. "I bet he's got Michael's shoes," Patty said. He probably did.

John

Our sixth child, John Daley Haggar, was born September 25, 1956. He was always a happy-go-lucky kid. John has been a terrific athlete all his life. When he was in the fourth grade, he volunteered me to coach his football team. "My dad went to Notre

My Wonderful Family, Special Friends, and Favorite Pastime 171

Dame and played football," he told everyone. Well, I couldn't argue with that, so I coached his team for a year. It was the worst job I ever had. All dads and moms are just furious when you don't play their sons. Like Eddie and Jimmy, John was a great runner and track star. Today he is an excellent golfer.

John began his schooling at Christ the King and graduated from Jesuit Academy in Dallas. His college education started at a small liberal arts college in Denver called Regis College and eventually transferred to Southern Methodist University and graduated with a degree in accounting.

John met his lovely wife, Diana, in the Redondo Beach, California, area while he was working for the company. They were married on June 11, 1983, on a romantic moonlit night, in the most beautiful setting. Shortly thereafter, another job opening in the sales department became available in the Denver area. Like Mary Alice, John just loves Colorado. He and Dianna built a home in Denver and have been up there since. They have one daughter, Shaina. Shaina's a beautiful girl — and tall. Both parents are tall, and Shaina is on her way to attaining great heights!

¤ ¤ ¤

We bought our first family home at 3709 Greenbriar in 1946 and in 1951 we built a home at 4945 Wedgewood Lane.

We had been in our first home about two years when Eula Grant came to work for us, accompanied by her eleventh child, Joe Nathan, who was about four. Eula was our loyal housekeeper for many years. She saw us through many happy times, and a few sad times. When our last child had "flown the nest," we "retired" Eula (much against her will). She is now in her 106th year, living with her daughter, Zadie Williams. Eula is an important part of our family — a wonderful lady!

I sometimes felt that Patty, as an only child, was a little overwhelmed by all the clamor and noise of twelve feet running through the house! One night she was preparing dinner, and Eula was helping. Patty was bent over, with her head in the oven, basting a roast, when all six kids came stampeding through, carousing and laughing. "Quit it!" Patty shouted. At that point, Eula said, "Mrs. Haggar, you ain't got used to them kids yet, have you?"

¤ ¤ ¤

Dad always loved traveling and spending time with the family — all his life. He traveled often to New York City and enjoyed many fine meals at Club 21, on West 52nd Street. Over the years, he befriended the owner. Subsequently, the owner's nephew, a fellow named Sheldon, managed a fine restaurant in Dallas, "The Mansion." Very shortly after the restaurant's opening, Dad called and invited Rosemary and me, along with our families, to dinner at the Mansion. We had a very nice dinner. Dad ordered Dover sole. When the check came, Dad called Sheldon over to the table. "Sheldon," Dad began, "the Dover sole was wonderful. But I'm surprised at the extremely high price!" Sheldon replied, "Mr. Haggar, we fly that fish in every day direct from Dover." Dad shook his head and finally said, "But do you have to fly it in first class?" One of the Dallas columnists got hold of the story, and it appeared the next day in the Dallas newspapers. We always had fun needling Dad about that Dover sole!

About a week after his eightieth birthday, Dad was driving to Preston Trail. A good friend, Bobby Folsom (former mayor of Dallas), was following Dad's car. The next time I saw Bobby, he said to me, "Ed, I've heard of people shooting their age in golf, but I've never heard of them driving their age! (80 mph) Ed, you and Joe better slow him down."

CHERISHED FRIENDS

Earlier I recalled some of my childhood friends. Now I would like to introduce some dear friends who came into my life later.

One of my greatest and oldest friendships began in Nashville, Tennessee, during World War II. Earlier, Paul Hazelrig had been a tactical officer at Officer's Candidate School in Miami Beach, Florida. But we really didn't get to know each other until I was transferred to Nashville. I always admired Paul, because he brought himself up the hard way. Before the war, he had a bread route for Colonial Baking Company in Atlanta, Georgia. Ironically, Colonial was owned by Campbell-Taggart Baking Company, which was headquartered in Dallas. In fact, they were located next door to our company headquarters on Lemmon Avenue. After the war, Paul and his family were transferred to Dallas, and our friendship continued.

My Wonderful Family, Special Friends, and Favorite Pastime 173

The CEO of Campbell-Taggart, Will Carrence, was a good friend of mine. Paul worked diligently and advanced through the ranks. When Mr. Carrence was ready to retire, Paul and another fellow, Bob See, were the two candidates opting for the position of CEO. Ultimately, Bob was chosen for the position and Paul was transferred to Oakland, California, as president of the Kilpatrick Baking Company. The next time I saw Mr. Carrence I asked him, "How come you shanghaied my boy to Oakland?" Mr. Carrence looked at me and said, "Don't worry about Paul. The Oakland job is like having a license to steal! Paul will do just fine." And he did.

Martha Hazelrig and Patty are very close. Patty recalls:

> Ed was still in the service in early 1945. We were living in Nashville, Tennessee. Our first child (Patty Jo) was due in July. Martha and Paul Hazelrig lived across the street from us. Martha had a new baby boy of her own, Paul, Jr. Being an only child, I was very nervous about the care and feeding of my impending arrival. In all seriousness, I called Martha and invited myself to her house, the purpose of my visit... to bathe her son!

Paul, Jr., grew up and became one of the most prominent orthopedic surgeons in San Francisco. Patty still kids him about that early bathing session in Nashville. Our families are still very close. Sadly, I attended Paul Hazelrig, Sr.'s funeral in December 2000. He was a good soldier and a very good friend.

I first met Ambassador Walter Annenberg about sixteen years ago at Castle Pines Country Club in Castle Rock, Colorado.

After graduation from college, young Walter Annenberg joined the family newspaper and eventually made his own mark in the publishing business with the creation of *TV Guide*. Ambassador Annenberg is one of the great philanthropists of this country. Many large universities have been endowed with an "Annenberg School of Communications." A great proponent of education and communication, his contributions have touched people in every walk of life. In addition, Mr. Annenberg represented his country with great distinction as ambassador to England.

I've played golf with President Bush three times at

Ambassador Annenberg's estate in Rancho Mirage, California, and on several other occasions. (Yes, the ambassador has his own private golf course.) Following the golf, Ambassador Annenberg always served luncheon on his patio. Sitting around the lunch table on this particular day, the ambassador said to me, "Ed, I'm going on a cruise with two of your favorite friends, Father Hesburgh and Father Joyce."

"I'd sure like to stow away on that trip," I replied.

"Why don't you call Ned Joyce and have him arrange accommodations for you and Patty?" I did just that. Our itinerary took us through the Scandinavian countries. We traveled all the way up to the Arctic Circle. One of the highlights was a visit to Knute Rockne's birthplace, the small town of Voss, Norway.

I am pleased and honored that Ambassador Annenberg offered his comments for this volume of memoirs:

> Unfortunately, I don't get to see Ed very often, because he lives in Texas, and I live in Pennsylvania. However, our paths do cross from time to time, and it's always a pleasurable experience.
>
> I respect Ed for his great citizenship, integrity and honesty. He's a 21-Karat Citizen.

Short, redheaded, and always ready with a witty quip, Bobby Russell is a major character. Bobby has always been one of the hardest working fellows I know. I soon learned that any phone calls to Bobby had to be made early in the evening. By 8:30 P.M., he fell apart like a Westclox.

We played a lot of golf together over the years. On the course or off, Bobby was always a big needler. For many years we played as partners. We won a lot of bets, but probably lost more than we won. Playing at Lakewood Country Club, we were even going into the last hole. We were betting heavy. Bobby missed his putt and then sank a practice putt. Our caddie said, "After death, up pops the doctor!" After losing the match, I kidded him saying, "Bobby, you must have some kind of tax write-off that I don't know about!"

When asked to recruit new members for Preston Trail Golf Club, the first person I called was Bobby Russell. At the time,

My Wonderful Family, Special Friends, and Favorite Pastime 175

Bobby was president of Floyd West Insurance Company in Dallas. "Big 'Un (Bobby always called me Big 'Un, and, in turn, I called him Lil' 'Un), I'm moving to New York," he told me. "Why the hell are you doing that?" I asked. Bobby's company had just merged with Crumm and Forrester, which, at the time, was the second largest fire and casualty insurance company in the United States. "I'm going in as an executive vice president. If all goes well, I'll be CEO in the next few years." And that's exactly what happened. Bobby had a marvelous career with Crumm and Forrester.

Bobby's retired now. He is still very active in golf circles. At one time, he was chairman of the USGA Foundation. Over the years he has remained a great character and a great friend.

Born in Spavinaw, Oklahoma, in 1931, Mickey Mantle became one of the greatest sluggers in baseball history. He played center field during most of his career (1951-68) with the New York Yankees. His 536 home runs placed him among the leaders in the game. He was named the American League's most valuable player in 1956, when he led the league in batting average, home runs, and runs batted in, and again in 1957, when he batted .365, his highest average. He was named MVP a third time in 1962, when he hit 18 home runs in World Series play.

Over the years, Mickey provided me with autographed pictures and baseballs, which I sent to my children and grandchildren. The kids were absolutely thrilled to receive them. And they were awed by the fact that I befriended Mickey. To be honest, at the time I didn't realize what a great celebrity and hero he was to kids.

I was on a business trip to the West Coast in the early 1960s, traveling with our regional sales manager, Bob Gugliehmi. We stopped at Bob's house for a few minutes and I stepped out to the backyard and started up a game of catch with Bob's two sons, who were were five and seven years old. I asked them, "Do you know who Mickey Mantle is?" and they said, "No, but we know Mickey Mouse!"

A few weeks later, I ran into Mickey at Preston Trail and relayed the story about Bob's kids. Mickey just shook his head and smiled, "A lot of my baseball friends' kids have said the same thing to their dads."

Mickey and I played a lot of golf together at Lakewood Country Club. When playing in a foursome, we had an agreement that we would bet $100 on the longest drives. Secretly, we settled for $1, rather than $100! He really was quite a rogue. One day, Mickey used a 5 Wood and really busted the ball. "Mickey, why don't you use your driver?" I asked him. "I *hoooook* the ball too much!" he replied.

I sponsored Mickey for membership at Preston Trail Golf Club. In the early days, one could join as a non-resident for $1,000 or become a full member for $4,000. I urged Mickey to take the full membership. "It'll be worth a lot of money someday," I advised him. At one time, that membership was worth $90,000. Mickey tells this story in one of his books.

Herb Durham and I won the Dallas 4-Ball Tournament at the Athletic Club of Dallas Golf Course in 1956. After our win, I always needled "Happy Herb" about the fact that he never got past the third round in any big tournament until I was his partner. Although I helped him on several crucial holes, my main function was keeping him calm. Herb was a great golfer — as long as he remained calm. In 1961 Herb won the Trans-Mississippi, one of the most prestigious amateur tournaments in the country.

Herb knew I was friendly with Mickey Mantle, and he was dying to play golf with this great sports legend. I arranged a game at Lakewood. On the fifth hole, which is a par 3, Mickey hit a great shot to the green; he was about ten feet from the pin. The others in our group were subtly needling him. I said, "You can't needle the great Mickey Mantle!... He's in Yankee Stadium... He's up at bat... Here comes the ball! (I made a popping sound, like a bat brutally striking the ball, followed by my interpretation of crowd cheers.)... And it's a home run!" (More crowd cheers.) Mickey never forgot that cheering, and we became even greater friends after that incident.

To his dying day, God bless him, Mickey always asked me, "How does it sound when I hit a home run?"

Congressman Marty Russo of Illinois is my favorite Democrat. I first met Marty at a Jerry Ford Tournament in 1981. He found out that I was slightly involved with the Bob Hope Tournament and asked if I could get him an invitation. I told him that I would be glad to try. I called my good friend

Congressman Jim Collins and asked him what he thought about Congressman Marty Russo. His reply: Marty is a good guy. A little on the liberal side, but he votes favorably on conservative issues as well. Well, I got Marty a celebrity invitation (a freebie) and he never forgot it. Anytime there was legislation on taxes, business, etc., Marty always called for my input.

I have been involved in many political campaigns, not for lobbying purposes but for good government. However, here is the one exception. I called Marty about the following and he went to work on it immediately. I was playing golf with Bill Hybl of the El Pomar Foundation (Broadmoor Hotel, Colorado Springs, Colorado) and he was telling me about some unfavorable foundation legislation: the Foundation in 1983 requested to be exempted from the Excess Business Divesture Rules. Unfortunately, the House Ways and Means Committee ruled that no exemptions would be made. Bill has just retired as president of the United States Olympic Committee.

¤ ¤ ¤

My sons Eddie, Jimmy, and John attended the Jesuit College Preparatory School in Dallas. Bob Higgins, a good friend who often assisted Father Robert A. Tynan, S.J., administrator at Jesuit, informed me that Jesuit needed a new sports stadium. He asked if the Haggar family could contribute to the cause. A few days later, Mother, Dad, Joe, Rosemary, and I were all driving together in the car. I raised the question about the stadium. Mother replied, "I think it's a great idea. I'd like to do something, while I'm still alive, and see the final outcome of this project." The new stadium was dedicated in November 1964. Mother passed away on All Saints' Day, 1965.

Shortly after the stadium was dedicated, Ross Perot purchased Rosemary's home. He had just taken his company public at the time and was really "the new kid on the block" in the Dallas business community. My entree to Ross was through Rosemary. I arranged a meeting with Ross, at which time I asked him to donate some money to Jesuit. His immediate reply was, "Ed, I'm not a Catholic."

"Ross, I know you're not Catholic. Religion isn't the issue. The issue is education," I responded.

Ross agreed to make a contribution for $150,000.

I first met Father Paul Schott in 1964. At the time, Jesuit College Preparatory School, like most private schools, was short of funds. Father Schott was sent to raise funds, as well as raise the academic standing of this institution.

A year after the dedication of the stadium at Jesuit, Father Schott asked me to be the first chairman of the Jesuit Foundation in Dallas. Of course, that meant raising money! I worked closely with Father Schott on several fundraising campaigns over the years. He became a close and wonderful friend.

I am pleased and honored that Father Schott offered the following recollections for this volume of memoirs:

> Ed was Chairman of the Board of Advisors at Jesuit at the time I arrived. It was essential to raise significant funds. If we didn't do that, the school would have been in deep trouble. At the time, Ed was a very prominent man in the Dallas business community. He did an awful lot of civic work. For that reason, he never turned his back on Jesuit, even though he was so busy doing so many other things. The most important contribution Ed made to me was through all his connections. Ed was able to open so many doors, which nobody else could.
>
> Ed's a very, very generous man and a very humble man. He's always been a good friend.

¤ ¤ ¤

The year was 1966. The Coors Beer Company of Golden, Colorado, announced they were going to expand their business by opening the first Coors distributorship in the state of Texas, right here in Dallas. Shortly after Coors made their announcement, some friends suggested that I organize a group of investors and obtain the distributorship. I called good friends and neighbors Bill and Marilyn Georges, who owned a beer distributorship in Houston, and asked them all sorts of questions. Bill suggested that Don Meredith and I apply for the deal together. I had never met Don before, and my friend arranged a meeting. It was the beginning of a wonderful friendship that continues to this day.

Our family will never forget the kindness of Marilyn Georges at the time. Within a three-month period we lost Mother and our son Michael. You can't believe how kind, helpful, and caring Marilyn was to us at this traumatic time.

There were at least 100 applicants for the distributorship. Don and I took several tests and were interviewed by the people at Coors. Coors refused our application because Don was still playing football and could only actively participate in running the business for six months each year. "Come see us again, when you're through playing football, and we'll be glad to find you another distributorship!" they told Don. Well, that became a very big and successful distributorship. Don quit playing football in 1968 and went right into a second marvelous career in broadcasting. He never did pursue another deal with Coors. You might say Don became a "tea-totaler"—for many years, "Dandy Don" was the official spokesperson for the Lipton Tea Company.

Johnny Lujack is considered one of the greatest T-formation collegiate quarterbacks of all time. He gained 2,080 yards in three seasons (1943, 1946, 1947) and 144 completions out of 282. The Notre Dame "Fighting Irish" were National Champions all three years. He won the Heisman Trophy in 1947. After graduation, Johnny went to the Chicago Bears and played four years. He was All-Pro in 1948 and 1950. He set an NFL passing record of 468 yards and six touchdowns in a single game. He retired from the NFL in 1954.

I first met Johnny in 1988, at my fiftieth reunion at Notre Dame. We've played a lot of golf together and enjoyed each other's company. We both spend our winters in Indian Wells.

The year was 1996. Dick Herman, a friend from Eldorado, invited me to a fundraising auction for the Boys and Girls Clubs. Johnny, who served as honorary chairman at the time, acted as auctioneer and master of ceremonies. Several autographed footballs were auctioned off during the course of the evening. Johnny personally auctioned off a Notre Dame football that had been autographed by all the Notre Dame Heisman Trophy winners: Leon Hart, Angelo Bertelli, John Lattner, Johnny Lujack, Paul Hornung, John Huarte, and Tim Brown. Well, mine was the highest bid. Holding said ball in hand, Johnny threw me a pass. I was seated at a table about twenty-five feet from the podium. The ball hurled over a field of fine crystal and china!

Fortunately, for me and everyone else at the table, I caught the pass. On future occasions, and just for laughs, I'll ask Johnny, "Who's your favorite receiver?" Johnny will smile and say, "Ed Haggar!"

Another great and dear friend to both Joe and me is Lank Smith, a nifty Notre Dame defensive back. Lank starred during the playing days of Army's Glen Davis and Doc Blanchard. He retired recently from a most successful career as an insurance attorney. Lank is a True Blue and Golden Domer and a walking encyclopedia on Notre Dame academics and athletics.

¤ ¤ ¤

ON THE LINKS

When I was about ten years old, Dad asked me to caddie for him at Oak Grove Golf Course. Oak Grove was a nine-hole course with sand greens. After putting, each player was required to roll out the sand. Players used wet sand to tee up the ball. The year was 1926, and it marked my first time on a golf course.

L.E. Guillot, a school chum from a very old and prominent Dallas family, called me one summer day when I was fifteen. "How would you like to join me on the golf course?" he asked. "I'm going to caddie for my mother, and her friend needs a caddie." That day marked my first exposure to eighteen holes of golf. I learned quite a bit about the game from watching L.E.'s mother and from several pointers I received from L.E.

In the early 1940s, I met a wonderful old Scotsman by the name of Arch Munn at Lakewood Country Club. Arch was about forty years older than me and spoke with a thick Scottish brogue. One time, after watching me take a powerful swing, Arch remarked, "What does it profit a mon to hit a ball 300 yords and take an 8 on the hole!"

Golf is a sport I've enjoyed sharing with Patty. Playing together, or in a mixed foursome, Patty is always a pleasure on the links—although, at times, she does too much coaching from the sidelines. She's always been a real student of the game. Patty loves to take lessons, especially when we play a course with a distinguished pro. Several years ago, while staying at the Broadmoor, I met Mary Lena Falk, a famous teaching pro. "Ed, is Patty coming to my seminar tomorrow?" she asked. "Confidentially, Mary Lena," I replied, "Patty is a 'Pro-aholic' and I'm sending her to Pro-aholic's Anonymous to get dried out!"

Patty and I went on several trips with the "People-to-People" golf team, a group of American businessmen who played similar groups in foreign countries. Over the years we played with businessmen in Portugal, Italy, France, Ireland, Scotland, and Mexico. At each match, we were paired with businessmen from our host country. Charles and Sadie Seay led the group.

One trip took us to Italy. Since my roots were planted on the Mediterranean Sea (albeit the opposite shore), I was the closest thing to an Italian on the team and was named team captain. Generally, the team captain was required to make a speech at the end of the match. The daughter of our travel agent spoke fluent Italian. She coached me, so that I was able to deliver most of the speech in Italian. "I was in the olive trees so many times today, you might have thought I was going into the olive oil business," I started. "We enjoyed playing with you. It doesn't make any difference if you win or lose, but how you play the game. We enjoyed your country, thank you very much." Following my speech, one member of the group, Billy Moore, asked one of the Italians if I was really speaking the language.

In Monte Carlo we had a shortage of businessmen, so several women played. Billy Moore was paired with Mademoiselle So-and-So. Dick Clark, one of my very good friends, was paired with Madame So-and-so. I was also paired with a Madame. Whenever Dick didn't want to play golf, he would always come down with a sore throat. After finding out he was paired with a Madame, Dick said to me, "Big Ed, I've got a sore throat and I'm not going to play!" I said, "Dick, you're going to create an international scene if you do this." I looked away from Dick for a moment and saw a beautiful, shapely brunette accompanied by a big dog walking toward our group. I approached her, hoping she was Madame. She said to me, "I am Mademoiselle So-and-So. Are you Mr. Moore?"

"No, I'm not Mr. Moore," I informed her. "He's right behind me. (I pointed toward Billy.) Would you ask him if he's Mr. Haggar? When he says he's Mr. Moore, please try and look disappointed!" At the time, Billy Moore called everyone "Stoop." The beautiful Mademoiselle approached Billy. He turned to me and said, "Hey, Stoop, you put her up to that, didn't you?"

Most of the caddies in Monte Carlo were German. I put a ball out of bounds and my caddie yelled, *"Kaput!"* Following that day, anytime I put one out of bounds, stateside or out of the country, someone in my group always yells *"Kaput!"*

Sam Snead is one of the greatest golfers of all times and one of the most colorful people associated with the sport. Born and raised in Hot Springs, Virginia, Sam won three PGA Championships (1942, 1949, and 1951) and three Masters (1949, 1952, and 1954). His professional career began in 1935. Sam spent most of his time at the prestigious Greenbrier Golf Resort in West Virginia. About forty years ago, Bobby Russell and I played the Greenbrier course. Sam was watching us on the practice tee. I was hitting the ball long and straight. "Man, you hit that ball a long way," Sam said to me. "What do you shoot on this course?"

I replied, "In the high 80s, low 90s."

"You must not be worth a shit around the greens!" Sam said.

Over the years, a lot of professional golfers endorsed Haggar slacks. From time to time, I was fortunate to play with some of these remarkable men. On this particular day, I was playing at Oakcliff Country Club with Dow Finsterwald, Art Wall, and Doug Ford. Sam Snead was playing behind us. A big gallery followed Sam down the fairway. I teed off. My ball sliced severely to the right and landed in a big grove of trees and debris. Sam witnessed this debacle and called out to Doug, "Hey, Doug, does that guy play for money?"

For many years I played at Lakewood Country Club. A big, burly fellow named "Big Mamma Jack" caddied for us quite often. Now, Big Mamma wanted to play professional football more than anything else in the world. At the time, Joe and I were very friendly with Lamar Hunt, who had started the American Football League with his team, the Dallas Texans. Hank Stram, one of the greatest coaches in the sport, coached the Texans. One day, we put together a foursome of Lamar Hunt, Hank Stram, my brother Joe, and myself. Big Mamma Jack caddied for us. Of course, we were all anxious for Coach

Stram to meet Big Mamma Jack. Now, Hank had this habit of nudging the ball a little bit. He did this a few times. The other members in the foursome didn't utter a word. But I noticed Big Mamma Jack watched Hank's every move. After our match, Big Mamma said to us, "Mr. Ed and Mr. Joe, if that little coach could move that football the way he moves the golf ball, he would make a first down every time."

Joe and Hank were friends for many years. They always enjoyed wagering on their shots. We decided to continue on and play a few more holes after the 18th. Lamar Hunt left to attend a business meeting. Joe excused himself for a few minutes. In the meantime, Hank started off by hitting a poor drive. I followed with an excellent drive. But as soon as my club hit the ball, I felt my back go out. I told Hank I couldn't continue. Joe joined us a few seconds later. So, it ended up that Hank played against Joe. After the match, I met up with Big Mamma Jack. He leaned toward me and whispered, "Mr. Ed, do you know which drive the coach used?"

"I've got a pretty good idea," I said.

Then Big Mamma Jack said, "Yes, sir... he played your ball!"

For many years, all the Haggar families were members of Lakewood Country Club. We had many enjoyable times on the golf course and met a lot of wonderful friends.

Joe Bailey, Allen Humphrey, Harold Miller, Henry Minyard, Joe Parrino (one of my dearest friends), Lonnie Pollock, Bobby Russell, Buster Shelton, Clyde Skeen, Earl Summers, Dan Thomas, and Dr. Raymond Thomason were all wonderful golfing buddies throughout the years at Lakewood. One particular day, when the balls were thrown into the air, I ended up being partnered with Dr. Raymond Thomason. We were playing against Joe and Dan Thomas. I was the poorest golfer of the four. Raymond just shrugged his shoulders and said, "We've got as much chance as a one-legged man in an ass-kicking contest!"

Henry Minyard, one of the family owners of the Minyard Grocery chain in Dallas, spoke with a thick and slow Texas drawl. He was excruciatingly slow on the course. Whenever it was his turn to hit, he'd walk over to the ball, do a few warm-up exercises, after which he stepped back a few paces... about three yards... and examined the ball from a different angle...

then he walked back, took a few practice swings... and finally hit the ball. One time I brought a yellow flag and a whistle. As Henry finally started his swing, Joe blew the whistle and I threw the flag and yelled, "Delay of game... ten-yard penalty!" Henry earned the nickname "Three Yard Minyard" because he always backed up three yards to examine the ball. We got the idea for the nickname from "Six Yard Sitko," a Notre Dame halfback who averaged six yards on most carries.

Clyde and Helen Skeen joined Lakewood shortly after they moved to Dallas from Seattle. I was always amused by the fact that the Skeens played golf rain or shine! Our families became good friends and good golfing buddies. We've enjoyed a long and endearing friendship with these wonderful people. Helen and Patty were the closest of friends. Sadly, Helen passed away in 1994, which added a sad note to our many, many happy memories, and Clyde passed away in late 2000.

Byron Nelson is a wonderful man, and his wife, Louise, was a magnificent lady. Several years after we met, Louise suffered a bad stroke. Byron devoted the next few years caring for Louise and stopped playing golf altogether. A few years after Louise passed away, Byron met a lovely girl, and an avid golfer from Toledo, Ohio, named Peggy. They were married, and Byron was back in the golfing groove again. Shortly thereafter, Byron called me. "Ed, when is the Jerry Ford Tournament in Vail? I'd sure love to play."

Byron and Peggy and Patty and I played together at Castle Pines the day before the start of the Jerry Ford Tournament. It was one of my most unforgettable games. After taking my third shot on a par 3, the ball holed out. Byron dourly said, "Ed, that was a hole in three!" I turned to Patty and said, "Why couldn't I make a hole in one playing with Byron Nelson?" If I had made a hole in one, I wouldn't be in Byron's book. In his book, *How I Played the Game*, one chapter is titled "Golfers I've Known." At the beginning of the chapter, there is an alphabetical listing of golfers. I am listed between Walter Hagan and Ben Hogan! Here is Byron's recollection of our game at Castle Pines and my hole in three:

> In nearly seventy years in the game, I've played with and watched quite a few golfers. From the best on the tour to the

40-handicappers, I've seen some amazing things and some just plain strange ones. Here are a few stories about some of my favorites... [He begins the chapter]

Ed's father started the Haggar clothing company in Dallas, and he and his wife Patty are very dear friends of ours. A few years ago we were playing golf with them at Castle Pines. Ed and I had a pretty big bet going, a dollar Nassau, and I had beaten him one down on the first nine. On the back, we came to the par three eleventh hole, which is all downhill. I put my tee shot on the green but Ed hit a bad shot to the right, into all this brush and trees. His caddie said, "You better hit another one Mr. Haggar," but Ed said, "No, we'll find it." Well, they went down in there and beat around in the brush awhile but didn't have any luck—which was a good thing, as it turned out. Because Ed went back to the tee, played another one, and this ball landed twenty feet back of the hole almost at the top of this big ridge that ran across the green. Then his ball starting rolling back down and sprang into the hole for a hole in three. It was the only time I ever saw that happen in all the years I've played golf.

By the way, I've made six holes-in-one during my golfing days—all good shots (no flukes)!

Patty was also an active participant in the Byron Nelson Open:

My dear friend, Ginger Harvey, was always active in Dallas women's golf. She was president of North Texas Women's Golf Association and the Northwood Club. When the Byron Nelson Tournament started, Ginger took an active role, chairing the women's division of the tournament. I worked alongside Ginger for many years. Subsequently, I followed Jane Munger as chairwoman of this special event in 1974.

Ginger had a very special interest in the Texas Kidney Foundation.

At the time, the foundation was in existence, but had become dormant. Through her zealous efforts, and with the help of Ed and several of his friends, Ginger was responsible for getting the Foundation off and running again.

After many years of fun on the links at Lakewood, I joined Northwood Country Club. Northwood was a great family club. The U.S. Open was played there in 1952.

We have enjoyed many golf outings with Ken and Elaine Langone and Tom and Carolyn Marquez—wonderful friends. Tom was Ross Perot's first employee. Ken, a great investment banker, brought Ross Perot's company public as well as Home Depot. He is, by far, that company's largest stockholder.

Patty and I have immensely enjoyed our memberships at the Eldorado Country Club in the desert, as well as Castle Pines, which is south of Denver, Colorado. Since joining Eldorado (in 1972) and Castle Pines, we've made a host of wonderful friends, too numerous to mention. Currently, we have more friends at Eldorado and Castle Pines than we do in Dallas!

What is especially wonderful about Eldorado is the great membership, made up of prominent and successful people. The club could be very snooty; however, it's anything but. At one time, new members were not allowed to sponsor other potential candidates for membership for a three-year period after joining the club. My good buddy from Dallas, Bill Braecklein, and I share many mutual friends in our hometown. When Bill was a new member, I was glad to sponsor several of our friends for membership, since he wasn't eligible to do so at the time.

I was pleased and honored when Jack Vickers, founder of Castle Pines, personally invited Patty and me to join. Florian Barth, a special friend and historian from Castle Pines, has teamed up with Bob Carlin and Rayburn Tucker to write a book about the history of this wonderful club.

In all the years I've played the game, I have to admit that Preston Trail Golf Club is my favorite place to play. It's a great course and never crowded, like so many of the other good Dallas family clubs. I was very involved in the early years of this club, and served on the original board from 1962 through 1968. Also, I was chairman of the Membership Committee for a couple of years. We had two members from each of these four clubs, that comprised most of our original members: Brook Hollow Golf Club, Dallas Country Club, Lakewood Country Club, and the Northwood Club.

For many years Preston Trail hosted the Byron Nelson

My Wonderful Family, Special Friends, and Favorite Pastime   187

Open. A tournament of this scope and magnitude required a million details. I, along with Toddy Lee Winn, Jr., was asked to oversee the marshals, and my good friend Joe Kern was asked to oversee the caddies. The event was a great success, and shortly thereafter Joe was elected president of Preston Trail. After Joe's term began, one of the caddies told a guest, "That Mother went from caddie-master to president in one year!"

Charlie Sifford was the first black man to make the pro golf tour. When Charlie was invited to play in the Byron Nelson Tournament being held at Preston Trail in the mid-1960s, I instructed Renfro, the locker room attendant at Preston Trail, to make sure Charlie had use of my locker. "Renfro, I want you to find the biggest ass box of cigars and put them in my locker for Charlie." Now, Charlie was a big fellow, kind of gruff and rough around the edges. He continued to play in the Byron Nelson in subsequent years, and each time he'd come to the club, he would summon Renfro: "Wer my locker and wer my cigars!" Charlie complained that he never made a dime in Dallas. However, in one of those early tournaments, he won $1,000. When he was presented with the check, I told him, "Charlie, I don't want to hear any more of this shit about you never making a dime in Dallas!"

Curtis Sifford, Charlie's nephew, qualified for the pro-tour several years later. Curtis was a very polished fellow, a real gentleman. I had the pleasure of being paired with him in two Bob Hope Classics. Curtis traveled with his own caddie, a short fellow with gray, cropped hair, called Pappy. On one occasion, Curtis conferred with Pappy about which club to use for his next shot. Pappy looked down the fairway and handed Curtis the club. Well, Curtis whacked the ball and completely flew the green. He scowled at Pappy. "I thought you told me that tree was 125 yards!" To which Pappy replied, "Curtis, that's right, but I must have had the wrong tree."

About three weeks before the start of the Byron Nelson, committee members were allowed to enroll players participating in a specific tournament. The year was 1973, and fellow committee member Eiband Wilshusen and I flew down to Deerfield Golf Club in Jacksonville, Florida. This was our opportunity to meet the pros face-to-face and invite them to

Dallas. Much to our chagrin, Eiband and I realized that while we knew several of the pros, we knew an inordinate number of caddies. Each handshake in the clubhouse was accompanied with a hard-luck story. "My car broke down. I need $100." Or, "My mother is in the hospital. I need $200 to get her out." Or, "My car was broken into and all my clothes were stolen. I need $100!" Upon our return to Dallas, Eiband and I were kidded that we recruited eight caddies, six rabbits, and very few pros!

An aside: Preston Trail has always been a men's-only club. The only two women who ever played the course were Stuart Hunt's wife, Jean, and Patty. About four weeks before the club formally opened, the four of us played the 13th and 14th holes, which were the farthest away from the temporary clubhouse. The ladies did us proud, but they never played the course again!

One day I was playing with Stuart Hunt (one of the club's original four founders, whom we always called "King Stuart"). He had earned the reputation of being a major needler on the course. It was during the height of the Vietnam War, and as usual, we were arguing about the war and other issues. Out of nowhere, Stuart started in on football: "The Americans just aren't trying to win the war, just as Coach Ara Parseghian didn't try to win the game against Michigan State last week and settled for a 10-10 tie." Stuart just ranted on and on about the game for the rest of the afternoon. The following spring, Ara came to Dallas and I arranged a game with Ara, John Murchison, Stuart, and myself. I told Stuart about the game, but didn't mention that Ara was joining us. We were having lunch in the clubhouse before the game. Stuart walked in. "Stuart, this is Ara Parseghian," I said. "Please tell him how displeased you were with the Michigan State vs. Notre Dame 10-10 game." Stuart turned red as a beet! Later, as we were coming in from the 18th hole, Stuart said, "Coach, what time are you going back?" Ara turned to Stuart and said, "On Braniff at 10:10!" We had a big laugh on this true reply.

It seems there is always an awful lot of kidding and needling going on at Preston Trail. Great camaraderie. However, if you are thin-skinned, Preston Trail is not the place for you. I should list the entire roster, but in lieu of this, let me name some very good friends that I play golf with: Tom Alexander, Adrian Alter,

Kirk Anderson, Dee Brown, Bob Carlin, Jim Chambers, Joel Cowdrey, Herb Durham, John Eulich, Bobby Folsom, Don Finn, Rawles Fulgham, Joe Geary, John Gourley, Dick Griffith, Bob Higgins, Ed Hoffman, Denny Holman, Bill Hooten, Allen Humphrey, Sherman and Stuart Hunt, Joe Kern, Graham Koch, Tom Landry, Jim Leake, Tom Marquez, Mike Massad, Kelly McCann, Pat McEvoy, Felix McKnight, Roger Meier, Eldridge Miles, Vance Miller, John Murphy, Tom O'Dwyer, Pat Patterson, Jean Patton, Dr. Ernest Poulos, John Strauss, Jack Stroube, Charles Summerall, Earl Summers, Stark Taylor, Rayburn Tucker, Eiband Wilshusen, John Wilson, Bob Wright, and Fred Zeder. Regarding Don Finn, he and my wife, Patty, like to coach from the sidelines. They not only obstruct justice, they obstruct my game—especially Finn's comment regarding my short game: "Too many moving parts!" I could tell you stories about these guys and many others at this club that could go on forever.

IT'S A WONDERFUL LIFE

My parents had a wonderful, loving relationship. Devoted, hard-working, and mutually respectful, their guidance and nurturing created a wonderful atmosphere for their children. We were loved, secure, and happy.

I've been extraordinarily blessed throughout my lifetime. Every night, before going to sleep, I thank God for three things. I am grateful for the good health God has granted to Patty and me. We won't be around forever, but we've been blessed for over eighty years. I thank God for our material blessings. And certainly, I thank God for having such wonderful children, grandchildren, and a great-grandson.

I think those are pretty good things to be thankful for. Don't you?

Appendix
AWARDS, HONORS, CIVIC AFFILIATIONS & DIRECTORSHIPS

J.M. Haggar
Awards:
Horatio Alger Award—1976
The Golden Torch Award—City of Hope Hospital in Los Angeles—1971
Knight of Malta
Knight of the Holy Sepulcher
Texas Business Hall of Fame—Inducted 1984
Honorary Degree-Doctor of Laws, University of Notre Dame—1976
Distinguished Salesman of the Year: The "Glory Award" from the Dallas Sales and Marketing Executives Club—1976

Member:
Dallas Citizens Council
Dallas Chamber of Commerce
University of Notre Dame Business Council
Dallas Serra Club
Honorary member, Dallas Sales and Marketing Executives Club

E. R. Haggar
Directorships—past and present:
Board of Trustees, University of Notre Dame (Life Member)
Chairman, Frederick Sorin Society (Fund Raising Arm), Notre Dame
Board of Trustees, University of Dallas

National Director, Boys & Girls Clubs of America
Board of Trustees, Dallas Children's Medical Center
Board of Trustees, Eisenhower Medical Center
Member, Dallas Citizens Council

Civic Activities — past and present:
Chairman, Boys & Girls Clubs of America, Southwest Region
Board of Directors and Founding Director, Thanksgiving Square, Dallas
Business Council, University of Notre Dame
National Alumni Board, First Vice President, University of Notre Dame
President, Notre Dame Club of Dallas
President, Dallas Serra Club (Catholic Businessman's club fostering vocation)
Advisory Board Member and Social Center Chairman, Salvation Army
Chairman, Mid-Texas Chapter of the Young President's Organization
Board of Directors, Chairman of Business Education Committee- Dallas Chamber of Commerce
Vice Chairman, Dallas Civil Service Board
Board of Directors, Metropolitan YMCA
Board of Directors and Treasurer, Dallas Services for Blind Children
Member, Dallas Assembly
Board of Directors, United Way of Metropolitan Dallas
Executive Board, Boy Scouts of America
First Chairman of the Board, Kidney Foundation of Texas

Former Business Affiliations:
Board of Directors, First National Bank of Dallas; Executive Committee
Board of Directors, Inter First Corporation (original board)
Board of Directors, Fidelity Union Life; member Executive Committee
Board of Directors, Policy & Conflict of Interest Committee and Audit Committee, Enserch Corporation
Metropolitan Chairman, National Alliance of Businessmen (a presidential appointment)

Awards:
Notre Dame Man of the Year

Jesuit Man of the Year
Humanitarian Award, National Jewish Hospital, Denver, Co., 1980
Herbert Hoover Award for Boys & Girls Clubs of America, 1991
Edward Frederic Sorin Award, 1988

Honorary Degrees:
1978 — Doctor of Laws, Philadelphia College of Textiles and Science
1996 — Doctor of Humane Letters, University of Dallas

J.M. Haggar, Jr.
Directorships — past and present:
Mercantile National Bank
Enserch Corporation
Brinker International

Civic Activities — past and present:
St. Paul Hospital Foundation of Dallas
The American Task Force for Lebanon
Board of Governors of St. Jude's Children's Hospital in Memphis, Tenn.
Chairman of St. Jude's $250-million Endowment Fund Drive
Board of Directors, Dallas Medical Action Group
Dallas Citizens Council
President, Dallas Serra Club
Business Council, University of Notre Dame
Trustee, University of Notre Dame — 1993
President's Development Committee, Notre Dame — 1993
Member, Notre Dame University's Relations Committee
Member, Notre Dame University Athletic Affairs Committee
Member and past Chairman, Notre Dame Club of Dallas
Chairman of the $175-million Dallas Crossroads Bond Program — 1967
Member, Dallas-Fort Worth International Airport Board of Directors
Chaired Retirement and Compensation Committees for D-FW Airport
Served two terms on Dallas City Council-beginning in 1979
Vice-Chairman of Texas Turnpike Authority
Past President, Dallas Manufacturers and Wholesalers Association
Board Member, Catholic Foundation of Dallas

Board Member, Dallas Summer Musicals
Board Member, Kidney Foundation of Dallas

Awards:
Honored by the Dallas Chapter of National Conference of Christians & Jews
The Lone Star Chapter of National Football Foundation Hall of Fame: Recipient of Distinguished American Award
Sales & Marketing Executives International Academy of Achievement
Man of the Year — Notre Dame Club of Dallas

J.M. Haggar, III
Directorships:
Board of Directors, Salesmanship Club of Dallas
Board of Directors, Presbyterian Healthcare Foundation
Board of Directors, Notre Dame Business Council
Board of Directors, Texas Commerce Bank

Civic Activities:
Young President's Organization
Salesmanship Club of Dallas

Frank D. Bracken, Jr.
Directorships:
Chancellor's Advisory Committee, University of North Texas
Alumni Board, University of North Texas
Academic Advisory Board, University of North Texas
College of Business Advisory Board, University of North Texas
Board of Directors, Dallas Big Brothers & Sisters
Board of Directors, Fashion Association
Board of Directors, American Apparel Manufacturers Association
Executive Committee Member, Trade Policy Committee, American Apparel Manufacturers Association
Board of Directors, Uniform Code Council

Awards:
Distinguished Alumnus Award, University of North Texas — 1955

Index

A
Abraham, Joe, 60
Acapulco, Mexico, 99
Adams, Nathan, 9, 10
Adolphus Hotel, 24, 53, 54
Advisory Council for the College of Business Administration, 57
Agua Caliente Casino, 7
Air Transport Command, 71, 72
Alban, J. Frederic, 12
Alban, Maggie, 11
Alexander, Gus, 35
Alexander, Tom, 188
Allan, Denny, 58-59
Alter, Adrian, 188
Alumni Hall, 41, 49
American Football League, 160, 182
American League, 175
Anchorage, Alaska, 154
Anderson, Kirk, 189
Annenberg, Walter, vi, 149, 173-174
Anthony, C.R., 65
Antlers Hotel, 164
Armstrong, Gordon, 121
Arrow shirts, 103
Ashe, Arthur, vi, 87
Athens, Texas, 70
atomic bomb, 72
Augusta National, 66
Austin, Texas, 37
Azar, Samir, 20

B
Baby First Program, 150, 155
Badin, Rev. Stephen, 39
Baer, Max, 46
Bailey, Joe, 183
Baker Hotel, 24, 53
Baloyan Greg, 128
Baltasrol, 99
Bantz, Fred, 99
bar codes, 101-102, 125
Barrett, Bob, 140
Barth, Florian, 186
Batroun, Lebanon, 12
Batts Hanger Company, 89
Baylor Hospital, 91
Bazoun, Lebanon, 11
Beall's, 67
Beattie, Ralph, 75
Beauchamp, Father William, 158
Beauty Control, 75
Becker, George, 43
Belk, Henry, 66
Belk, John, 66
Belk Stores, 65
Bell Hotel, 67
Bell, Pat, 38

Ben Hogan Company, 86
Benthal, Jerry, 62
Bentsen, Lloyd, 141
Bertelli, Angelo, 179
Betty Ford Clinic, 140
Beverly Hills, California, 7, 37
Big Bertha, 116
"Big Mamma Jack," 182-183
Big Six Oil Company, 42
Bing Crosby Classic, 138
Blanchard, Doc, 180
Bob Hope Classic, 86, 87, 176-177, 187
Boland, Father John, 38, 44, 47, 49
Bolt, Tommy, 86
Bomer, Weldon, 10
Bon Marché, 93
Borden's Milk, 83
Borg, Bjorn, vi, 87
Boston, Massachusetts, 36
Bowie, Texas, 80
Box, Cloyse, vi, 84
Boys and Girls Clubs of America, 158-159
Bracken, Frank, 75, 112, 123-124, 155
Braecklein, Bill, 186
Braniff Airways, 162-163
Braniff, Tom, 162
Brinker International, 75
Brinker, Norman, 75
Bristow, Oklahoma, 5, 15, 24, 60
Broadmoor Golf Resort, 164
Broadmoor Hotel, 177
Broadway, The, 85, 93
Brook Hollow Golf Club, 99, 186
Brooklyn, New York, 21
Brothers of St. Joseph, 39
Brown, Dee, 189
Brown, Tim, 179
Brownsville, Texas, 79, 80
Brownwood, Texas, 118
Bryan, George, 19
Bryan, Marion Haggar, 19
Buckalew, Don, 18
Buckalew, Joanne, 18
Buckalew Ranch, 18
Bunyan, Shorty, 118-119
Burlington Mills, 115
Bush, Barbara, 142, 146, 148

Bush, George H., v, vi, 3, 141-149, 151, 158, 173-174
Bush, George W., v, 147, 149, 150-151
Bush, Jeb, 148
Byron Nelson Open, 87, 138, 185, 187

C

C.R. Anthony Department Stores, 65
C-Zone, 111, 126
Cadillac, 83
Calhoun, Mr., 2
Callahan, Charlie, 49, 52
Callaway, Ely, 115-116
Callaway Golf Clubs, 116
Calloway, Cab, 45
Campbell, Dolores, 20
Campbell, Glen, 87
Campbell-Taggart Baking Company, 172
Caolo, Patty, 165
Capital theater, 29
Capone, Al, 12
Carlin, Bob, 186, 189
Carr, R.N., 62
Carrence, Will, 173
Carrollton, Texas, 152, 159
Castle Pines Country Club, 66, 173, 184, 185, 186
Castleman and O'Neill Oil Company, 43
Castleman, Billy, 42-43
Catholic Charities, 14
Cavanaugh, Father John J., 39, 52, 54, 55
Cave of the Winds, 31
Celanese Corporation, 105
Center for World Thanksgiving, 157
Central Intelligence Agency, 141
Chambers, Jim, 189
Chapel of Thanksgiving, 157
Charisse, Cyd, 54
Charlie Farrell's Racquet Club, 22
Chevigny, Jack, 38, 50, 52
Chez Paree, 53
Chicago Bears, 179
Chicago Board of Trade, 43
Chicago, Illinois, 42, 82
Chisholm, Kevin, 75

Christ the King, 167, 169, 170, 171
Cincinnati, Ohio, 72
City of Hope Hospital, 91
Clark, Dick, 181
Clements, Bill, 141
Cleveland Municipal Stadium, 48
Club 21, 172
CNN, 122, 154
Cobra, 116
Cochran, Joe, 41, 53
Colliers, 84
Collins, Jim, 135, 140, 177
Colonial Baking Company, 172
Colorado Springs, Colorado, 164
Columbian Club, 157
Columbus, New Mexico, 24
Coney Island, 30
Congregation of Holy Cross, 39
Connally, John, 95, 135
Connally, Nellie, 95
Constantine, Eugene, 155
CooCoo Gang, 12
Coors Beer Company, 178-179
Cooter, 33
Corsicana Company, 94, 124
Corsicana, Texas, 80, 124
Covington, Kentucky, 161
Cowden Brothers, 68
Cowdrey, Joel, 189
Cox, Ed, 141
Crazy Horse Hotel, 154
Crossen, Dan, 56
Crouere-Denechoud, Pat, 165
Crow, Trammel, 38, 141
Crum, Paul, 168
Crumm and Forrester, 175
Cullum, Bob, 156
Cummings, E.E., 36, 78
Custom Fit Suits, 106
"cut-make-trim," 61, 65

D

D.M. Oberman & Company, 1, 5, 25, 60
Daily News Record, The, 83, 99
Daley, James Joseph, 161
Daley, Kathryn, 161
Daley, Patricia Ann, 161
Dallas 4-Ball Tournament, 176

Dallas Baptist College, 91
Dallas Citizens Council, 156
Dallas City Council, 19-20, 125, 149
Dallas Country Club, 30, 186
Dallas Cowboys, 84, 85, 169
Dallas Fire Department, 33
Dallas/Fort Worth Airport, 19
Dallas Gas Company, 153, 156
Dallas Golf Course, 176
Dallas Morning News, 167, 168
Dallas Opera, 14
Dallas Pants Company, 93, 94
Dallas Symphony, 14
Dallas Texans, 182
Dallas, Texas, 5, 8, 24, 80, 87, 121, 152-157
Dallas University and Academy, 31
Danna, C.D., 38
Davis, Glen, 180
De Ore, Mary Lynn Vaughan, 23
Dean, Daffy, 8
Dean, Dizzy, 8
Debs, Rose, 11
Deer Trail, Colorado, 169
Deerfield Golf Club, 187
Deering Milliken Company, 101, 115
Delta Mills, 113
Denver Broncos, 169
Denver, Colorado, 127, 157-158, 171
DeSoto, Texas, 33
Detroit Lions, 84
Devlin, Bruce, 87
Diamond, Monsignor, 28
Dillon Hall, 40, 41, 46, 49
Dillon, Terry, 56-57
Dominican Republic, 104
Donohue, —, 46
double-knit fabrics, 98-99, 106, 113-114, 116
Doyle, Joe, 52
Dr Pepper, 83
Duncan, Ola, 62
Duncan, Walter, 43
Duncan, Texas, 79, 80
Durban, South Africa, 153
Durham, Herb, 176, 189

E

E. Magrath, 126, 168
Ed Haggar Family Foundation, 91, 155
Edinburg, Texas, 79, 80
807 Program, 104
Einstein, Albert, 24
El Pomar Foundation, 177
Eldorado Country Club, 66, 115, 116, 186
Electronic Data Interchange (EDI), 102
Ely & Walker Company, 1-3
Emporium, 85, 93
Enserch, 153-154
Esquire, 84
Eulich, John, 189
Evans, Jack, 20
Evans, Ray, 75
Everett, Edward, 161

F

factory outlet malls, 115
Fair Park, 19
Fairmont Hotel, 37
Falk, Mary Lena, 181
Farah, 82, 100-101, 125
Farmers Branch, Texas, 33
Farrell, John, 99-100
FBI, 43
Ferguson, Roland, 90
Ferguson, Tim, 76
Finn, Don, 189
Finsterwald, Dow, vi, 86, 182
"First Impressions," 155
First National Bank, Dallas, 9, 108, 141, 152
558th Air Force Army Base, 72
Flemming, Walter, 43
Flitewate, 110
Florence, David, 157
Florsheim, 53
Floyd West Insurance Company, 175
Folsom, Bobby, 20, 172, 189
Foot Joy, 53
Ford, Betty, 139-140
Ford, Doug, vi, 86, 182
Ford, Gerald R., v, vi, 87, 135-140, 149, 151, 184

Ford, Henry, 64
Forecast Flannels, 93
"Forever Pressed," 110, 111
Formula 5000 Road Racing, 86-87
Forrest Avenue High School, 33
Fossil Creek, 114
Fowler, Archie, 17, 119
Fox Deluxe Beer, 42
Fox, Kenny, 42
Fox, Nellie, vi, 84
Frankfurt Distilleries, 41
French, Bob, 149
Frick, James, 56
Fulgham, Rawles, 189

G

Gallagher, Chick, 41, 43, 53
Garrett Park, 29
Geary, Joe, 189
Geiberger, Al, 139
George Bush Presidential Library, 148
Georges, Bill, 178-179
Georges, Marilyn, 178-179
Gerber Cutting Machine, 122
Gifford, Frank, vi, 84
Gilmer, Texas, 66, 67
Girls Clubs of America, 159
Gladewater, Texas, 66
Glasgow, Scotland, 1
"Golden Rule Store, The," 63
Goldman Sachs, 108
Goodstein, Arthur, 67
Gore, Al, 150
Gourley, John, 189
Grace Corporation, 166
Grace, Peter, 166
Grace, Steve, 166
Graham, Otto, vi, 84
Grand Lake, Colorado, 164
Grant, Eula, 171
Green Grass Golf Shops, 126
Greenbrier Golf Resort, 182
Greenville Pants Manufacturing Company, 94
Greenville, Texas, 79, 80, 81, 121
Griffith, Dick, 189
Grunsfeld, Clarence, 7, 63, 77, 119, 127
Grunsfeld, Herbert, 7, 77, 93

Gugliehmi, Bob, 175
Guillot, L. E., 180
Gutowski, Dennis, 58-59

H

Hagan, Walter, 184
Haggar, Ann Rogers, 166
Haggar, Barbara, 27
Haggar, Daley Christie, 167
Haggar, Diana, 171
Haggar, E. R., Jr., 75
Haggar, Eddie, 58, 103, 107, 108, 124-125, 166-167, 177
Haggar, Edmond R. "Big Ed": awards/honors, 157-158, 191-193; birth of, 15, 24; children of, 165-172; education of, 26, 27, 28, 31-33, 39-52; endowments/gifts by, 53-54, 56-57, 90-91, 155, 157; on Enserch board, 153-154; on First National Bank board, 152; as football player, 33, 38, 47-52; and founding of Haggar Co., v; and gambling, 44-45; and golfing, 87, 99-100, 135-136, 138-139, 149, 158, 164, 173-176, 180-189; on Haggar board, 75; marries, 164; and Notre Dame, 39-59; organizations/community involvement, 53, 57, 97, 107, 142, 150, 152-159; real estate partnership of, 159; in sales/marketing, 36, 66-68, 78, 81-82, 83, 93, 99, 101-102, 105, 117, 120, 122; on Univ. of Dallas board, 154-155; in U.S. Army Air Force, 71-73; and U.S. presidents, 97-98, 133-151; works at Haggar plant, 34
Haggar, Isabell, 10, 19, 20, 95, 139
Haggar, James Joseph "Jimmy," 9, 18, 126, 167-168, 170, 177
Haggar, Jayne Frederick, 123
Haggar, Jennifer, 123
Haggar, Jessica, 123
Haggar, Joanne, 123
Haggar, Joe, III, 10, 18, 19, 57, 58-59, 75, 108-110, 123, 133, 155
Haggar, John, 127, 170-171, 177
Haggar, Joseph Marion (Joe), Jr., iv, 9, 10-11, 16-20, 26, 31, 32, 35, 43, 57, 61, 75, 76, 78, 81, 86, 87, 92, 95, 101, 102, 108, 109, 110, 117, 120-122, 125, 133-134, 139, 140, 149, 154, 155, 159-160, 182-183
Haggar, Joseph Marion, Sr.: iv , 75, 76, 95, 117, 172; awards/honors, 155, 191; birth of, v, 4; birthplace of, 4, 20; called "Jim," 5; death of, 11; with D.M. Oberman, 25, 60-61; education of, 4, 20; with Ely and Walker, 1; endowments/gifts by, 52-59, 90-91, 157; and founding of Haggar Co., v, 1, 61; and gambling, 7-9; as hunter, 9, 17-18; and IRS, 77-78; marries, 5; in Mexico, 4; in oil business, 42; and pricing, 117-118; and sales/marketing, 5-7, 15-16, 60-66, 78, 96, 98, 118; and U.S. presidents, 133-134, 140, 149
Haggar, Lee Davidson, 168
Haggar, Lydia, 19, 57, 58, 133-134
Haggar, Marc, 168
Haggar, Marion, 19, 57
Haggar, Mary Alice, 85, 168, 169-170
Haggar, Melissa, 168
Haggar, Michael, 168, 170
Haggar, Nicholas, 4
Haggar, Nick, 27
Haggar, Patty, 41, 116, 138, 139, 141, 142-143, 146, 148, 151, 161-165, 167, 170, 171, 173, 174, 180- 181, 184, 185-186, 188, 189
Haggar, Patty Jo, 57, 165-166
Haggar, Rose Mary Wasaff, iv, 5, 8, 11-15, 31, 75, 95, 157, 177
Haggar, Rosemary, iv, 8, 21-23, 26, 31, 35, 61, 76, 172; also see Vaughan, Rosemary
Haggar, Shaina, 171
Haggar Black Label, 116
Haggar Casuals, 111
Haggar College Center, 53
Haggar Corporation: additional products of, 103, 104-107, 116, 125; and advertising, 77, 82, 83-88, 99- 100, 105, 106, 111, 112-113, 117, 122; and Belk Stores, 65-66; board of directors of, 75, 109, 123; and C.R.

Anthony Co., 65; and civic contributions, 90-91, 155-156; data processing, 90, 101-102; employees (longtime), 128-132; fabrics of, 78, 88, 93, 98-101, 105, 106, 110-111, 113, 114, 122, 124; facilities of, 61-62, 68-70, 74, 76, 79-80, 93, 104, 114, 121; 50th anniversary of, 117-118; founded, v, 1, 61; and internet sales, 115; and J.C. Penney stores, 63-64, 67, 68, 78, 96, 122; labels of, 74, 86, 96, 122, 123; manufacturing innovations of, 121-122; and merchandising, 88-89, 105, 111-113, 115-116, 127-128; name of, 116; and offshore manufacturing, 102-104, 107, 125; pants line of, 61, 68, 82, 87, 88, 93, 98-101, 103, 105-106, 110-114, 115, 122, 124, 126; and pre-pricing, 97; profit sharing program of, 92, 104; as publicly owned corp., 75, 107-110, 113; regional sales offices, 82; sales force of, 63, 67, 70, 76-77, 81-83, 107, 113, 115, 119, 122; 75th anniversary of, 151; shareholders of, 65, 108; shirt line of, 79; and straight line production, 64; stores of, 115; textile lab, 111, 113, 166; trucking fleet, 80-81; and unions, 93-95; women's wear division, 106-107, 108, 125; in WWII, 70-71; zones of, 121

Haggar Customer Service Center, 114, 115, 123
Haggar Expandomatic, 106
Haggar EZ's, 111-112
Haggar Fitness Center, 53
Haggar Foundation, 22, 90-91
Haggar Hall, 91
Haggar Hall of Psychology, 53
Haggar Hangers, 89
Haggar Harmony Chart, 84
Haggar Imperials, 103
Haggar Order Transmission (H.O.T.) Program, 102, 122, 154
Haggar Profit Sharing Program, 92, 104
Haggar vs. Helvring, 77

Haggerty, Pat, 134, 155
Hajjar, Kahlil Abou Chacra El, 4
Hajjar, Kalil Maney, Mrs., 4
Hajjar, Yousef Maroun, 20
Halaby, Mr., 141
Hale Center, Texas, 6-7
Haley, Art, 56
Hallmark Cards, 75
Harris and Frank, 93
Hart, Leon, 179
Hart-Shaffner and Marx, 100
Harvard Advocate, The, 167
Harvey, Ginger, 185
Hatbox Field, 13
Hazelrig, Martha, 173
Hazelrig, Paul, 172-173
Hazelrig, Paul, Jr., 173
Heath, Dick, 75
Heisman Trophy, 31, 179
Helvring, Guy, 77-78
Henry Miller and Company, 165
Henson, Jake, 17, 67, 119
Hercules Pants Company, 64
Herman, Dick, 179
Hesburgh, Father Theodore M., vi, 52, 54, 55, 57, 158, 174
Hewins, Doris Johnson, 164
Hickey Freeman, 100
Higgins, Bob, 177, 189
High Y, 37
Highland Park, 30
Higuey, Texas, 80
Hill, Dr., 36
Hilliard, Bohn, 50
Hills of Adonis, The, 3
Hiroshima, Japan, 71, 72
Hite, Morris, v, 19, 83, 88
Hobbs, David, vi, 87
Hockaday, 167
Hoffman, Ed, 189
Hogan, Ben, vi, 86, 184
Hogan, Carl, vi, 87
Holdreth, Father George, 41
Holman, Denny, 189
Holy Cross Brothers, 39
Holy Trinity, 28
Home Depot, 186
Hong Kong, 102

Hoosier Manufacturing Company, 64, 105
Hooten, Bill, 189
Hoover, Herbert, 159
Hope, Bob, vi, 54, 86, 87, 138, 176-177, 187
Horany, Johnny, 18
Horizon Group, 123
Hornung, Paul, 179
Host Pajamas, 103
Hot Springs, Virginia, 182
Hotel New Yorker, 21
How I Played the Game, 184
Huarte, John, 179
Huff, Sam, vi, 85
Hugh Perry and Company, 65
Humphrey, Allen, 183, 189
Hunt, Jean, 188
Hunt, Lamar, 87, 160, 182-183
Hunt, Sherman, 189
Hunt, Stuart, 188, 189
Hussein, King, 141
Hussein, Saddam, 142
Huston, Clay, 103
Hutchinson, Kansas, 161
Hybl, Bill, 177

I
IBM, 89-90
Indian Wells, California, 115
Internal Revenue Service, 77
Interstate Folding Box Company, 105
Interstate Theater, 54

J
J.C. Penney Company, 14, 36, 63, 66, 67, 68, 78, 96, 99, 105, 122
J.L. Stifle & Company, 68
J.P. Coats Company, 1-2
J.P. Stevens, 85, 98
J-Mar Ruby, 100, 105
Jacksonville, Texas, 67, 70
Japan, 102-103
Jefferson City, Missouri, 60
Jerry Ford Invitational Tournament, 87, 139, 184
Jesuit Academy, 166, 171

Jesuit College Preparatory School, 84, 123, 177, 178
Jesuit Foundation, 178
Jezzeen, Lebanon, v, 3-4, 20
Jezzeen Partnership, 159
Jockey, 103
Joe Haggar Family Foundation, 91
Johannesburg, South Africa, 153
Johnson, Eric, 155
Johnson, General, 7
Johnson, Lyndon, v, 10-11, 133-134
Johnston & Murphy, 53
Joiner, Dad, 66
Jones and Vining Shoe Last Company, 53
Jordan, 141
Joseph, Meled, 34-35
Joseph, Monsignor Milam, 155
Joyce, Father Ned, 158, 174
Justice Department, 97-98

K
Kadane family, 42
Kansas City Junior College, 162
Kansas City, Missouri, 161
Kappa Gamma, 36
Keeling, Raymond "Tessy," 31
"Keen Built" pants, 61
Kemmerer, Wyoming, 63
Kennedy, Jackie, 95
Kennedy, Joe, 54
Kennedy, John F., 95
KERA, 155
Kern, Joe, 187, 189
Kerry, Norma, 12
Kidney Foundation of Texas, 15
Kilpatrick Baking Company, 173
Kilroy, Tom, 158
King, Aaron, 166
King Brand Overalls, 5, 6, 60
King, Devon Haggar, 166
King, Larry, 139
King, Maxwell Edmond, 167
Kissinger, Henry, 140
KMA Field, 42
Koch, Graham, 189
Korean War, 73
Korth, Colonel, 72

Ku Klux Klan, 13
Kuhlman, Jack, 43

L
La Romana, 104
Lacadena thread, 1-2
Lademon, Raymond, 67
Lahey, Father, 40
Lake Erie, 30
Lakewood Country Club, 8, 17, 30, 174, 176, 180, 182, 184, 186
Lalier, Jack, 38
Lalla, Bill, 38, 164
Lalla, Oscar, 38
Landau, Sylvan, 119, 127
Landry, Tom, 189
Lane, Bobby, vi, 84
Langone, Elaine, 186
Langone, Ken, 186
LaRomana, 80
Lattner, John, 179
Laver, Rod, vi, 87
Lawton, Oklahoma, 79, 80
Layden, Elmer, 49-50, 51, 52
Layden, Mike, 54
"LBJ Cut," 11
LBJ Ranch, 10, 133
Leake, Jim, 189
Ledbetter, Cal, 71
Lee James Co., 168
Lehman Brothers, 165
Leisure Suits, 105
Leon, Mexico, 80, 104
Leonard, Ada, 51
Levi Dockers, 88, 111, 112, 126
Levi Strauss, 82, 88, 111, 126
Levy, Gus, 108
Liberia, 138
Life Magazine, 83-84, 122
Lindbergh, Charles, 29
Linskie, George, 26
Lipton Tea Company, 179
Liston, Tom, 43
Lombardo, Guy, 45
Long, Lawson, 30
Longview, Texas, 66, 67
Look, 84
Looking Forward, 3

Los Angeles, California, 82, 85
Louisville, Kentucky, 41, 42
Love Field, 71
Love, Lucille, 38
Luce Weils Biscuit Company, 163
Lujack, Johnny, 179-180
Lyne, Fritz, 94
Lyon's Hall, 41

M
M.A.G.I.C., 21
Macmillan, Harold, 138
Magee, Bob, 43
Magee, Jim, 43
Magnolia Building, 24
Magrath, Edmund, 126
Maher, Edward, Sr., 155
Maher, Louis, 38, 155
Maher, Tommy, 38
Mailhes, Al "Tubby," 41-42, 67
Majestic theater, 29-30
Make Room for Daddy, 159
Malloy, Father Edward, 158
Manhattan, New York, 30
Manicchi, Charlie, 26
Manitou Springs, Colorado, 31
Mansion, The, 172
Mantle, Mickey, vi, 84, 85, 175-176
Maris, Roger, 84
Maronite church, 4, 5
Marquez, Carolyn, 186
Marquez, Tom, 186, 189
Marsh, Major, 26
Martin, Charlie, 87
Martin, Tony, 54
Massad, Mike, 189
Mathews, Eddie, vi, 84
Matthews, Frank, 66
Mazziotti, Tony, 49
McBee System, 89
McCallister, Mac, 48
McCleod, Fran, 22
McCord, Bill, 153
McCullough, Mr., 44
McElvaney, Gene, 9, 10
McEvoy, Pat, 189
McKinney Pants Manufacturing Company, 94

McKinney, Texas, 79, 80, 121
McKnight, Felix, 189
McMahon, Ollie, 44
Measurement of Intelligence, The, 24
Meier and Frank, 93
Meier, Roger, 189
Mel Rose Manufacturing Company, 64
Melba theater, 29
Memphis, Tennessee, 159
Men's Wear Magazine, 83, 99
Mercantile Bank, 152
Meredith, Don, vi, 84, 85, 178-179
Merrill Lynch, 108
Mesquite, Texas, 33
Methodist Hospital, 91
Metropolitan Museum of Fine Arts, 91
Metzger, Charlie, 44
Mexico City, 21
Miami Dolphins, 49, 159, 160
Miami Dolphins, 159
Michigan City, Indiana, 105
Micro Khakis, 105, 114
Micromatics, 105, 114
Miles Avenue Grill, 43
Miles, Eldridge, 189
Miller, Harold, 183
Miller, Vance, 189
Miller, Vicki Vaughan, 23
Milliken, 98
Milliken, Roger, 101
Millner, Wayne, 49
Mineral Wells, Texas, 71
Minyard Grocery, 183
Minyard, Henry, 183-184
Mix, Tom, 29
Monte Carlo, 181, 182
Moore, Billy, 181
Moran, Mary Lou, 162, 163
Moroney, James M., 155
Morrison, Ray, 33
Morrissey Hall, 41
Moses, Fred, 38
Mrs. Baird's Bread, 83
Muleshoe, Texas, 25
Munger, Jane, 185
Munn, Arch, 180
Murchison, John, 188
Murchison, Mary Noel, 169

Murphy, John, 189
Muskogee, Oklahoma, 13
"Mustang Pants," 87

N

Nagasaki, Japan, 71, 72
NASDAQ, 108
Nashville, Tennessee, 72, 165, 172
Nastase, Ille, vi, 87
National Alliance of Businessmen, 97, 134, 144
National Bank of Commerce, 68
National Football League, 160
National Highway Act, 80
National Industrial Recovery Act (NIRA), 77-78
National Jewish Hospital, 157
National Recovery Act, 7, 36
NBC, 87
Nelson, Byron, vi, 138, 184-185, 187
Nelson, Louise, 184
Nelson, Peggy, 184
Neuhoff, Barbara, 165
Neuhoff, Joseph, 157
New Orleans, Louisiana, 5
New York City, 16, 36, 82
New York Giants, 85
New York Yankees, 175
Newcombe, John, vi, 87
Niagara Falls, 30, 36
Nichols, Bobby, vi, 86
Nieporte, Tommy, vi, 86
Nixon, Richard, v, 97-98, 134-135, 137
Nogales, Arizona, 26
North Pole, 154
North Texas Women's Golf Association, 185
Northwood Country Club, 185, 186
Notre Dame Alumni Association, 52, 54, 57
Notre Dame Board of Trustees, 52, 57
Notre Dame Business Council, 123
Notre Dame Club of Dallas, 53
Notre Dame d'Liban, 20
Notre Dame, University of, vi, 14, 20, 21, 38, 39-59, 91, 123, 124, 158, 166, 179, 188
Novakov and Davis, 19

Novakov, Dan, Jr., 59
Novakov, Dan, Sr., 19, 59
Novakov, Isabell, 59
Novakov, Lydia Haggar, 19

O
O'Brien, Davey, 31
O'Brien, John "One Play," 38, 51
O'Brien, Neil, 155
O'Donnell, Bob, 54
O'Donnell, Father Hugh, 38, 47, 52
O'Dwyer, Tom, 189
O'Grady, Father, 27
O'Malley, Frank, 50, 51
O'Neil, Joseph I., III, 151
O'Neill, Joe, 42, 46, 54
O'Rourke, James S., 45
Oak Grove Golf Course, 180
Oak Lawn, 31
Oakcliff Country Club, 182
Oakland, California, 173
Oklahoma City, Oklahoma, 79, 80
Old Mill theater, 29
Old Orchard Beach, 36
Olmstead Kirk Paper Company, 65
Olney, Texas, 18, 80
Operation Headstart, 144
Orthodox church, 4
Osborne, Super Dave, 88, 112
Otterville, Missouri, 25
Our Sunday Visitor, 49
Owens, Arch, 99
Oxxford, 102-103

P
Paducah, Texas, 25
Palace Theater, 29, 51
Palm Springs, 87
Palmer, Arnold, vi, 86, 87
Palmer House Hotel, 42
Palms, Roberta, 38
Pappy, 187
Paris, Texas, 67
Parkland Hospital, 15
Parrino, Joe, 183
Parseghian, Ara, 58-59, 188
Patterson, Pat, 189
Patton, Jean, 189

Pearl Harbor, 70
Pebble Beach, California, 138
Peerless Touring Car, 29
Penney, James Cash, 14, 63
Pennsylvania Hotel, 16
Penrose, —, 164
"People-to-People" golf team, 181
Perot, Ross, 177, 186
Pershing, John J., 24
Persian Gulf crisis, 142
PGA, 86, 139, 182
Philadelphia College of Textiles and Science, 91
Pike's Peak, 31
PIMALON pants, 10
Ping, 116
"Pinpoint the Pigskin," 89
Pitsinger and Laine, 68
Plano, Texas, 33
Pojman, Hank, 49
Pollock, Lonnie, 183
Poulos, Dr. Ernest, 189
"Pre-Line," 82
Presbyterian Healthcare Foundation, 123
Presbyterian Hospital, 91
Preschool Educational Programs, 155
Presock, Patty, 142, 146
Prestige, 111
Preston Trail Golf Club, 8, 138, 174, 176, 186-187, 188-189
price fixing, 97
Price, Stan, 41
Prince, Harris and Company, 76
Private Label, 123
Prudhoe Bay, Alaska, 154
Pugh, Alice Marie, 161
Pugh, Ed, 161, 162, 163-164
Pugh, Minnie Bell Stevens, 161

Q
Queen Noor, 141
Queen Theater, 29

R
Rancho Mirage, California, 140, 149, 174
Ranger, Texas, 11

Razook, Bill, 34-35
Reagan, Dan, 56
Reagan, Ronald, 141, 145
Reed St. James, 103, 123, 125
Reflections in the Dome, 45
Regis College, 171
Republic Bank, 152
Retail Marketing Associates Program, 124
Reynolds Aluminum, 43
Richardson, Texas, 33
Rio Grande Valley, 79-80, 121
Rizzuto, Phil, vi, 84
Robbie, Joe, 160
Roberts, Robin, vi, 84
Robstown, Texas, 79, 80
Rockne, Knute, 50, 158, 174
Rogers, Bob, 155
Rogers, Dick, 155
Rogers, Ralph, 155
Rogers, Will, 30
Roosevelt, Franklin D., 7, 70
Rose Brothers, 64
Rose Clothing Company, 121
Rosemary Haggar Vaughan Foundation, 91
Rosie's Restaurant, 43
Rough Rider Pants, 64
Rumble, Martha Ann, 23
Russell, Bobby, 99, 174-175, 182, 183
Russo, Marty, 176-177

S

Saba, Solomon, 26
Sacred Heart Cathedral, 26, 28, 49, 61, 164
Salesmanship Club of Dallas, 123, 138
Salloum, Isabell, 19
Samuel, Dr., 36
San Diego, California, 151
San Francisco, California, 7, 85
San Francisco longshoremen, 37
"Sans a Belt," 105
Santa Fe Building, 61, 62, 65, 68, 69, 93, 114
Sarasota model, 93
Saratoga Springs, New York, 44-45
Saturday Evening Post, The, 84

Schepps, Julius, 157
Schmidt, —, 64
Schnitzius, Philip, 38
Schott, Father Paul, vi, 178
Scurry County, Texas, 43
Seay, Charles, 181
Seay, Sadie, 181
Secret Service, 136, 139
Sedalia, Colorado, 169
See, Bob, 173
Sexton, Bill, 56-57
Shadid, Joe, 10, 25
Shakespeare, Bill, 49
Shakespeare, William, 120
Shanghai Weave, 93
Shelton, Buster, 183
Shepherd, Ira "Snag," 33
Shewmaker, Jack, 101
Shortall, Jack, 161
Shreveport, Louisiana, 66, 67
Shreveport Times, 42
Shula, Don, 160
Sidor, John, 61-62
Sifford, Charlie, vi, 187
Sifford, Curtis, 187
Silverwoods, 93
Sisters of Divine Providence, 32
Skeen, Clyde, 135, 183, 184
Skeen, Helen, 184
Skouras, Spyro, 5
Slack Suits, 104-105
"slacks" (term), 88
Smith, Emma Barn-Hill, 164
Smith, Jack, 75, 127
Smith, Lank, 180
Smith, Masio, 156
Smith, Stan, vi, 87
Snead, Sam, 182
"Snug Duds," 87
Solis Engineering and Diving Company, 153
Sorin, Rev. Edward, 39, 57
Sorin Society, 57, 142
South Bend Tribune, 52
Southern Methodist University, 21, 22, 33, 53, 54, 91, 171
Southern Pacific Railroad, 32
Southland Hotel, 5, 60

Southwest Business Graphics & Forms, 19
Southwest High School, 162
Spavinaw, Oklahoma, 175
Sports Illustrated, 84
St. Clair, June, 51
St. Edward's University, 27, 38, 45, 47, 50, 51
St. Joseph's Academy, 17, 32-33, 40, 47
St. Jude's Children's Research Hospital, 91, 139, 159, 160
St. Judes/FEDEX Tournament, 139
St. Louis Cardinals, 8, 12
St. Louis, Missouri, 5, 11, 12, 24, 61
St. Mark's, 59
St. Mary's College, 21, 22, 57, 53, 91, 165
St. Paul's Hospital, 11, 14, 15, 85, 91
St. Rita's Grammar School, 165
St. Scholastica, 169
Stanford University, 165
Stans, Maurice, 98
State Dinner, 138, 141
Staubach, Roger, vi, 84
Stay Prest, 111
Stedillie, Anthony, 169
Stedillie, Mary Alice, 169
Stedillie, Steven, 169
Stedillie, Terry, 169
Stem Beach, 13
Stevens, Joe, 37
Stewart, Bobby, 107, 141, 152
Stewart, Earl, Jr., 86
Stewart, Peter, 157
Stone, Justice, 78
Stram, Hank, 182-183
Strauss, John, 189
Stroube, Jack, 189
Sullins, Ted, 125, 127
Summerall, Charles, 189
Summerall, Pat, vi, 84
Summers, Earl, 8, 183, 189
Sun State Slacks, 86
Super Bowl, 88, 159, 160
Swift, Jim, 54
Sydney, Australia, 153
Syrian-American-Lebanese Educational Association (SALEA), 14

T

Tansil, Beryl, 62, 63, 128
Task Force for the Rebuilding of Lebanon, 20
Tasman Sea, 153, 154
Taylor, Stark, 189
Tehan, Hal, 127
television, 74
Temple, Texas, 79, 80, 124
Terman, Lewis Madison, 24
Texarkana, Texas, 66
Texas Christian University, 31
Texas Commerce Bank, 123
Texas Instruments, 134
Texas Kidney Foundation, 185
Texas Power and Light Company, 90
Texas Tech, 126, 168
Texfi, 98
Thanksgiving Square, 157
Theisman, Joe, 59
Thomas, Dan, 183
Thomas, Danny, vi, 159, 160
Thomason, Dr. Raymond, 183
Thompson Company, 64
Thornton, Ramona Myers, 164
Three Beall Brothers, 67
Thurbron, Colon, 3
Tijuana, Mexico, 7
Tolbert, President, 138
Torreon, Mexico, 2
Toyoba, 103
Tracy-Locke Advertising Agency, 19, 83
Trans World Airlines, 162
Trans-Mississippi Tournament, 176
Tucker, Rayburn, 186, 189
Turner, Garrett, 59, 148, 166
Turner, John, 166
Turner, Patty Jo, 165-166; also see Haggar, Patty Jo
TV Guide, 173
Twain, Mark, 30
Twentieth Century Fox Films, 5
Tygart, Barger, 96
Tyler, Texas, 66

Tynan, Father Robert A., 177

U
U.S. Army Air Force, 71
U.S. Supreme Court, 77
Unis, Tom, 155
United Fund Drive, 91
United Nations, 10
United States Hotel, 45
United States Olympic Committee, 177
United States Quartermaster Corps, 70, 71, 115
University of Dallas, 91, 154-155
University of North Texas, 91
University of Texas, 31, 37, 38, 45, 50
Ursuline Academy, 21, 165, 169
USGA Foundation, 175
USS *Missouri*, 50
USS *Sicily*, 19
Utsey, George, 65, 66

V
Vail, Colorado, 87, 139
Van Hollenbec, Al, 43
Vaughan, Eddie, 22, 95
Vaughan, Eddie, Jr., 22
Vaughan, Jimmy, 22-23
Vaughan, Martha (Marty), 22
Vaughan, Mary Lynn, 22
Vaughan, Rosemary Haggar, iv, 14, 21-23, 91, 95; also see Haggar, Rosemary
Vaughan, Vicki, 22, 57
Veeneman, Kenneth, 41
Vickers, Jack, 186
Villa, Pancho, 2, 24
Vincentian Fathers, 31
Vogel, Harry, 61-62
Voss, Norway, 174

W
Waggoner family, 26
Wal-Mart Stores, 101, 103
Walker, Doak, vi, 84, 89
Wall, Art, Jr., vi, 86, 182
Walsh, Jim, 84
Wasaff, Alex, 12, 13, 61
Wasaff, Amil, 12
Wasaff, Fred, 12
Wasaff, Harry, 12, 13, 63, 75, 119
Wasaff, Kalil George, 11
Wasaff, Marie, 12, 13
Wasaff, Rose, 5; also see Haggar, Rose Mary Wasaff
Wasaff, Sam, 11, 12
Wasoff Pants Company, 13
Watergate, 98
Waxahachie Garment Company, 70, 94
Waxahachie, Texas, 79, 80, 121
Wembley Ties, 103
Wendover, Utah, 71, 165
Weslaco, Texas, 79, 80
White House, 135, 141-142
White House State Dinners, 138, 141
White Rock Lake, 38
Whitsel, Carl, 68, 69
Wichita Falls, Texas, 42
Wiley, Texas, 33
Williams, Zadie, 171
Wilshusen, Eiband, 187-188, 189
Wilson, James K., 38
Wilson, John, 189
Winchell, Walter, 29
Windsor, Duke of, 99-100
Winn, Toddy Lee, Jr., 187
Woodrow Wilson High School, 37, 38
Woolworth Building, 30
World Championship Tennis, 87
World's Fair, 36
Wright, Bob, 148, 189
Wright Field, 73
Wright, Rev. Sam, 156
Wrinkle Frees, 88, 106, 111, 112-114, 116, 124

Y
Yellowstone Park, 36-37
Young Presidents Organization (YPO), 107, 123
Young Street Café, 35

Z
Zachary, Father, 33
Zeder, Fred, 141, 149, 189